X-Planes of
Europe II

Military Prototype Aircraft
from the Golden Age
1945 – 1974

Tony Buttler AMRAeS

HIKOKI
PUBLICATIONS

Published in 2015 by Hikoki Publications

ISBN 9781902109480

Printed in Bulgaria by Multiprint

Hikoki
1a Ringway Trading Estate, Shadowmoss Rd,
Manchester M22 5LH
www.crecy.co.uk

Contents

Acknowledgements

Yet again my thanks must go to the following for their help in researching and preparing this book, and for supplying a large number of rare photographs. I apologise if I have left anyone out.

Jens Baganz; Adrian Balch; Prof Brian Brinkworth; The National Archives, Kew; Michel Bénichou; JC Carbonel; Fabrice Cario (Camosine); Cyril Chick; Michel Cristescu; Ernie Cromie and Paul McMaster (Ulster Aviation Society); the late Sidney Dix; Ken Ellis; José Fernandez (*Air Magazine*), Nicolas Gauthier; Chris Gibson; Albert Grandolini; the late Peter Green; Derek James; Tim Kershaw (Jet Age Museum); Yves Laurençot (Société Lyonnaise d'Histoire de l'Aviation et de Documentation Aéronautique Association (SLHADA), Lyon Aeronautic History Society); Paul Martel-Mead; Henry Matthews; Heather Midwinter; Jacques Moulin; Wolfgang Muehlbauer; RAF Museum; Thomas Mueller; Alain Pelletier; Brian Riddle (Royal Aeronautical Society); Alexis Rocher (*Le Fana de l'Aviation* magazine); Angelo Romano; Alberto Trevisan; Achille Vigna; Guy Warner; Malcolm Wild.

Extra special thanks must go to Phil Butler for finding so many photos and for dealing with numerous other requests, Chris Farara for editing some of the text, Terry Panopalis for, in particular, supplying some rare and astonishing colour shots, and Mike Kirk for his great help with all matters relating to Swiss aircraft. Also to Paul Eden for his considerable editing skills and, finally, once more my great appreciation goes to Jeremy M Pratt, Gill Richardson and the team at Crécy. It is always a pleasure to work with you all.

Tony Buttler
Bretforton, United Kingdom

The first volume in this brace of titles looking at the military X-Planes of Europe concentrated on types that had introduced for their respective countries features and elements of aircraft design for the first time. This second work is an effort to bring together most of the 'rest', those experimental aeroplanes which perhaps duplicated work done elsewhere or might have been built as prototypes for planned production runs, but which for whatever reason failed to progress further. There was not enough space for these in Volume I, but they are no less important – indeed the BAC TSR.2 is perhaps the most controversial aeroplane ever produced in the UK.

The list of types chosen to go in Volume I created argument among readers, a good sign since it showed that many enthusiasts are still passionate about this subject. The parameters for inclusion in this work were as follows:

1. Types that actually flew. Designs that were only part built do not merit separate chapters, although where and when appropriate the opportunity has been taken to describe them within a chapter covering an associated aircraft. A few unbuilt designs related to a chapter's subject have also been included.

2. Transport and trainer, helicopter and rotary-wing prototypes are omitted. The aircraft described are in general all fighters or bombers, or research aircraft designed with the objective of furthering the knowledge of these two categories (or the 'high performance' areas of aviation).

3. Aircraft that entered service, however briefly or if in just very small numbers, were ignored. Of course designs such as the de Havilland DH.110 and English Electric P.1 proved to be prototypes for what became successful production aeroplanes, but the considerable level of redesign required for them to arrive at a production configuration was enough for the author to want them in.

For British subjects the coverage includes as much new information as possible from original papers. For those of France it has not been possible to access many original reports and documents, but several authoritative secondary sources have been referred to. The selection is presented in order of first flight date and we are lucky that at least some of the aircraft featured are now on view within the permanent collections of aviation museums (see *Surviving airframes*). I have endeavoured to include as many previously unpublished photographs as possible, but in some cases the photographic material is minimal, especially for certain French prototypes.

Writing about the situation in France has been fascinating! The speed at which the French aircraft industry got moving after the end of the German occupation in World War II was remarkable! Less than a week after the Allies had entered Paris in 1944 the French Air Minister organised a meeting to assess whether the industry could be revived. The first orders were placed at the beginning of September, but the cessation of hostilities resulted in cuts to wartime orders after January 1946.

The four nationalised airframe factories, SNCASO, SNCASE, SNCAN and SNCAC, and the national aeroengine works SNECMA, left about 25% of the industry in the hands of private firms including Breguet and Morane. A system of rivalry was established, but with many projects there was an under-estimation of the problems associated with modern aeronautical design. This, coupled with a need to keep factories at work, meant many new types were hampered by unforeseen difficulties and was a factor in why some early French prototypes failed. The late 1940s was a difficult period for France's aircraft industry, but within a decade it would turn itself into a powerful force on the international stage.

Events that again feature regularly in the narrative are the Farnborough and Paris Air Shows, which served as shop windows for the British and French aircraft industries. The Paris show was first held as a complete and separate event in 1909, at the Grand Palais des Champs-Elysées, and from then on was staged regularly, except for the interruptions resulting from the two world wars. With the end of the second conflict, the show restarted in 1946, and from 1949 has been held every odd year. The early post-war shows continued to be held at the Grand Palais, but from 1949 flying demonstrations were also staged at Paris's Orly Airport. In 1953 the show was relocated from the Grand Palais to Le Bourget.

It has been very enjoyable writing about these aeroplanes and, like the previous volume, the list of contents embraces several favourites. I do hope that readers enjoy the results.

Tony Buttler, Bretforton, UK, March 2015

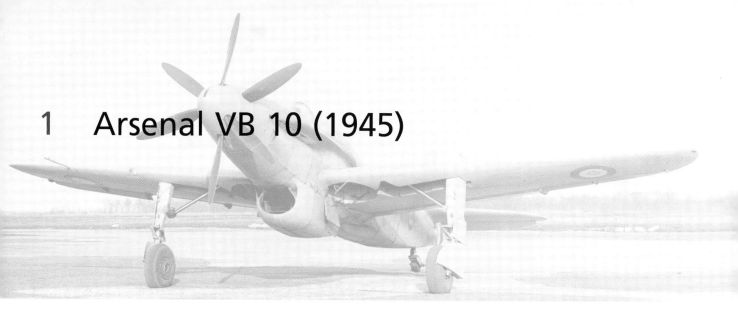

1   Arsenal VB 10 (1945)

Arsenal VB 10

Type: single-seat medium- and high-altitude day/night fighter, fighter-bomber and reconnaissance aircraft

Span: 50ft 10in (15.49m)

Length: 42ft 7in (12.98m)

Gross wing area: 381.72sq ft (35.50sq m)

Gross weight: 20,613lb (9,350kg)

Powerplant: 2 x Hispano-Suiza HS.12Z piston engines

Max level speed: 323mph (520km/h) at sea level, 447mph (720km/h) at 29,200ft (8,900m)

Service ceiling: 36,090ft (11,000m)

Climb rate: time to 32,800ft (10,000m), 21 minutes 20 seconds

Range: normal fuel 1,057 miles (1,700km), max fuel 1,616 miles (2,600km)

Armament: 4 x 20mm Hispano cannon, 6 x 0.5in (12.7mm) Browning machine guns, 2 x 500kg (1,102lb) or 250kg (551lb) bombs, or 8 x 60lb (27kg) rocket projectiles

Design of the Arsenal de l'Aéronautique VB 10 can be traced back to the late 1930s when the manufacturer's director, Ingénieur-Général Michel Vernisse, became keen on the idea of a twin-engine fighter with its engines mounted in tandem, one in front of the cockpit and the other behind, driving counter-rotating co-axial tractor airscrews. The outcome was a proposed experimental wooden aircraft designated VG 10, 'VG' relating to the project's co-designers Vernisse and Jean Galtier, which would serve as a lead-in to a fighter designated VG 20.

The growing threat from Germany altered these plans and by the first months of 1939 work on the full fighter prototype was under way, the VG 10 having been abandoned. The VG 20 would have been a larger aircraft with a wing area of 387.1sq ft (36sq m) compared to the VG 10's 279.6sq ft (26sq m), and to begin with it would have used two 910hp (679kW) Hispano-Suiza 12Y-29 engines. Later, however, the VG 20 was to have received two 1,200hp (895kW) 12Z units, which offered a possible maximum speed of 404mph (650km/h).

By mid-1939 Galtier had moved on to the VG 30-series fighter programme, leaving the VG 20 in the hands of another Arsenal engineer, Robert Badie, who concluded that such an advanced aeroplane as the VG 20 needed an all-metal structure. It was thus redesigned in metal and with this input the fighter became the VB 10 (for Vernisse-Badie). A production order for 40 aeroplanes for the Armée de l'Air (French Air Force) was awarded off the drawing board in May 1940, a move helped by the fact that the VB 10's wing and tail surfaces were near identical to those of the single-engine VG 33 (apart, that is, from being scaled up). However, before any metal had been cut the signing of the Armistice with Germany in June brought immediate cancellation.

In the meantime, Arsenal had moved from its Villacoublay home south west of Paris to Villeurbanne, near Lyon, which came inside the territory ruled by the Vichy French government. With the permission of the German Air Ministry (the Reichsluftfahrtministerium, RLM) in April 1942 the firm was permitted to resume work on the twin-engine powerplant and proceed with a VB 10 prototype. Before construction had begun, however, in November 1942 German

A series of walkaround photos of the first Arsenal VB 10 prototype, taken in 1945. In the first view the aircraft has no guns, but in the final image the full ten-gun armament appears to have been installed.

forces entered Vichy-controlled southern France. Nevertheless, the project was cleared to continue, Vernisse having stated that the VB 10 was purely an experimental aeroplane.

Flight data for the Hispano-Suiza tandem engine powerplant was acquired by fitting an example in the Latécoère 299 torpedo-bomber prototype, the aircraft's entire forward fuselage having to be rebuilt to turn it into a test bed as the 299A. In its new form the aircraft first flew late in 1943, but it was destroyed on 30 April 1944 by an Allied air attack on Bron airfield, where it was based. However, by then the concept of the tandem-mounted engine configuration had been proved.

Construction of the first VB 10 began in 1943, but the work moved forward (as intended) quite slowly. With the end of the German occupation of France the rate of progress accelerated until, in 1944, an Allied bombing raid destroyed the aircraft. Work on a second prototype, designated VB 10-01 and now classed as a fighter/fighter-bomber, began immediately after the Arsenal factory had been liberated and this made its maiden flight on 7 July 1945 from Bron, piloted by Modeste Vonner, Arsenal's chief test pilot. Early test flying gave good results, including a speed at sea level of 304mph (490km/h), and in December a production order was placed for 200 aeroplanes under contract 430/45. These were to be built by SNCAN (Société Nationale de Constructions Aéronautiques du Nord), with final assembly at Nord's Méaulte factory using major sub-assemblies produced by several other Nord facilities.

In the meantime, in late 1944 Arsenal had moved again, this time to Châtillon-sous-Bagneux, where the first prototype was completed, and on 13 September VB 10-01 was sent to Brétigny, home of the CEV (Centre d'Essais en Vol) test facility. In November 1946 the VB 10 was exhibited at the Paris Air Show (Salon international de l'aéronautique et de l'espace, Paris), mounted against the wall of the Ministry of Armament exhibition, with its fuselage opened up to show the structure.

By this time, however, the Air Force had declared that production machines would be used only as photographic-reconnaissance aircraft, and the order had been cut to just 50 aeroplanes, still to be manufactured by SNCAN. Deep cuts to France's military spending were being made at this time and there were also plenty of cheap surplus Allied aircraft on offer. Nevertheless, Arsenal's aircraft attracted plenty of interest at the Paris show

and it was claimed to have attained on test a speed of 435mph (700km/h) at 22,965ft (7,000m). One report understood that the first VB 10 was now regarded purely as a flying test bed for the tandem powerplant.

VG 10-02 first flew from Villacoublay on 21 September 1946 with 1,150hp (858kW) 12Z-12/13 engines installed; it also featured an all-round vision canopy, modified undercarriage doors and had all ten guns. Unfortunately, both prototypes were plagued by mechanical problems and engine overheating, which delayed the flight test programme. Although generally connected with the engines, more often than not the technical issues came about through the use of unsatisfactory or incorrect equipment chosen to save money. The airscrews, for example, did not have their necessary full range of pitch. A July 1947 report on the first prototype added that the VB 10's handling was 'clearly inadequate' and it was slow to enter a turn. Its general its stability was fine, but the stall came suddenly, the control surfaces were not balanced and at indicated speeds above 311mph (500km/h) there was a small amount of flutter at the tail.

The first production machine flew on 3 November 1947 (the original plans had expected to see this aircraft flying before the end of 1946). Changes for the production run included a taller, reshaped fin and deletion of the six machine guns (the first six production aircraft were built with the original fin), but speed performance from series aeroplanes proved to be no better than that of the prototypes. The third prototype, VB 10-03, served as the photo-reconnaissance prototype with provision for the camera fitting, and flew on 30 June 1948, but again the lack of performance meant that it fell short of current piston-powered reconnaissance aircraft. A two-seat version, with the second crewman placed behind the rear engine, was also considered.

On 10 January 1948 VB 10-01 was lost during a speed test after its propeller suddenly

Note the engine exhausts on the sides of the first VB 10's fuselage.
Le Fana de l'Aviation

The first production VB 10 with the taller fin and rudder, plus redesigned main undercarriage doors and just the four 20mm gun armament. This front-angle photo provides good comparison with the similar view of the prototype. *Alain Pelletier*

switched from coarse to fine pitch, forcing rods from the aft power unit to break through the crankcase and ignite the oil. Before he escaped by parachute, test pilot Pierre Decroo kept his burning aircraft in the air long enough to take it beyond the village of Antony, near Paris. Decroo suffered leg and head injuries, and severe burns. For his bravery he was awarded the Officer's Cross of the Legion of Honour later that month. VB 10-01 crashed in an open field, while prototype 02 suffered a similar problem in March 1948, but without such serious consequences. Then, on 15 September that year, the third production machine was lost at Méaulte while also under test. Henri Koechlin, a SNCAN test pilot, died when the VB 10 hit the ground.

These events gave the VB 10 something of an unfortunate reputation, but it was the aircraft's mechanical and aerodynamic weaknesses that brought the end. The

programme was cancelled on 21 September 1948 (the decision to abandon the VB 10 had in fact been taken the previous 18 February), with many airframes at an advanced stage of assembly. At 1 March 1948, ten airframes had been completed, twelve were 70% finished and another fifteen had reached 50%. At final cancellation the first, second and fourth production aeroplanes had accumulated thirteen, four and three test flights, respectively, and these, plus the surviving prototype, were scrapped. Some accounts indicate that the number of completed airframes eventually totalled between twenty-five and thirty, but in most cases they were still short of certain equipment and the majority were scrapped without ever having flown.

As a concept the VB 10 powerplant, with its engines set in tandem and driving, via concentric shafts, contra-rotating propellers, was very advanced for the early war years. But by the time it actually flew, almost all piston-engine fighter designs, no matter how ingenious their powerplants may have been, had been rendered outdated by the arrival of jet-powered aircraft. In fact the VB 10 design as a whole was hampered by the complexity of its powerplant. It also suffered problems of poor aerodynamic flow around the tail and its flying qualities were such that only very experienced pilots were allowed to fly it.

Airframe

The VB 10 was a low-wing, cantilever, all-metal monoplane. Construction of the semi-monocoque fuselage comprised four longerons and a straightforward braced structure, the frame in welded steel tube and then covered in a skin of non-stressed contreplaqué metallique, which was smooth Dural sheet welded electrically to a corrugated-sheet base. A single large radiator was mounted centrally beneath the centre section. The same contreplaqué metallique was used to cover the two-spar wing and tail surfaces, except for these it was stressed. Built in one piece, the wing had constant taper from the root in both chord and thickness, and featured split flaps; thickness/chord ratio at the root was 18%, at the tip 9%. The guns were housed in the middle wing section (cannon inboard of machine guns) and fired outside the airscrew arc.

The unarmed first prototype's Hispano-Suiza 12Y-31 12-cylinder, liquid-cooled engines, mounted in tandem and geared together, each provided 860hp (641kW) of power. The second prototype had two 1,150hp (858kW) 12Z engines, while the first production machine received a pair of 12Z-15/16 units maximum rated at 1,300hp (969kW). The 12Z two-speed supercharged engines drove two, three-blade counter-rotating, co-axial, constant-speed Ratier metal airscrews. The arrangement was that the forward unit drove the rear propeller, with the rear engine driving the forward prop, the shaft for the latter passing through the axis of the former. Either engine could be shut down for cruising flight.

The pilot's seat was mounted over the interconnecting shaft, and between the coupling-shaft tunnel and radiator were two fuel tanks containing 77 Imp gals (350 litres) in total. A 123-Imp gal (560-litre) tank was housed in each inner wing, inboard of the gun bays. Production fighter-bombers had the four

Some of the team that worked on the VB 10. *Michel Cristescu*

20mm cannon and provision to carry one 500kg bomb under each wing. With the machine guns deleted and the change to reconnaissance duties, internal fuel load increased to 365 Imp gals (1,660 litres). Two cameras were installed in the aft fuselage for reconnaissance.

The first prototype had a flush, sliding canopy that obstructed visibility to the rear, while the second machine introduced a bubble canopy for an improved view out. With its late 1930s' heritage, the VB 10 retained a tailwheel undercarriage, the main legs retracting inwards into wing centre-section recesses. The tailwheel was fixed and unfaired and the main gears were unusually large, with a travel of more than 21in (53cm), a feature specified by the French Air Ministry following experience with American and British undercarriages which, in general, were considered weak.

The VB 10's powerplant and contra-rotating propeller. *Michel Cristescu*

2 Aérocentre NC 1070 and NC 1071 (1947 and 1948)

Aérocentre NC 1070 and NC 1071

Type: three-seat naval bomber

Span: 65ft 7.5in (20m); NC 1070 24ft 7in (7.50m) folded

Length: NC 1070 33ft 6in (10.21m), NC 1071 35ft 3in (10.75m)

Gross wing area: 537.63sq ft (50sq m)

Gross weight: NC 1070, ship based 23,448lb (10,636kg), land based 23,907lb (10,844kg); NC 1071 30,313lb (13,750kg)

Powerplant: NC 1070 2 x Gnome-Rhône 14 R-25 piston engines each 1,600hp (1,193kW); NC 1071 2 x Rolls-Royce Nene turbojets each 5,180lb (23kN)

Max level speed: NC 1070 359mph (578km/h); NC 1071 497mph (800km/h)

Diving speed: NC 1070 307mph (494km/h)

Service ceiling: NC 1070 32,645ft (9,950m); NC 1071 42,650ft (13,000m)

Climb rate: NC 1071 2,950ft/min (900m/min) at sea level; time to 13,125ft (4,000m), NC 1070 6 minutes 50 seconds, NC 1071 5 minutes; time to 26,739ft (8,150m), NC 1071 17 minutes 30 seconds

Range at 13,125ft (4,000m): NC 1070 2,115 miles (3,400km); NC 1071 622 miles (1,000km)

Armament (not fitted to NC 1070): 2 x 20mm fixed forward firing guns, 2 x 20mm in rear turret, 4,409lb (2,000kg) of bombs or torpedoes. NC 1071 same, except no rear turret

The end of the Second World War allowed the French to begin looking towards the acquisition of new military aircraft for the first time since 1940. One category to come under consideration was a carrier-based 'multi-mission' aeroplane for delivering bombs or torpedoes and the studies resulted in two prototypes, the Nord 1500 Noréclair covered in the next chapter and the Aérocentre 1070. Neither type entered production.

NC 1070

Although France was still occupied by the Germans, in 1943 the Marine Nationale (French Navy) began a clandestine programme for a new dive-bomber, torpedo-bomber and anti-submarine aircraft. After the liberation, a number of studies were opened for this type of aeroplane in 1944. It had been retained as part of a planned rearmament programme and the project that was to become the NC 1070 was first produced by SNCASO (Société Nationale de Constructions Aéronautiques du Sud-Ouest) as the SO 1070. Sud-Ouest's Issy les Moulineaux office in Paris's western suburb, headed by chief engineer Charles Pillon, was responsible for the work and the facility had previously specialised in carrier-based bombers. The factory had been part of SNCAO (Société Nationale des Constructions Aéronautiques de l'Ouest), but in mid-1945 the project was moved to SNCAC, the Société Nationale de Constructions Aéronautiques du Centre (or Aérocentre), the aircraft now becoming the NC 1070.

The French Navy predicted that it would require at least 100 new aircraft in this category and requested an order of fifteen prototypes, twelve to operate from land bases only and three equipped for carrier operation.

In fact, only three were ordered (on 20 August 1945, under Contract 4193/45) and the first of these made its maiden flight on 23 May 1947. In the cockpit for the initial flight was Fernand Lasne, Aérocentre's test pilot, and the flight test programme revealed that the NC 1070 exhibited good flying qualities, but not especially good performance, in part because the engines did not supply sufficient power.

During a test flight on 9 March 1948 the NC 1070, known as the 'Tabouret' (Stool), suffered undercarriage failure during an emergency landing near Toussus-le-Noble. Although the aircraft was not badly damaged, the decision was taken not to repair it since interest in putting the piston type into service had passed. Also, work was now under way on building the second airframe with a jet powerplant, as the NC 1071. The NC 1070 never received its full armament and in fact its rear turret was only ever installed for trials purposes while the aircraft was on the ground. By May 1949 the NC 1070 had been stripped of its radial engines and was thought to be awaiting modification to 1071 standard, which in the event also never happened.

Aircraft Engineering magazine for April 1949 reported that Aérocentre had claimed that the NC 1070 possessed some of the advantages of both the tailless and normal aeroplane, though the article noted that it was difficult to see where the tailless virtues had been retained. The large fins and high tailplane had ensured longitudinal and directional control, but it was considered that the type's relative aerodynamic cleanness was debatable.

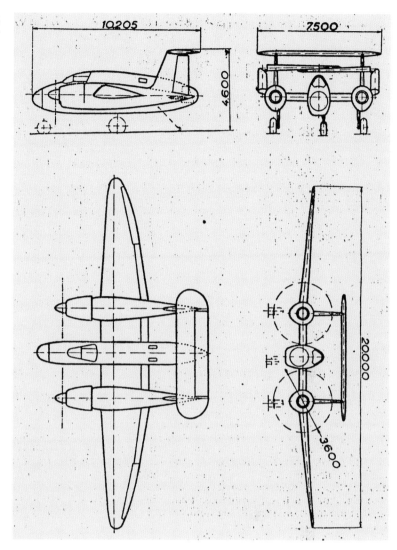

Three-view drawing of the NC 1070. *Aircraft Engineering, April 1949*

Here the Aérocentre NC 1070 has its long fuselage bomb bay open.

17

The Aérocentre
NC 1071,
jet-powered
prototype.

NC 1071

Work on the follow-on NC 1071 continued because it was a relatively easy change to have two jet engines in place of the piston units. The Nenes were built under licence by Hispano-Suiza and the switch to all-jet powerplant was covered by an amendment to the CN 1070 contract dated 24 November 1949, though the decision to go ahead with this had been made much earlier, on 23 October 1947. As such the type became France's first twinjet aircraft, but the cost of the project ensured that there would be no series production; however, the opportunity to test a twinjet aircraft would be of great value to the industry as a whole. Lasne took the NC 1071 on its first flight on 12 October 1948, accompanied by flight engineer Marcel Blanchard, the aircraft taking off from Toussus-le-Noble and landing at CEV Brétigny.

By the time of the Paris Salon in May 1949 the NC 1071 had, according to *The Aeroplane*, only completed ten to fifteen flights since its maiden sortie. The 20 May 1949 issue of the British magazine described the air display at Orly Airport that followed the Salon on 14 May. Its comment on the NC 1071 noted: "It accelerated quickly, the nosewheel was pulled up, and at a high angle-of-attack the aircraft climbed into the air. There then followed a few runs at about 350mph. This grotesque-looking aircraft fails to give any impression of efficiency. Its one good feature is that with huge round intakes both Nenes can breath well." The equivalent issue of *Flight* magazine noted: "The bizarre-looking twin-Nene NC 1071 possesses unusual slow flying qualities; it seemed happiest, in fact, at the lower end of its speed range, approaching and touching down with becoming sobriety."

CEV's evaluation of the NC 1071 began during 1949 with some of the flight testing apparently being undertaken by Roger Receveau (another test pilot heavily involved with the aircraft was Claude Dellys). The assessment came to a halt on 27 July, however, after the fourth flight, when the NC 1071 suffered damage the aircraft became uncontrollable and overran the runway. Repairs lasted eighteen months but several modifications were also introduced, including smaller, high-pressure tyres; a longer and more heavily glazed nose; and fuel tanks in the wings, providing more space in the fuselage for test equipment.

Frequent incidents and consequent repairs brought further interruptions until the programme came to an end in June 1951. During a high-speed run at Mach 0.7 on 8 May 1951, the 1071, piloted by Jean Sarrail, suffered damage around the engine nacelles after the onset of flutter and, although it was not severe, the decision was made not to make repairs. Later, on the NC 1071 went to the maintenance school at Rochefort for use in ground instruction.

In the air the NC 1071's rudders were effective but heavy, giving only adequate control throughout, especially at speeds below 124mph (200km/h). Below 249mph (400km/h) the aircraft was longitudinally unstable and quite rough riding, especially in the landing configuration, and had little stability above these speeds (the NC 1071 experienced vibration at high speeds). Although handicapped from being

a design incompatible with the approach of transonic speeds, and also by the method of its construction, the heavy NC 1071 presented a very reasonable performance for an aircraft whose thrust/weight ratio fell below 0.4. However, its flight characteristics at low speeds meant that significant changes to the airframe were needed to make it suitable for operation from aircraft carriers.

In 1948/49 a fighter version, designated NC 1072 was considered, featuring wings swept slightly at the leading edge. A model of this project was displayed at the May 1949 Paris Salon, but any ideas for a go-ahead were given up due to a predicted lack of performance – new jet bombers would have outclassed the design.

Airframe

The NC.1070 was an all-metal, twin-engine aircraft with mid-position wings, a fuselage nacelle, and engine nacelles that formed tail booms to carry twin fins (in effect, it was a three-fuselage aircraft). The tailplane was mounted on top of the fins. The large, tubby, oval-section centre fuselage was made using normal semi-monocoque construction and there was a bomb bay running almost its whole length to provide space for a torpedo, bombs or depth charges. Its nose had glazed panels to allow the pilot to sight his target and the prototype had glazing at the rear for a turret

The NC 1071's substantial size is confirmed by the presence of two ground staff.

In this view the NC 1071 is thought to be at CEV. The photo was taken prior to the aircraft's July 1949 crash, since it has the original observer's glazing and a nose pitot. *Mike Kirk*

The great majority of views of these aircraft were taken on the ground. This pair shows the NC 1071 in its original form and with engine nacelle covers in place.
Michel Cristescu

(which, if fitted, would have had a reasonable all-round field of fire). The crew stations were completely separated, the pilot entering the cockpit by way of a door in the starboard side and the gunner through a port side door.

The wing structure was divided into five parts – a centre section joining the two nacelles (and passing through the fuselage) and two outer portions on each side. These outer sections were hinged to each other and double folded hydraulically, and the section inboard of the outer fold had a span of only 3.28ft (1m). The port wing folded first, just outboard of the nacelle, and the starboard would lie above it. The final folded width was exactly the same as the tailplane span. The land-based coastal patrol version did not have wing folding and the removal of the associated equipment and arrestor hook reduced tare weight by about 176lb (80kg). Frise-type

ailerons with balance tabs were fitted, while the wing was made in light alloy with stressed metal covering for the wing and flaps, but fabric on the ailerons.

The horizontal tail surfaces were similar to the wing in that the tailplane was metal while the elevators, which had a balance tab, employed fabric covering. Between the rear fuselage and nacelles there was a small and quite unorthodox adjustable tailplane used for tail trimming, resulting in a 'biplane' tail configuration. In their design and manufacture the rudders were similar to the elevators, while the tall fins were built integrally with the ends of the two nacelles.

The Gnome-Rhône 14 R-25 engines had neat close cowlings that blended well into the nacelles, and were of opposite rotation (in the early 1930s France had been the first country to seriously adopt opposite-rotation airscrews

The NC 1071's extremely bulky appearance is accentuated in this view, which also provides detail of the wing and fin. *Michel Cristescu*

on multi-engined aeroplanes). They drove three-blade, constant-speed, fully-feathering airscrews of 11ft 10in (3.6m) diameter, but apparently they did not supply the quoted maximum 1,600hp (1,193kW) of power. All of the fuel, 319 Imp gals (1,450 litres), was housed in the centre section and the heavy tricycle undercarriage had double main legs (although single legs might have been fitted on production machines had they gone ahead). The nose leg was offset to port in order to clear the bombsight windows.

Apart from the switch to jet engines with larger nacelles for the jet pipes, the NC 1071 showed few differences from the piston version. The tail turret was replaced by an observer's position and there was a simplified undercarriage, and, as described, fuel was subsequently housed in the wings.

A possibly unique photograph showing the NC 1071 after its nose had been modified with additional glazing.

3 Nord 1500 Noréclair (1947)

Nord 1500 Noréclair

Type: two/three-seat navy bomber

Span: 64ft 7.5in (19.70m)

Length: 46ft 9in (14.25m)

Gross wing area: 494.62sq ft (46sq m)

Gross weight: 26,431lb (11,989kg)
(25,033lb/11,355kg without armament)

Powerplant: 2 x Gnome-Rhône 14 R-28
and R-29 piston engines each 1,600hp
(1,193kW)

Max level speed: 336mph (540km/h) at
9,843ft (3,000m) – CEV testing never
exceeded 261mph (420km/h)

Ceiling: 32,810ft (10,000m)

Max range in still air: 2,145 miles
(3,450km)

Armament: 2 x 20mm fixed forward
firing guns, 2 x 20mm guns in rear turret
(not fitted to prototype); 1 x 45cm (17.7in)
torpedo; 4,409lb (2,000kg) of bombs or
depth charges

The Nord 1500 Noréclair was the second type produced and flown against the French Navy's requirements for a new dive-bomber, torpedo-bomber and anti-submarine aircraft. The first prototype (ordered under Contract 4242/45 of September 1945) was constructed between 1946 and early 1947, in the Issy-les-Moulineaux experimental workshop under the direction of Mr Vicat.

It began its test programme with a first flight from Mureaux on 29 August 1947, with Roger Janin, Nord's chief test pilot, at the controls. There were problems almost immediately, including severe instability that eventually required a new vertical tail. Some sources have indicated that the Noréclair's maiden flight took place on 7 September 1948, but it seems likely that this was the date when the prototype returned to the air after modification; by October the white-painted machine had accumulated several hours of flying.

A formal assessment of the Nord 1500 Noréclair began at CEV Marignane (the home of the CEV before it completed its move to Brétigny) on 8 July 1949. It had arrived the previous day (the original date for delivery to the CEV had been February 1949), but found to be in poor condition with, in particular, very dirty undercarriage hydraulics. As a result, the second CEV sortie did not take place until 25 August. Two more trips were made over the next four days, but then a hydraulic failure halted test flying until 10 September.

CEV discovered that the aircraft was incapable of carrying sufficient stores and was short of equipment. In terms of performance, in clean configuration with the engines running at 800hp (597kW) at 7,546ft (2,300m), the measured climb rate was 1,412ft/min (348m/min) at 131mph (210km/h). The stall occurred at 110mph (177km/h) and with 'everything down', 91mph (147km/h). The control surfaces were found to be well balanced, effective and in harmony, but at times they required considerable effort from the pilot.

Once the hydraulic and some other problems had been cured, CEV was able to report that for normal service use the Noréclair would not present any major difficulties to its pilots. However, there had not been sufficient time to assess the prototype in bad weather or at night. The 10th and last CEV flight took place on 22 September 1949, to give a final total of 11 flying hours in CEV hands. The following day all of the test and monitoring equipment was taken out and a CEV pilot ferried the Noréclair to the Commission d'Etudes Pratiques d'Aéronautique (CEPA, Commission for the Practical Study of Aviation) at Saint-Raphael for further assessment, but there was little enthusiasm for the aeroplane among the pilots who flew it here.

Even at the time of the Noréclair's first flight it was clear that this type of piston-powered aeroplane was somewhat out of date and that production orders were never going to be placed. In mid-1946 Nord had been hoping to win a contract to build 105 machines, and indeed the design attracted quite a lot of interest when the incomplete prototype was displayed at the November 1946 Paris Salon, but by October 1947 it was being reported that the aircraft was unlikely to go into production, at least in its present form. Had any been built for the Navy they would have featured arrestor hooks and rearwards-folding wings.

Given the unreliability of the 14 R engines, consideration was given to fitting the Bristol Hercules as an alternative, but nothing came of this. A further proposal looked at fitting a Nene turbojet in place of the rear turret, the project becoming the Nord 1510, but again it was not followed up. Installing the Nene, for use as required on take-off and for emergency combat performance, would also have required a degree of fuselage redesign (some

sources indicate that an entirely new fuselage would have been needed). With all three power units running, however, it was estimated that a speed of about 480mph (772km/h) would have been possible.

Finally, when the second prototype was apparently around 65% complete, the decision was made to convert the airframe into a specialised coastal surveillance aircraft. The first flight of the second Noréclair was planned for 1 October 1948 and it was envisaged that an order for 35 aeroplanes in this category could be forthcoming in the 1949 Navy budget. A start was made on converting the second airframe, but all work was halted on 15 December.

It is unknown if the construction of a planned third prototype was begun while the first prototype, the only Noréclair to fly, was condemned in July 1950. Prior to that date it had been commissioned into Escadrille 10S with the number 10S-36, although nothing is known of its subsequent time with the unit. In May 1950 it was still classed as 'airworthy', but by then spares were running short and components had been taken from the incomplete second machine to keep it serviceable.

The mediocre 14 R-25 type engines proved to be an Achilles heel for the Nord 1500 Noréclair, but potential customers of the type were also critical of its modest warload. It also retained features of wartime aircraft, making it look rather outdated for 1947.

Detail of the Noréclair's forward fuselage and canopy, and the large engine nacelles. *Michel Cristescu*

The Nord 1500 Noréclair. Note the large main undercarriage wheels. *Collection Jacques Moulin*

Airframe

The Nord 1500 Noréclair was an all-metal, twin-engine monoplane. The inner sections of its single-spar gull wings were fixed, while the outer sections folded outboard of the engine nacelles for stowage aboard carriers. The wings had relatively thick skins and were built as box structures while the fuselage, of ovoid section with flattened sides, was much deeper than it was wide. The tail was also of single-spar box structure and the ailerons, rudder and elevators were all aerodynamically balanced.

Reports indicate that the Gnome-Rhône 14 R engine generated only 1,200hp (895kW) of power, contributing to the Noréclair's lack of performance. Each of the two engines drove a metal, three-blade, variable-pitch, 12ft 1.5in (3.7m) diameter Ratier airscrew; the 14 R-28 and 14 R-29 units differed only in their direction of propeller rotation. The combined internal fuel and oil load amounted to 2,690lb (1,220kg).

The pilot was seated near the nose behind heavily-framed cockpit glazing (it was reported that the pilot's view seemed inadequate) and there was a separate glazed enclosure over the observer's seat, in the fuselage between the wings and fin. The mainwheels of the tailwheel undercarriage retracted into the engine nacelles and there was a novel retractable arrestor hook immediately to the rear of the tailwheel. The long fuselage bomb/torpedo bay was divided longitudinally and its doors were in sections to accommodate the curved shape of the lower fuselage. A tail turret with twin 20mm guns was to have been fitted to production machines.

The Nord 1500, showing the rear crew station. *Collection Jacques Moulin*

Here the 1500 is on public display. *Michel Cristescu*

| A nose view of the Noréclair, with an open access door. *Michel Cristescu*

| The wing junction, fuselage shape, engine nacelle and French Navy roundel are evident in this view. *Michel Cristescu*

4 Gloster E.1/44 'Ace' (1948)

Gloster E.1/44 'Ace'

Type: single-seat jet fighter prototype

Span: 36ft (10.97m)

Length: TX145 38ft (11.58m), TX148 38ft 11in (11.86m)

Gross wing area: 254sq ft (23.62sq m)

Max weight (analysis on TX145 on 26 March 1947): 13,550lb (6,146kg) with 300 Imp gals (1,364 litres) of fuel

Powerplant: 1 x Rolls-Royce B.41 Nene 5,000lb (22.2kN) thrust

Max level speed: 620mph (998km/h) at sea level

Service ceiling: 44,000ft (13,411m)

Absolute ceiling: 48,000ft (14,630m)

Climb rate: time to 40,000ft (12,192m): 12.5 minutes

Range: approximately 650nm (1,204km)

Armament: 4 x fixed 20mm cannon in nose. Planned underwing stores detailed below

Gloster Aircraft will forever be remembered for producing Britain's first jet-powered aircraft, the E.28/39 research prototypes and the Meteor jet fighter. The Meteor dominated the firm's workload from 1943 onwards, but Gloster still had time to produce more jet fighter designs, and these led to a prototype that was never officially named, but unofficially christened 'Ace'. However, when the aircraft's flight test programme began in 1948 its configuration was already out of date and it possessed little or no development potential. In terms of British fighter design, the 'Ace' would become one of the relatively unknown 'also-rans'.

The first official flight by a British jet aircraft, the Gloster E.28/39, was made on 15 May 1941 and Gloster quickly followed it with a twin-jet fighter that flew in March 1943 and entered service as the Meteor. However, using the single-jet experience gathered from the E.28/39, Gloster also moved ahead with a new single-engine fighter design covered by Specification E.5/42, as featured in Hikoki's *British Experimental Combat Aircraft of World War II*, published in 2012.

Three E.5/42s were ordered, but the programme quietly faded away and sometime in late 1943 or early 1944 the E.5/42 project was replaced by a new design. By 7 February 1944 the E.5/42 prototypes had been cancelled and on that day their SM-series serial numbers were re-allocated to the new Gloster type. There was a new specification, E.1/44, the E.5/42's unofficial name 'Ace' was carried through to the new aircraft and a brochure describing the project was completed in late January 1944; 'Ace' was probably a Gloster nickname since contemporary magazine articles always refer to E.1/44.

The powerplant was to be a de Havilland Halford H.2, which was expected to give 4,000lb (17.8kN) of static thrust at sea level and later entered service as the Ghost. Gloster felt that it would offer the new fighter a very high level of performance and the brochure described the aeroplane as "a compact and aerodynamically exceptionally clean machine", with the predicted levels of drag reduced very considerably to about half those of the Meteor. Estimates suggested a maximum speed from sea level to high altitude approaching 600mph (965km/h), at the time a very impressive figure that corresponded to a Mach number of 0.80 at sea level and 0.90 at 40,000ft (12,192m) – and this would be complimented by an excellent rate of climb.

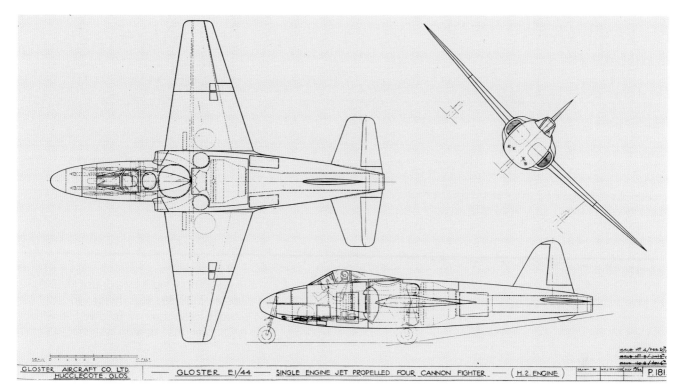

Specification E.1/44, first raised in February 1944 and embracing official Operational Requirement (OR) 157, covered the design and construction of a 'single seat jet-propelled interceptor fighter'. For a short period it was actually designated F.1/44 ('F' for Fighter), but a switch was made to experimental status; the prototypes themselves were always looked on as combat aircraft, however. Three prototypes,

Gloster drawing P.181 of 20 February 1945, showing how the E.1/44 design with the de Havilland H.2 engine looked at that stage. *National Archives*

TX145, TX148 and TX150, were ordered in January 1945 as additions to the airframes left over from the E.5/42 plans.

Gloster drawing P.190 of 20 February 1946, showing the Rolls-Royce B.41 Nene-powered version of the E.1/44. *National Archives*

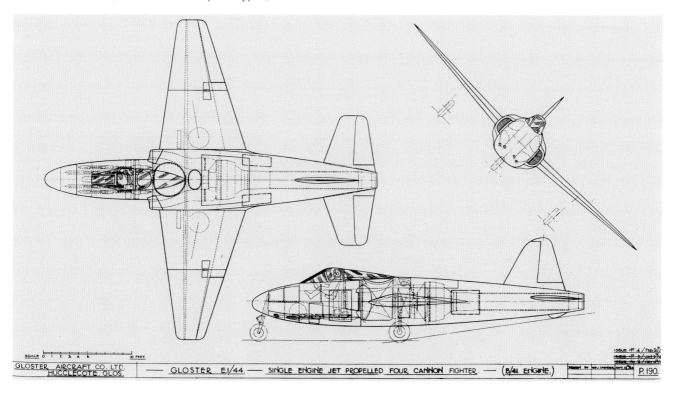

Official photographs of the unmarked prototype SM809, which never flew. This aircraft had a rudder horn balance at the tip of the fin whereas the next prototype, TX145, had the rudder hinge extended to the tip, the only difference between the two airframes. Note also the box-like anti-spin parachute housing beneath the rudder. *Peter Green Collection*

Although the type would never be supersonic, E.1/44 stated that the effects of compressibility had to be allowed for in the airframe's stress calculations. The maximum speed was to be at least 560mph (901km/h) rue airspeed (TAS) at all heights up to 30,000ft (9,144m) and the altitude where the rate of climb would drop below 1,000ft/min (305m/min) (the service ceiling) was to be as high as possible, and certainly not less than 45,000ft (13,716m). Armament was four 20mm Hispano cannon.

In due course the aircraft grew a little in size, but by early July 1944 it had pretty much reached the layout that would be built. However, in September a proposal was made to fit a single Rolls-Royce B.41 Nene engine which, in the event, would become the primary powerplant. This move was brought about by potential delays with the H.2, but it was not a simple case of switching from one engine to the other because the two exhibited fundamental differences. The H.2 consumed high-velocity air passing through ducts connected directly to the compressor casing, but Rolls-Royce's power unit needed the air to be expanded to a relatively low velocity before it entered the engine.

Creating a suitable arrangement of ducting that would work for a Nene in the E.1/44 presented problems because it used up space that was already in short supply. On the H.2-powered model the ducts passed straight through the spar at constant cross section and fed directly into the impellor of the engine. In the case of the Nene the solution was to split each duct so that it ran over and under the straight through spar, with the cross section being increased gradually until entry to the plenum chamber surrounding the engine impellor. An outcome of these separate air supply arrangements was that the H.2 had two fuel tanks placed behind the main spar, whereas the Nene initially had just the one central tank; it meant that no individual airframe could take both engines.

28

With SM809's wing stubs protruding so far outside its trailer it is hardly surprising that the prototype suffered damage in an accident during the road trip to Boscombe Down. The journey was a long one via Filton and had to contend with narrow roads. The second photo was taken in 'Vicarage Street', but just where that was has not been established. In both cases the photographer was Fred Cheshire, an electrician working at the Gloster company. *Heather Midwinter/Jet Age Museum*

Under a new standardised system of designations introduced by the Society of British Aircraft Companies (SBAC), Gloster allocated G.A.2 to the E.1/44 (although this may have applied to the Ghost prototypes, with G.A.3 for the Nene machines – G.A.1 had been the E.5/42). In early December 1944 Gloster estimated that the first prototype would be completed in August 1945, but in May 1945 discussions were still ongoing as to whether to fit the aircraft with a de Havilland Ghost 10 or a Nene. The line up was eventually decided as: SM809, TX145, TX148 and TX150 (a 'strength test' airframe) would get Nenes, with SM801 and SM805 having the Ghost, but on 7 September 1947 SM801 was cancelled and a decision made to use its wings on SM805. The sixth prototype was intended to test some of the operational equipment and would also receive an ejector seat (something not originally specified in E.1/44).

From 9 July 1946 there were discussions about fitting the upgraded Nene II to give an 'Ace' Mk 2, but at a meeting held at the Ministry's Thames House on 8 August, attended by Sir Alec Coryton, S Scott-Hall, Ralph Sorley and RN Liptrot from the Ministries; George Carter and other Gloster staff; and Messrs Lovesey and Hendrey from Rolls-Royce, it was decided to drop the Nene II variant and proceed with the Nene I alone. On 29 April an order was placed for twenty pre-production aeroplanes with serials VP601 to VP620 and covered by Specification 23/46/P of 15 November 1946. Published sources have indicated these would have been designated G.A.4, while another twenty pre-production

aeroplanes were ordered on 2 July 1946 to the same contract as VR164 to VR183. However, nine days later this second set was cancelled, but the plan was still to run an E.1/44 production line in parallel with the Meteor's.

Another July 1946 report noted how at that stage George Carter, the E.1/44's chief designer, was hoping that airflow over no part of the airframe would become critical until a Mach number for the aeroplane of 0.95 had been attained. Indeed, there was some hope on the part of the technical staff that the machine might actually be able to dive through the transonic region and thus provide data on transonic and supersonic operation. However, the rate of climb was not expected to meet interceptor requirements.

Then a revised issue of Specification 23/46/P disclosed that the 'Ace' was to operate as a low-level 'ground-support' fighter-bomber. Its span was to be reduced to 32ft (9.75m), an ejection seat was to be standard, and external stores would be carried on the underwing pylons – two 500lb or 1,000lb bombs, or two drop tank incendiary stores (napalm). Another alternative for the production aircraft would be eight 95lb (43kg) or 135lb (61kg), or four 305lb (138kg) rocket projectiles, and all of this would require a stronger structure to handle the higher aerodynamic loads associated with low-level operations, which again pushed up the weight and reduced the performance. As a result, on 27 November 1946 the Air Council agreed that the type "would not be accepted for service" – the E.1/44 would now be used for research and experimental purposes only.

SM809 back at the factory after its road accident. Chalk lines below the air intake and above the wing indicate damage to the airframe.

Gloster proposed further schemes for alternative E.1/44 versions, usually with different engines and without major changes to the airframe (except for the tailplane). For example, the P.199 project of 1945 had a 6,500lb (28.9kN) thrust Rolls-Royce AJ.65 (Avon) axial engine. But once the likelihood of production had passed Gloster showed relatively little enthusiasm for the aircraft itself, progress in general was slow and the expected first flight dates were pushed back several times.

Assembly of SM809 in the Bentham Experimental Department was finally completed in July 1947 and it was taken by road to Aeroplane & Armament Experimental Establishment (A&AEE) Boscombe Down for its maiden flight. However, during the journey the Queen Mary vehicle was used to transport SM809 apparently jack-knifed when descending a hill and crashed into a stone wall, damaging the first prototype so badly that it had to be written off as beyond repair (no official reports describing the crash have been traced). SM809's loss accelerated work on the next airframe, TX145, helped in part by having SM809's forward fuselage incorporated into TX145 while the rest of the damaged airframe was used for spares. The accident also first alerted the public to the existence of this second fighter type from Gloster.

TX145 undergoes ground testing at Gloster's Moreton Valence airfield, most likely in November 1947.
Jet Age Museum/ Bill Baldwin

TX145 at Moreton Valence in mid-1948. The aircraft has the rear section of its canopy removed.
Ted Currier

TX145 and ground crew in mid-1948. Access panels have been removed in some photos, but the cockpit canopy is now complete. *Jet Age Museum/ Bill Baldwin*

Mid-1948 views of TX145 show what a clean design the E.1/44 was. *Jet Age Museum/ Bill Baldwin*

TX148 in mid-1948, showing detail of the elevator and rudder.

| This is the only air-to-air image of TX145 known to the author. *Ted Currier*

Having arrived safely at Boscombe Down, TX145 recorded the E.1/44's first flight on 9 March 1948, flown by Gloster's chief test pilot WA 'Bill' Waterton. This was the first time Waterton had taken a brand new prototype up and he eventually christened the aircraft the 'Gormless', because he found that the airframe was just too heavy for its single Nene engine. Even before the first flight, in September 1947 he had experienced trouble during taxiing trials, a nosewheel 'shimmy' at first and then, at 140mph (225km/h), ferocious nosewheel oscillation that resulted in substantial damage to the front end. The prototype had to go back into the workshops for the winter and did not resume its taxi trials until the end of February 1948. On the ground, Waterton's first impressions were of slow acceleration, the elevators seeming heavy and the rudder poor, and the E.1/44 took a lot of stopping. Compared to the "lively Meteor" the 'Ace' was not impressive.

| TX148 during a test flight. *Jet Age Museum*

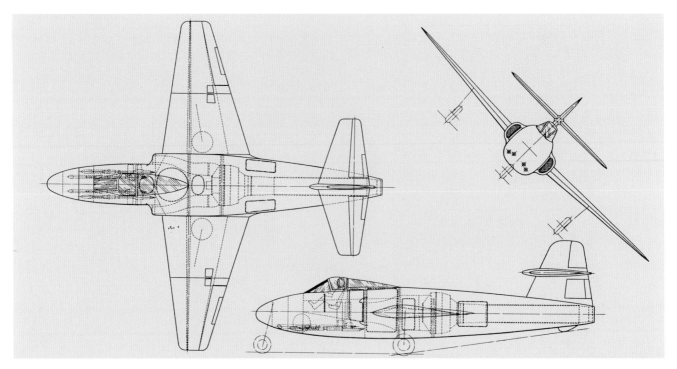

Gloster drawing P.212 of 2 September 1946, showing the E.1/44 fitted with the new high-position tailplane, a modification envisaged well before the first prototype's maiden flight.

Soon afterwards TX145 returned to Gloster's airfield at Moreton Valence to begin manufacturer's development flying. Early sorties showed that it could reach 620mph (998km/h) but there were handling problems, in part due to the horizontal tail's fuselage mounting position. However, prior to TX145's first flight plans were already under way to fit one prototype with a tailplane in a new position slightly more than halfway up the fin. This alternative rear fuselage and tail arrangement had first been drawn as the P.212 on 2 September 1946 and, although TX145 was initially expected to receive it, in fact it was TX148 that introduced the change.

The second aircraft to fly also had slightly larger air intakes than TX145 and its brake chute housing stretched back beyond and above the jet pipe. At one point the intention was to have TX148 allocated to armament work; TX150 was still scheduled for destruction in static tests, while SM805 would undertake more aerodynamic flying, but was cancelled in January 1949.

TX145 was accepted off contract on 22 November 1949, and on 2 December it flew to Farnborough from Moreton Valence to begin operating with the Royal Aircraft Establishment. On 2 November 1950 it suffered an engine flame-out in flight and crash landed, but was repaired within a couple of months. Further damage was suffered on 18 May 1951 when the starboard undercarriage leg collapsed on landing, and TX145 may not have flown again. It was

Struck Off Charge on 2 August and subsequently went to the Proof and Experimental Establishment (PEE) at Shoeburyness. During its Farnborough career TX145 had managed to make a brief appearance in the 1951 feature film *No Highway in the Sky*.

TX148 first flew in 1949. The exact first flight date is unknown, but it was also made from Boscombe Down and the aircraft's handling with the new tail was found to have improved considerably. TX148 was accepted off contract on 3 February 1950 and flew from Moreton Valence to join TX145 at RAE on 14 February, and the roles allocated to the two aeroplanes at Farnborough included parachute-braking tests and research into flying controls systems. Struck Off Charge on 24 August 1951, TX148 also went to Shoeburyness and, like TX145, served as a ground target; it is understood that both prototypes had been broken up by July 1952.

TX150 was cancelled before it was completed. The airframe was accepted off contract on 8 November 1949 and after that date it was used for structural tests up to proof load. On 15 May 1950 TX150 was declared surplus and sold to Cranfield College of Aeronautics for instructional purposes. It was delivered to the College in sections and some parts are known to have survived until at least 1966. An outer wing was at one stage held in the College's 'Library of Flight' and is now with the Midland Air Museum at Baginton. All of the E.1/44s were given a silver finish and none of them ever took part in a Farnborough show.

Official views made in February 1949 of the second E.1/44 prototype TX148 with its high tail. Note also the slightly larger air intake. It is possible that these images were taken at Gloster's Experimental facility at Bentham, around 1 mile (1.6km) from the company's airfield at Brockworth. *Peter Green Collection*

Another official picture of TX148 showing the new tail and modified parachute housing. Note the open plenum chamber doors. *Peter Green Collection*

It is understood that the maximum speed achieved by TX145 in flight was indeed 620mph, although one source quotes 550 knots (633mph; 1,019km/h) but this may have been for TX148. The rate of climb was apparently reported as satisfactory, but handling problems with the original empennage had been a weakness. These appeared to be caused by turbulence around the tailplane, the position of which initially was only a fraction higher on the rear fuselage side than the wing, putting the two surfaces almost in line. Testing with the subsequent mid-fin tailplane position was one area where the E.1/44 'Ace' played a most valuable role.

At this time Gloster's most important fighter was still the Meteor, now long in production, and developed into and manufactured in a number of versions. However, from a performance point of view the early marks were out of date and in 1947 Gloster began modifying the Meteor F.Mk IV, the RAF's standard fighter variant, into the more capable F.Mk VIII (the system for allocating aircraft mark numbers remained in a state of flux during 1947, but from 1948 all Roman numerals were replaced by Arabic equivalents, thus the Meteor F.Mk VIII became the F.Mk 8, its more familiar designation).

Key changes to the airframe included a longer nose that pushed the heavy cannon armament forward, plus additional fuel capacity, both of which affected the centre of gravity (CofG). As the gun's ammunition was used up, the CofG moved aft, an undesirable situation that the old Mk IV tailplane could not compensate for. The 'worst condition of stability' would occur at take-off when the fuel tanks were full and no ammunition was carried, but there was also an acute danger when the Meteor was taken into a turn or out of a dive, where the unstable aircraft would 'tighten' into the manoeuvre. There were also problems of stability and damping with increased altitude and a new tailplane was urgently needed.

Eventually the Gloster design office worked out that TX148's fin and fin-mounted tailplane would be ideal. In fact, by a very fortunate coincidence the E.1/44's 'high tail' had the correct area and gave the requisite lift and control to manoeuvre and stabilise the new, longer-nosed Meteor. Trials showed that the prototype Mk VIII with the E.1/44 fin and tail delivered performance well above that of the old Mk IV. The new mark went on to enjoy a long production run; the long nose and the 'Ace's' high tail had complimented each other perfectly!

Right: A small selection of air-to-air photographs of TX148 exists. Gloster took this one, probably before the aircraft's departure to RAE Farnborough in February 1950. *Peter Green Collection*

Below: TX148 with the modified tailplane. *Copyright Pete West*

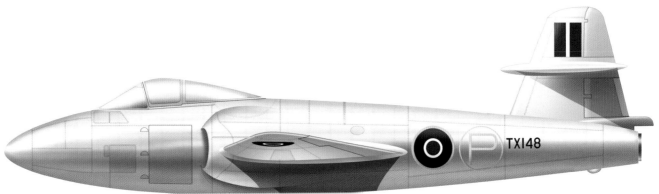

TX148 banks away from the camera, in perhaps the most well known photo of the aircraft in the air.

In contrast, this photo of TX148, taken during a test sortie, has only recently been rediscovered. *Phil Butler Collection*

The adoption of the later tail position for the Meteor fighter was the Gloster E.1/44's greatest contribution to aviation in. VT150 in the foreground was a Meteor Mk IV converted as a full F.Mk 8 prototype with the new tailplane. As such it made its maiden flight on 12 October 1948. *Jet Age Museum*

In spite of extensive searches in many archives and enquiries to a number of people who worked on the aircraft at the time, a full flight test report for the Gloster 'Ace' has never been found. All that is available are the contemporary recollections. Former Gloster employee Cyril Chick remembered that although Bill Waterton made the first flight, it was Jan Zurakowski, the famous Polish test pilot who had joined Gloster in 1945, who did most of the manufacturer's flying (and wrote the reports). Chick suggested that the 'Ace' was a bit of a disaster, in part because it was underpowered. Basically it was too heavy for its engine (one element being the quantity of heavy steel used in the wing spar), which resulted in a rather pedestrian performance. The E.1/44 was a little faster than the Meteor, but to show off its speed Zurakowski had to dive the 'Ace' "to try and get something out of it".

TX148 in a hanger at Farnborough on 7 September 1950, showing the split rudder and main undercarriage. The wing of Avro Lincoln RE284 is visible just above the jet. *Peter Green Collection*

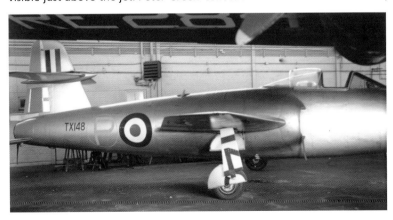

In the RAE archives at the Farnborough Air Sciences Trust (FAST) there is a high-speed wind tunnel test report on the E.1/44 from November 1945 (prior to the first flight). This showed that there was no sign of shock stall at low values of lift coefficient (a measure of the lifting effectiveness of the wing) up to speeds of Mach 0.8, but with nacelle-type drop tanks on the wing there was a considerable increase in drag above Mach 0.65. As the Mach number increased from 0.3 to 0.75 at low lift coefficients the model became increasingly unstable, but it would become stable again at about Mach 0.8. The longitudinal instability that was prevalent between Mach 0.75 and 0.8 may also help to explain why the aircraft's performance was so disappointing.

However 'modern' the E.1/44 may have appeared when it was first designed, by the time it made its maiden flight it looked quite out of date when other British prototypes already had swept wings. The lack of drive and effort by Gloster to keep the project moving, coupled with the loss of SM809 before it had the opportunity to fly, meant that progress was usually quite slow throughout. Overall, the E.1/44 'Ace' must have been a disappointment.

Airframe

The E.1/44 had a mid-position straight wing tapering in plan and thickness, a very broad fuselage and a tricycle undercarriage of exceptionally wide track. The wing thickness ratio varied from 11% at the root to 6% at the tip and its centre-section was formed using a

Since there are so few air-to-air images of the E.1/44 'Ace', photos showing certain angles of the aeroplane are not available. These photographs of an original manufacturer's model of TX148, belonging to the Cheltenham Art Gallery and Museum, provide alternative aspects.

single spar and an auxiliary rear spar with a stressed skin structure built around it. Attached to the centre section were split flaps with 75° maximum deflection, the main undercarriage, dive-recovery flaps and inboard airbrake flaps. A single steel main spar stretched throughout the wing except for the extended (about 5ft/1.5m) tips, which almost constituted outer panels. Chrome molybdenum steel was employed here and for all of the aircraft's internal steel structure, while high tensile steel sheet was used for the wing skinning aft of the main spar (the auxiliary spar was made in light alloy).

Four 20mm Hispano cannon were mounted on the bottom longerons and the outer webs, to give two guns on each side just below the fuselage nose. The centre fuselage housed the Nene engine and also provided the attachment points for the centre wing sections. Detachable 'nostril'-type air intakes fitted with boundary layer bleeder ducts were built into the sides of the centre fuselage and each intake was then divided to pass around the wing spar and lead into a plenum chamber (or pressure casing) that enclosed the complete power unit, the engine exhausting into a 12ft (3.66m) long tailpipe. Fuel was housed directly behind the cockpit in two small and one large tank between the intake ducting. Another fuel tank was placed to each side of the exhaust pipe just rearward of the engine, making five in all for a total capacity of 428 Imp gals (1,946 litres). Provision was also made for two 100-Imp gal (455-litre) underwing drop tanks as alternative loads to ground-attack weapons.

The rear fuselage and detachable tail portion employed semi-monocoque construction. The tail unit components, with the exception of the upper portion of the fin, which was built in wood to insulate the surface aerial, were all-metal stressed skin structures. Both of the elevators had a spring tab and a trimmer tab, while the rudder had a balance tab. The elevator's range of movement on the ground was 25° up and 20° down (TX148, with its tailplane mounted on the fin, had its rudder divided into two sections). All of the control surfaces were internally mass-balanced and a tail parachute (installed for experimental flying only) was housed in a fairing beneath and just behind the rudder. Dive-recovery flaps were placed on the upper surface of the wing just behind the leading edge, close to the fuselage, and the airbrakes (which opened both above and beneath the wing) were in the mid position ahead of the trailing edge. Both the dive-recovery flaps and airbrakes had an angular movement of 60°. A non-steerable nosewheel retracted rearwards, while the two main inward-retracting undercarriage units were attached to the centre-section spar.

5   Aérocentre NC 270 and NC 271 (1948)

NC 270

Type: jet bomber
Span: 65ft 7.5in (20m)
Length: 71ft 2.5in (21.70m)
Gross wing area: 835.48sq ft (77.70sq m)
Gross weight: 61,706lb (27,990kg)
Powerplant: 2 x Rolls-Royce Nene turbojet each 5,000lb (22.2kN)
Max level speed (estimated): 539mph (867km/h) at 29,530ft (9,000m)
Cruising speed (estimated): 513mph (826km/h)
Service ceiling (estimated): 41,010ft (12,500m)
Climb rate: time to 29,530ft (9,000m) (estimated) 5 minutes
Max range at 29,530ft (9,000m) (estimated): 2,360 miles (3,800km)
Armament: 4 x 15mm or 20mm guns in rear turret, up to 11,023lb (5,000kg) of bombs

NC 271-02

Type: single-seat aerodynamic research aircraft
Span: 24ft 11in (7.60m)
Overall length: 26ft 8.5in (8.14m)
Gross wing area: 123.01sq ft (11.44sq m)
Gross weight: 7,496lb (3,400kg)
Powerplant: NC 271-02 1 x Walter 109-509A rocket motor 3,420lb (15.2kN)
Max level speed (estimated): 559mph (900km/h)

A French military aircraft design entirely of the post-war period, the Aérocentre NC 270 jet bomber was never completed. However, for the purpose of finding potential problems with the full-size machine, and in a similar way to the UK with its flying scale models for the V-bombers from Avro and Handley Page, it was decided to build and test a pair of piloted aerodynamic models that received the designation NC 271. One of these made it into the air, contributing to France's first attempt to acquire a heavy jet bomber.

NC 270

In January or February 1946, the Société Nationale de Constructions Aéronautiques du Centre (SNCAC, or Aérocentre) was notified of an intent to order a new jet bomber design designated NC 270, which had been proposed by the company in response to a programme set up in September 1945. The order was made official on 23 May 1946 under contract 5116/46, covering one full-size prototype and parts for a second, plus two 0.4-scale flying models.

Maxime Robin led the design work and during the development process it was realised that the 270's wing loading would be excessive, so the wingspan had to be increased from the original 62ft 4in to 65ft 7.5in (19m to 20m) with the area going up from 768.8sq ft to 835.5sq ft (71.5sq/m to 77.7sq m). A model of the NC 270 was shown at the 1949 Paris Salon and it was reported that it was hoped that a first flight would occur in August or September of that year. In fact there had been further problems due to excessive weight and other factors, and the NC 270 prototype (under construction at Aérocentre's Boulogne-Billancourt factory) had been cancelled by the Armée de l'Air in October 1947. Quite why the NC 270 model was displayed at Paris in 1949 is unknown, but work on the scale models had been permitted to continue.

NC 271

The two NC 271 scale models of the NC 270 were also built at Boulogne-Billancourt. The first faithfully reproduced the NC 270's shape and proportions, except that it retained the bomber's original tail and fin configuration (the full-size aircraft had since been

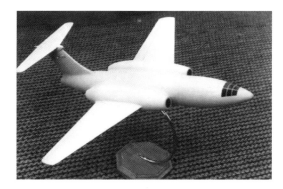

Manufacturer's model of the NC 270 in the configuration in which it was to be built, with a T-tail.

redesigned with a T-tail). In an emergency the 271's nose could be released to parachute its pilot to safety.

The first example, the NC 271-01 glider, piloted by Claude Dellys, was carried aloft aboard an Sud-Est SE 161 Languedoc transport a dozen times between 19 October and December 1948, in each case without release from the carrier aeroplane. It was intended for low-speed trials and sat on the Languedoc's back on two forward masts and a rear bracket. The composite flights were made at altitudes around 14,765ft (4,500m), which allowed an aerodynamic assessment to be made, and load measurements to be taken, of the NC 271's true characteristics compared to estimates made previously in a wind tunnel; in fact the amount of lift provided proved to be a little higher than predicted.

Dellys achieved the first separation from the Languedoc and subsequent free flight above Orléans-Bricy airfield on 28 January 1949, the Languedoc being piloted as previously by Marcel Perrin, a specialist in this kind of flying. Two more separations were made, on 16 February and again in early March, the procedure being to make the release when the required speed had been reached in a dive from 16,405ft (5,000m).

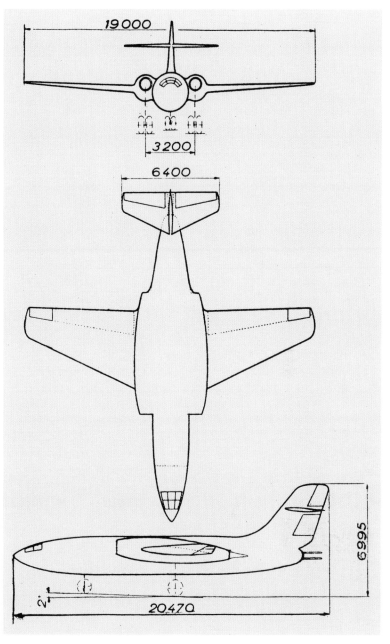

Manufacturer's three-view drawing of the NC 270 in its original form. At this stage the bomber had a span of 62ft 4in (19m) and length 67ft 2in (20.47m).

Below Left: The NC 271 scale model aircraft loaded aboard its Languedoc carrier aircraft. *Fabrice Cario*

Below: The NC 271 shortly before release on a trials flight. *José Fernandez*

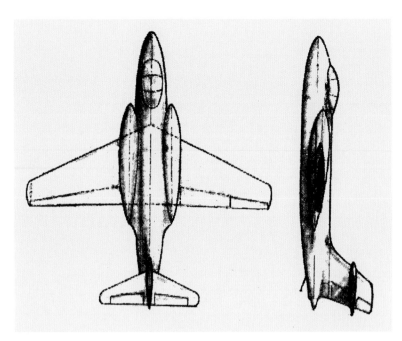

Above: The NC 271 on view in Paris in 1946.
JC Carbonel

Left: Manufacturers drawing of the NC 271.

The Aérocentre NC 271 was displayed on a pedestal at the November 1946 Paris Salon. *Flight* magazine mistakenly described the aircraft as the mock-up of a jet fighter.

The NC 271-01's glide back to ground level did not take long, about 6 to 7 minutes flying at almost 140mph (225km/h), but the results obtained from the first two drops confirmed the design's good aerodynamic characteristics. It was considered that changes to the flying controls would be unnecessary, and it is also understood that for the third release the NC 271-01 had received some alterations to its wing.

The second NC 271 introduced a rocket motor, a German bi-fuel Walter HWK 109-509 providing 3,420lb (15.2kN) of thrust for 53 seconds, and also featured the 270 bomber's T-shaped fin and tail. At one stage the factory was expected to have completed NC 271-02 by 1 March 1949 and a first release was then planned for 1 July, but in the event the bright red painted aircraft was only completed shortly before the closure of Aérocentre.

The powered high-speed research machine was transferred to Orléans-Bricy early in May 1949, with first flight now expected during September. It was to be carried to 32,810ft (10,000m) by an ex-German Heinkel He 274 four-engine bomber, and in free flight was

expected to reach a speed of 559mph (900km/h). However, the second NC 271 never flew – the abandonment of the NC 270 bomber had hastened the end of Aérocentre; the firm was liquidated in October 1948 and the factory closed in June 1949.

It is understood that both NC 271s were handed over for disposal soon after the closure. Having been stripped of useful equipment the NC 270 prototype, which had reached 85% completion, was released for scrapping on 14 December 1950.

In 1949 a study had been made for a rocket-powered interceptor fighter based on the NC 271-02 and designated NC 272, but this never left the drawing board (neither did a proposed rocket fighter version of the SNCASO SO M1 project covered in the previous volume in this series, which was apparently proposed at around the same time).

Airframe

The NC.270 was a large, very clean mid-wing monoplane with Nene turbojets installed at the sides of its circular fuselage. The wing was swept 26° at the leading edge. Fowler flaps occupied much of its trailing edge and spoilers were also fitted. The tailplane was mounted on top of the single fin and there was a large fairing acorn at the junction of fin and tailplane to reduce interference drag.

The tricycle undercarriage featured double main and nose wheels, while the lower fuselage

Heinkel He 274

Two German-designed Heinkel He 274 piston bomber prototypes were built at Suresnes in France but did not fly before the end of the war. Ateliers Aéronautiques de Suresnes, a company previously known as Farman, subsequently made them airworthy and they were first flown on 27 December 1945 and 27 December 1947, respectively, as the AAS 01A and AAS 01B. The aircraft were used for high-altitude research and as 'mother planes' to carry several different types of test aeroplane in readiness for their first flights. The NC 271-02 never got that far, but the He 274 did take some Leduc research aircraft *(Volume I)* and the SO M1 aloft.

contained a 29ft 6in (9m) long bomb bay. The crew station was located at the extreme nose, and a tail turret was to have been fitted to production machines, housing four 15mm or 20mm guns. When the NC 270 project was abandoned the method of control for these guns had still to be clarified.

The low speed NC 271-01 glider was of composite construction (wood and metal), but the NC 271-02 was all-metal since, it was intended to achieve rather higher speeds and consequently experience much greater loads. The NC 271-01 had its tailplane placed high on the fin, but on the NC 271-02 it was on top of the fin. Bulges to each side of the fuselage represented the 270's powerplant installation. Differences from the NC 270 included a bubble-type canopy, single main wheels and a tailskid replacing the nosewheel.

6 Sud-Ouest SO 6020 Series (1948)

SO 6020

Type: single-seat jet fighter prototype
Span: 34ft 9.3in (10.60m)
Length: 49ft 2.5in (15m)
Gross wing area: 270.96sq ft (25.20sq m)
Total weight (interceptor): 16,433lb (7,454kg)
Max weight: 17,778lb (8,064kg)
Powerplant: 2 x Rolls-Royce Nene turbojets each 5,000lb (22.2kN)
Max level speed: 601mph (967km/h) at sea level, 609mph (980km/h) at 32,800ft (10,000m)
Service ceiling: 39,370ft (12,000m)
Rate of climb: 5,920ft/min (1,804m/min) at sea level; time to 32,800ft (10,000m) 9 minutes 13 seconds
Range: 950 miles (1,530km)
Armament: 6 x 0.5in (12.7mm) machine guns, or 4 x 15mm or 20mm cannon

SO 6021

Span: 34ft 9.3in (10.60m)
Length: 49ft 2.5in (15m)
Gross wing area: 284.95sq ft (26.50sq m)
Total weight (interceptor): 15,146lb (6,870kg)
Max weight: 18,408lb (8,350kg)
Max level speed: 534mph (860km/h) at sea level
Max Mach number: 0.96
Climb rate: 5,313ft/min (1,619m/min) at sea level; time to 32,800ft (10,000m) 8 minutes 20 seconds
Service ceiling: 42,650ft (13,000m)
Armament: 6 x 20mm cannon

SO 6025

Type: single-seat tactical reconnaissance aircraft prototype
Span: 34ft 9.3in (10.60m)
Length: 49ft 2.5in (15m)
Gross wing area: 284.95sq ft (26.50sq m)
Max weight: 19,929lb (9,040kg)
Powerplant: 2 x Rolls-Royce Nene turbojets each 5,000lb (22.2kN) and 1 x SEPR 251 rocket motor 3,310lb (14.7kN)
Max Mach number in level flight: In excess of 1.00 at altitude with rocket lit

For its time a sizeable fighter, the fearsome-looking the Société Nationale de Constructions Aéronautiques de Sud-Ouest (SNCASO) SO 6020 Espadon was an unusual design with a remarkably large fuselage and relatively small, sharply swept wings. The first prototype was criticised for its air intake position, which was revised for the second example, while the third introduced supplementary rocket power. The type did not reach production, remaining as one of France's 'industry of prototypes'.

SO 6020

Lucien Servanty's design team opened studies for the SO 6020 in 1945 and an order for three prototypes was placed on 28 June. The work was performed against the first post-war French fighter programme and the aeroplanes were covered by Contract 4484/45. Developed from the SO 6000 Triton (the first French jet aircraft to fly) described in Volume I, the SO 6020 had several unusual features. In particular there was a ventral air intake to feed its

44

Nene engine (which was to be built by Hispano under licence from Rolls-Royce), a rather strange framed cockpit structure and a tricycle undercarriage with what the aviation press described as an excessively wide undercarriage track. As first proposed the underfuselage intake was placed level with the cockpit; on the first prototype it was further back, but there were constant problems in finding the best way of supplying air to the engine, SNCASO testing many different air intake positions.

The first prototype was registered F-WFDI and made its initial flight on 12 November 1948, piloted by Daniel Rastel, Sud-Ouest's chief test pilot. A report from December 1948 noted that the SO 6020 was intended for quantity production to equip Armée de l'Air fighter squadrons (although only three prototypes had thus far been ordered) and flight testing with the solitary prototype was continuing at Orléans-Bricy. At that stage the aircraft was named Gerfaut, but by the time of the Paris Salon in May 1949 it had been given a new name, Espadon (Swordfish).

In May 1949, Britain's *The Aeroplane* magazine described the SO 6020 as "a huge ungainly creature with a very long nose and cockpit with a vast transparent canopy." The article added: "The designers have swept all of the surfaces and it has a sharp nose almost suitable for supersonic flight. Then behind they have put an intake which must excite all of the shockwaves in the district." Another report covered the June 1949 Orly air display in which the SO 6020 took part. It described the Espadon in the air: "The machine was flown at speeds up to 450mph (724km/h), it did some steep climbs until it hit the cloud layer, but was otherwise flown carefully and without dash." Earlier that month the second prototype had been put on display at the Paris Salon where it showed three gun ports on each side of the fuselage nose, with magazines for the ammunition visible in the lower part of the fuselage centre section between the undercarriage mainwheel wells (the Espadon also took part in the Orly Air Display in June 1950).

By the time of Paris in May 1949 the SO 6020 had completed twenty flights totalling 12 hours of flying time. A wind-tunnel model, displayed at the show with the second prototype, had also been tested at the Royal Aircraft Establishment at Farnborough, England. In fact the Espadon's unusually large fuselage and cockpit led many Salon visitors to think that the type was a two-seater.

The original SO 6020-1. Note the long pitot. *Michel Cristescu*

By the time of the 1949 Paris Orly display the SO 6020's fin area had been increased. This angle also shows the original air intake design and the aircraft's French civilian registration F-WFDI. Note the heavily framed canopy.

The first SO 6020 Espadon, with the original fin.

The SO 6020's large canopy made it appear that the aeroplane was smaller than it actually was. *Phil Butler*

Below: The air of dereliction about this photo suggests it was taken after the first Espadon had been retired. The fourth Sud-Ouest SO 6000 Triton, F-WFDH, stands behind, with what looks like the Aérocentre NC 1071 beyond that.

The air intake proved to be a difficult problem. The original underfuselage position on SO 6020-01 was exposed to stones and dirt thrown up by the undercarriage tyres and on several occasions repairs had to be made (it reached the stage where ground crew would sweep the tyres to release stones trapped in the grooves). This arrangement was clearly flawed and when the famous mathematician and engineer Theodore Von Karman inspected the Espadon he reportedly said, "If you make this work well, then you make fools of us!"

In the air, however, the SO 6020 flew perfectly well up to a speed of Mach 0.72, but above that figure the engine began to suffer from an insufficient supply of air and would eventually flame out. On one occasion when test pilot Jacques Guignard experienced this very problem he was only able to successfully relight the Nene at the very last moment – less than 985ft (300m) above the ground! At the 1949 Paris Salon there had been general criticism of the original intake position, and the designers soon appreciated that the first example was underpowered and accordingly offered insufficient performance.

Consequently, the second Espadon (6020-02) had the ventral intake replaced by unusual buried NACA-type lateral air inlets positioned in the fuselage sides aft of the wheel wells. Jacques Guignard took this aircraft, F-WFOV, on its maiden flight on 16 September 1949. In June 1950 it went to CEV Brétigny for its first official evaluation. This revealed a mix of good qualities and design flaws, but it proved difficult for the pilots to make a full assessment since the Espadon's fuel use per sortie had to be kept to a maximum of 264 Imp gals (1,200 litres) to ensure

SNCASO photographs of SO 6020-2 F-WFOV. Note the air intakes just to the rear of the main undercarriage wells. *Alain Pelletier*
Stills from a cine film showing SO 6020 F-WFDI being displayed at Orly in May 1949. *Alain Pelletier*

Above: The SO 6021 in November 1955 during its test bed career, with small engines fitted to the wingtips and the letter 'A' on the fuselage.

SO 6021 F-WFKZ, showing the new fuselage side air intakes.
Michel Cristescu

investigation of high loads at low speeds, or at speeds high enough to produce compressibility was carried out.

The Espadon's longitudinal and transverse stability were found to be poor, but considered acceptable at this stage of the aircraft's development. Handling was also poor – the rudder was effective but quite heavy and the speed brakes were not very effective, with a speed reduction of 15mph (25km/h) taking 12 seconds. The Espadon's qualities as a gun platform were adequate up to speeds of 373mph (600km/h), but above that speed they were not good because of the effort required on the stick to correct deviations in flight. The flaps were rated as good, and on the final approach at 162mph (260km/h) the landing did not pose any particular problems

On 1 December 1949, prototype 01 suffered an electronic failure that forced its pilot to make a belly landing. As a result, prototype 02 took on some of the tasks previously earmarked for the first machine.

that a minimum 88 Imp gals (400 litres) was available if an overshoot had to be made on landing. This left only a short time for specific tests during a sortie and, in addition, because of the unreliability of the aircraft's Heinkel ejection seat at altitude, flight tests were made at heights up to only 22,966ft (7,000m), rather than the desired 29,528ft (9,000m). As a result little

Left: The SO 6021's faired over gun ports are obvious in this view. The large port side main undercarriage also stands out, as does the cut out in the fuselage ahead of the intake to take the main wheel. *Michel Cristescu*

Below: British Ministry of Defence photo of the SO 6021, the fourth and last Espadon built. The aircraft's new fin design is well shown, as is the addition of the letter 'B' to its markings.
Phil Butler

SO 6021

The SO 6021 was a revised version retaining the side intakes and is thought to have been the intended production model. As such it featured a reduction in armament and the quantity of armour plate carried, plus a smaller cockpit, which resulted in a weight reduction of around 882lb (400kg) over the first SO 6020 and formed part of an effort to improve the Espadon's performance. In fact the changes went further in that the lightweight SO 6021 introduced additional wing area, an all-new vertical tail and the addition of servo controls on all three axes (small hinged devices fitted to its control surfaces to provide assistance in their movement). The armament plans now included four 30mm guns, although alternative arrangements included the six 20mm weapons (which were apparently tested).

This fourth Espadon, F-WFKZ, first flew on 3 September 1950, again piloted by Guignard, and had a SNCASO ejector seat, but the air intake arrangement remained unsatisfactory and provided little improvement in performance. In a dive it proved possible to reach Mach 0.96, but on the level serious buffet was experienced at Mach 0.75. Flight testing showed that these changes had not provided any real improvements in the Espadon's handling and the type still lacked manoeuvrability.

Two US pilots flew the Espadon and surprisingly stated that it had some "excellent flying qualities", but they especially criticised its lack of engine power, the buffet at high speed, lack of comfort for the pilot and complex landing gear. In conclusion they declared the Espadon was not good enough to merit future development. Consequently, from 5 July 1951 the Espadon was no longer officially considered as a future combat aircraft – it had proved a failure from a military point of view and a serious financial failure for Sud-Ouest.

However, in February 1951 it was decided to use the Espadon in a trials role for a new programme covering the SNCASO SO 9000 Trident interceptor fighter described in *Volume I*. The SO 6021 was modified with wingtip-mounted, lightweight Turbomeca Marboré II jet engines for work that kept the aircraft flying until 1956. The turbojets were mounted in tip nacelles similar to those on the Trident, firstly without and then with afterburning, and it was also planned at one stage to mount Marboré III engines and then British Armstrong Siddeley Vipers built under license. However, in July 1955 priority was given to the Gabizo engine, which by then seemed to be the most promising of the new engines under development to power lightweight interceptors. The SO 6021's part in the Trident programme came to an end in 1956 after it had flown with different engines in the wingtip nacelles, a Gabizo on one side and a Marboré on the other.

SO 6025

The designation SO 6025 was given to the third Espadon (SO 6020-3), which was designed as a tactical reconnaissance variant and introduced an SEPR 251 liquid-fuel booster rocket to complement the Nene turbojet. It featured double ventral orifices with the rocket placed between them, the additional engine used primarily to improve the aircraft's take-off performance; it also had the larger wing of the SO 6021.

The SO 6025 first flew on 28 December 1949 from Melun-Villaroche and SNCASO claimed, despite the extra weight, that climb performance had benefited 'considerably'. The rocket motor provided 3,310lb (14.7kN) of thrust at sea level and could also (for a few seconds) produce 3,750lb (16.7kN) at 65,615ft (20,000m). Some of the SO 6020's original kerosene fuel capacity was used to accommodate the rocket's furaline fuel (a mix of 41% furfuryl alcohol, 41% xylidene and 18% methanol) while new wingtip tanks contained its nitric acid oxidant.

Below and overleaf: SNCASO photos of SO 6025 F-WFRG, with the additional rocket motor. Camera ports have been cut into the nose.
Michel Cristescu

The dorsal extension of the original fin on the SO 6025 is evident here, as it the type's less extensively glazed cockpit. *Phil Butler*
Sud-Ouest's SO 6025 at the 1955 Paris show, now with the code 'C' painted on its fuselage. *Nicolas Gautier*

The SO 6025 using rocket power for take off.
Phil Butler, Mike Kirk

The SO 6025's first flight employed only the Nene, since at that stage the challenges of operating the rocket had not been met. It was not until 10 June 1952, after a great deal of detailed planning, that Jacques Guignard made the first rocket-powered flight recorded in France. Guignard took the SO 6025 into the air using the rocket motor for 15 seconds on the take-off run and then, during the flight, ran it for another three minutes. Well over a year later, on 15 December 1953, Charles Goujon took the SO 6025 supersonic in level flight, making it the first European aeroplane to fly supersonically on the level. In June 1953 the 6025, registered F-WFRG, took part in the Paris show, *Flight* reporting the Espadon's routine, with its SEPR rocket in action, as "One of the most fearsome spectacles yet seen (and heard) at a flying display".

Most of the SO 6025 fuselage survives today at the Ailes Anciennes Toulouse (Toulouse Old Wings Association Museum), having been recovered from the Suippes firing range near Bourges in 1971, where it had been used as a target. It joined the Museum's collection in 1987.

SO 6026

In order to make a further contribution to the SO 9000 programme, the 6020-2 prototype was turned into the SO 6026 test bed. As such, this second Espadon was fitted with tip tanks and a SEPR 25 rocket mounted right in the aft end of the fuselage (corresponded to the rocket position on the Trident). It first flew with the rocket fitting on 15 October 1951 but, after a series of thorough ground tests, the first rocket-powered flight did not take place until 26 March 1953, the sortie again being made from Melun-Villaroche.

The 6026 displayed the motor at that summer's Paris show and cutting the rocket in after a preliminary flypast allowed the aeroplane (according to *Flight*) to "accelerate straight up out of sight". However, in its mixed powerplant form the SO 6026's flying career was relatively short, embracing just 28 flights, of which only 13 saw the rocket fired. The need for this particular test aeroplane gradually faded away and in early 1955 the SO 6026 was placed into storage.

The SO 6025 during a flypast, probably at the Paris show.

The Sud-Ouest SO 6026, coded 'N' and with the auxiliary rocket motor mounted beneath its rear fuselage. *Mike Kirk*

In terms of production orders, all of the Espadon development effort proved in vain because the contract for France's first indigenous jet fighter design to enter service went to Dassault, with a private venture aircraft designated MD.450 Ouragan (another type powered by the Nene). One report indicates that the French at one time had hopes for a production run of 355 Espadons.

Nevertheless, the four prototypes between them tested early jet engines and first servo-controls in France, swept wings and auxiliary rocket power. Despite their weaknesses they provided SNCASO with a rich harvest of data on high-speed flight. None of the prototypes survives completely intact.

Airframe

The first SO 6020 was powered by a single Nene turbojet fed by an underbody air intake located just forward of the wing root trailing edge; subsequent prototypes had lateral intakes and two of them also received a rocket motor. The Espadon had a swept-back, single-spar, mid-position cantilever wing. All metal, it had stressed skinning and hydraulically operated slotted flaps; ailerons were provided, as were leading edge slots.

The fuselage was all metal, with a 2mm thick skin and no stringers, as was the tail section, which again was of the cantilever type. The Nene was situated in the rear fuselage and four fuel tanks provided a total capacity of 473 Imp gals (2,150 litres). A proposed photo-reconnaissance variant would have featured additional fuel in two supplementary tanks in the area of the wing-fuselage join, containing 175 Imp gals (796 litres) each. No external fuel tanks were to be carried.

The 6020's fuselage was capacious enough to house heavy armament. Initially this comprised six 20mm guns, with the belt boxes for the guns placed approximately over the aircraft's centre of gravity. They were mounted fore-and-aft so that to feed the guns the belts had to be twisted. A small slot above and below each gun port in the fuselage nose allowed muzzle blast to escape, providing a muzzle-braking effect.

An unusually high cockpit enclosure (the result of a French Air Ministry decision to fit an ejector-seat parachute) meant the top of the canopy had to be raised by 6in (15.24cm) compared to the original design. The rather large mainwheels retracted inwards towards the fuselage centre section beneath the wing roots, while the nosewheel folded backwards into the forward body. The Espadons were painted silver.

7   Hawker P.1052 and P.1081 (1948 and 1950)

(Note: Sources vary considerably on maximum speed)

P.1052

Type: single-seat research aircraft

Span: 31ft 6in (9.60m)

Length: 37ft 7in (11.46m) with the original tail, 38ft (11.58m) with the swept tail

Gross wing area: 258sq ft (23.99sq m)

Wing thickness/chord (t/c) ratio: 10% constant

Max weight: 13,550lb (6,146kg)

Powerplant: 1 x Rolls-Royce Nene RN.2 5,000lb (22.2kN)

Max speed: 683mph (1,099km/h) at sea level

Max Mach: 0.87 at 36,000ft (10,973m) with the swept tail in level flight; 0.90 in a dive

Service ceiling: 45,000ft (13,716m)

Absolute ceiling: 49,500ft (15,088m)

Climb rate: time to 30,000ft (9,144m) 9.3 minutes

Radius of action: 310nm (574km)

Armament: provision for 4 x fixed 20mm cannon in nose (never fitted)

P.1081

Type: single-seat jet fighter prototype

Span: 31ft 6in (9.60m)

Length: 37ft 4in (11.38m)

Gross wing area: 258sq ft (23.99sq m)

Max weight: 14,480lb (6,568kg)

Powerplant: 1 x Rolls-Royce B.41 Nene 5,000lb (22.2kN). Installation 1 x Rolls-Royce Tay (Nene IV) rated at 6,250lb (27.8kN) with 20% reheat was planned, but the engine was not installed

Max speed: 696mph (1,119km/h) at sea level

Max Mach: 0.89 at 36,000ft (10,973m) in level flight

Speed/Mach data measured on 15 September 1950 at 12,350lb (5,602kg) take-off weight: max speed 635mph (1,022km/h) or Mach 0.84 at sea level; 601mph (967km/h) or Mach 0.89 at 30,000ft (9,144m)

Service ceiling: 45,600ft (13,900m)

Climb rate: 6,100ft/min (1,859m/min) at sea level

Radius of action: 380 miles (611km) at 35,000ft (10,668m)

Armament: provision for 4 x fixed 20mm cannon in nose (never fitted)

The straight-wing P.1040 land-based prototype first flown in September 1947 was Hawker Aircraft's first jet-powered aeroplane and eventually became the very successful Sea Hawk naval fighter. Two P.1052 prototypes followed, combining the Sea Hawk's fuselage with a new swept wing, but retaining the straight tailplane and split bifurcated jet pipe to either side of the rear fuselage. Eventually, one P.1052 was rebuilt as the P.1081 with swept empennage and all-through jet pipe, and these attractive aeroplanes filled the gap between the earlier types and Hawker's first production swept-wing fighter, the Hunter.

Charles E. Brown photographed VX279 in its original P.1052 configuration on 28 June 1949. *RAF Museum*

Hawker photo showing the P.1052 in planview. Note in particular the bifurcated jet pipe.

P.1052

Hawker's initial P.1052 brochure, submitted on 13 June 1946, commented that since it was "…important that the flight results from this conversion should be obtained with the least delay, as much as possible of the existing design has been retained." The Ministry confirmed on 27 August that it wished to go ahead with the swept-wing variant and the urgency for a quick conversion was the reason why the fuselage and bifurcated air intakes remained almost as per the P.1040.

The outer wing was swept back at 35° at quarter chord (40° at the leading edge). The tailplane was cut down in span from that of the P.1040. The balanced controls of the straight-wing aircraft were retained and although the P.1052 was intended primarily for experimental flight, it could be modified fairly easily for operational use, having been laid out to be equipped with four 20mm guns.

Owing to a national fuel crisis in the UK and the cutting of all heat and light to industry during a ferocious winter, Hawker's entire works was shut down from 10 to 28 February 1947,

although P.1052 design work continued. Two examples were ordered in May 1947, under Contract 6/Acft/1156, after Specification E.38/46 had been written around Hawker's swept P.1040 design. The wings had been assembled by August 1948 and the completed airframe (serial VX272) left Kingston for Boscombe Down on 14 November. It was taxied and then flown for the first time from Boscombe on 19 November 1948.

During a period of lay-up in January 1949, chord was added to the rudder trailing edge to 'heavy up' the rudder. Subsequent flying proved that this modification had greatly improved the aeroplane's lateral handling at low speeds, although the pilot stated the rudder was 'rather heavy'. High-speed flight tests revealed severe tail unit vibration and tailplane incidence was altered to +1° from the previous +0.5°, which proved quite satisfactory and enabled higher speeds and a higher degree of manoeuvrability to be obtained. The test programme now moved forward with some speed and during March a considerable amount of flying was completed.

VX272 in its original natural metal finish.

Left and spread overleaf: It is not well known that A&AEE Boscombe Down was responsible for many superb photos of British military aircraft. These show VX272 off the south coast of England, the aircraft displaying service roundels but lacking fin flashes. *Air-Britain via Phil Butler*

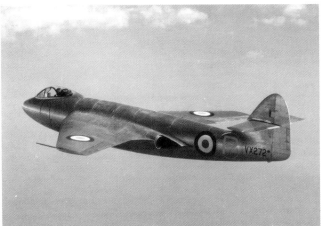

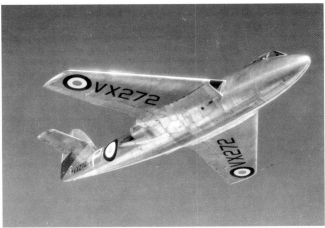

On 13 May 1949 VX272, piloted by Hawker Chief Test Pilot Sqn Ldr Trevor Sydney 'Wimpy' Wade AFC DFC, set a new London-Paris speed record of 21 minutes 27 seconds for the 221 miles (356km) distance. On 29 September the aircraft had to make a wheels-up landing after suffering engine failure, after which, on 4 October it was taken back to Hawker for repairs and the intended fitting of a variable incidence (VI) tailplane.

However, tests on a third structural test airframe had revealed a need to reinforce the wing spars and fuselage mounting frames up to a weight of 12,500lb (5,670kg), so the VI tail had to wait until later. Repairs were finally completed in March 1950 and the aircraft flew again on the 24th, wing-mounted airbrakes and a bullet fairing for the fin/tailplane junction having also been fitted by this time.

On July 1950 it crashed once more, this time on approach to land following another engine failure. The starboard wing suffered damage and as a consequence VX252 made no more flights until 4 September 1951. That month it attended the Farnborough show, where it was flown by Neville Duke, *The Aeroplane* noting that in his demonstration he performed loops and aileron-turns at each end of the airfield to complete a high-speed 'spectacles' manoeuvre.

The first P.1052 makes a carrier landing on 27 May 1952.

The preserved P.1052, pictured in July 1968 in a view that shows how close the pilot's cockpit was to the nose. The aircraft now also sports a bullet fairing at the fin/tail junction.

In March 1952 the first P.1052 was converted to 'high-speed condition' and the bullet fairing fitted in the tailplane junction delivered much improved high Mach number characteristics. On 19 April it was delivered to RAE for high-speed research, and on 27 and 28 May 1952, VX272 performed successful carrier deck trials aboard HMS *Eagle* (the Supermarine 508 (Chapter 17) completed its preliminary trials aboard *Eagle* on 28 and 29 May – a busy time for the carrier). Long-stroke Sea Hawk-type oleos had been fitted for these trials and the aircraft had also been repainted in grey/duck-egg green Navy colours. It arrived back at Dunsfold for 'reversion to standard' on the 29 May.

Almost a year later, on 27 May 1953, it was despatched to the RAE again. This was after the variable-incidence swept tailplane had, at last, been fitted (from June 1952, increasing overall length by 5in/12.7cm), but another

forced landing in September 1953 brought VX272's flying career to an end. On 8 February 1955 it was despatched to RAF Halton to begin a career as an instruction airframe (with maintenance serial 7174M). Later it was displayed outside RAF Cardington in a blue 'ground equipment' colour scheme. Today, PX272 is in the hands of the Fleet Air Arm Museum at Yeovilton.

The second P.1052, VX279 became airborne on 13 April 1949 and in July it performed brief handling trials at the Aeroplane & Armament Experimental Establishment at Boscombe Down, which became involved because of the P.1052's potential as an interceptor fighter. The aircraft was well liked by pilots, generally considered pleasant to fly and free from any vices likely to endanger its safety. Compared to the P.1040, the swept wings had produced the desired effect of a high useable Mach number (0.9), but directional disturbance could result in a lateral and directional oscillation known as 'Dutch roll'. This could be started by turbulent air if the pilot was hands and feet off – it was always 20° both ways and could be damped by the pilot.

Stalling characteristics were good and the only major criticism was the elevator, which was much too heavy for a fighter and tired the pilot rapidly during combat manoeuvres. Mock combat had been made with a Meteor Mk 4 at heights between 12,000ft and 25,000ft (3,660m and 7,620m), with the P.1052 in the attacking role throughout. Immediately combat was joined it was confirmed that the elevator control was too heavy and lacking in response

At the beginning of its flying career VX279 was also left in a natural finish, as shown in picture from 22 April 1949.

and effectiveness. However, Boscombe Down reported that the ailerons were "delightfully quick throughout the speed range", although rather heavy at high speeds. The rate of roll was good and could be further boosted by using the rudder. Taken all round the P.1052 was reasonably pleasant to handle in combat manoeuvres and the increase in critical Mach number and performance over current fighter types gave the pilot greater freedom of manoeuvre. Brief performance measurements made at a weight of 8,750lb (3,969kg) gave a maximum level speed of 515 knots (954km/h) TAS between 20,000ft and 25,000ft (6,095m and 7,620m).

Earlier, in May 1949 VX279 had been displayed at the Paris Air Show, and on 28 June it flew from Langley to Boscombe Down for an assessment by the Royal Australian Air Force (RAAF); it completed 22 hours of flying during the process. Also in July VX279 performed a brief preliminary deck landing trial using the airfield dummy at Boscombe and the resulting report summarised that the P.1052 "was found to be a very easy and pleasant aircraft to fly in simulated deck landings" and "was at least as good as the P.1040 at a similar weight".

The most comfortable approach speed for airfield dummy deck landings was 100 knots (185km/h) indicated airspeed (IAS) (at a weight of approximately 9,100lb/4,128kg). The aircraft touched down in a nose-up attitude and immediately sank forward on to three

points. All pilots agreed that the P.1052's slow-speed handling characteristics were superior to those of the P.1040 – the ailerons in particular were much more effective than on the earlier straight wing aircraft and there was adequate control right down to the stall (although at the stall a sharp wing drop could not be countered by the aileron). 'Dutch roll' was experienced on the approach, but the approach and landing characteristics were considered very good for "a present day jet powered aircraft".

A Hawker publicity photo of the second P.1052, VX279, after it had been painted duck-egg green. The aircraft did not receive a bullet fairing.

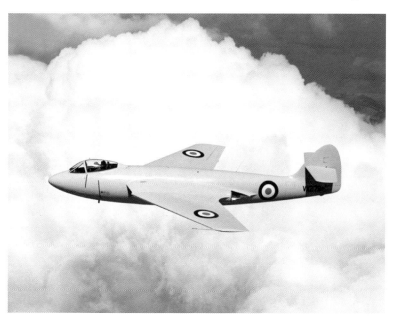

Underside detail of VX279.

On 30 July 1949, VX279 took part in the National Air Races at Elmdon and in early September attended the Farnborough show. From spring 1950 it was converted to P.1081 standard, having already had its metal finish covered over by duck-egg green paint, the lovely colour used for several Hawker prototypes in the 1940s and 50s.

In June 1951, and in response to a Ministry request, Hawker's design team submitted a brochure covering conversion of the P.1052 to take a 4,000lb (17.8kN) thrust Armstrong Siddeley Screamer rocket motor. The original P.1040 prototype, VP401 had already been converted to a mix of jet and rocket power by the addition of an Armstrong Siddeley Snarler rocket and as the P.1072 it first flew in this form in November 1950, the first British mixed-power prototype to fly.

The modifications required to install the rocket in the P.1052 were very considerable. A lengthened front end with pressure cabin would be necessary in addition to a completely new rear end aft of the wing trailing edge, while alterations to the centre section would be required to accommodate fuel, etc.

The object of the conversion was to obtain aerodynamic data at Mach 1 in level flight and to provide a high-speed test bed for the Screamer. However, in its present form the P.1052 was limited by longitudinal and lateral trim changes, and tail vibration, to speeds well below those possible with the rocket motor. Experience with the P.1081 gave some hope that the present limitation of Mach 0.93 or so might be raised, but the P.1052's wing was too thick to be representative of future practice, while the forthcoming Hawker P.1067 (Hunter) would quite likely exceed Mach 1 within two years. In the end the aerodynamic case was not a strong one and the project was abandoned, but serves as an example of the many ideas and proposals that were forthcoming in the 1940s and 1950s to research high-speed flight.

| Comparative 'before and after' photos of VX279 as P.1052 and P.1081. The earlier shot shows VX279 over Thorney Island in 1950.

P.1081

Design work for a sweptback tailplane for the P.1052 began at Hawker in August/September 1949 and on 4 November the company proposed to the Ministry of Supply, as a private venture, a modification of the aircraft with this and a straight-through jet pipe. The Ministry gave full support and Contract 6/Acft/5965 was issued to cover the work. In April 1950, before the aircraft was broken down for conversion into what was now the P.1081, VX279 was fitted with a swept back tail so that experience could be acquired into the affects of this new feature in flight.

On 11 May it went back to Hawker's Experimental Shop for the full conversion. In due course the old rear fuselage was adapted for carrier deck operation and fitted to VX272 for that aircraft's naval trials, while the P.1081 plans also included fitting a more powerful Rolls-Royce RB.44 Tay engine instead of the Nene. The Tay was Rolls' ultimate centrifugal jet engine but it never went into service in a British production aircraft; however, it was built under licence for production types in France and America.

The P.1081 was classed as an interceptor and by the end of January 1950 there was a proposal to build a special prototype for Australia, which by now was showing considerable interest in the new aircraft and its Tay powerplant. Fitting the Tay would involve only a small redesign of the centre fuselage, since the rear fuselage could accommodate a jet pipe suitable for the Tay with reheat. At this stage, however, the Tay was not in production,

Hawker photo showing the P.1081's all-swept configuration.
VX279 following rebuild to P.1081 standard, and after the jet pipe had been enclosed and a fillet added to the fin trailing edge.

a prototype engine would require a year to complete and in the end a planned second P.1081 with the Tay was never built.

However, even the addition of afterburning to the Nene would boost the fighter's potential quite considerably since thrust could be increased for short periods. This would result in improved all-round performance, especially in rate of climb and time to altitude, and predictions made by Hawker in October 1950 indicated that the aircraft's combat ceiling with reheat lit would be around 46,000ft (14,021m) –with no reheat the estimate was 40,500ft (12,344m). Again, although an afterburner was earmarked for the Nene it was never installed. On 26 April it was decided to fit VX279 with the jet pipe used on the Supermarine Attacker fighter.

On 19 June 1950, in its new P.1081 configuration and at an all-up-weight of 11,048lb (5,011kg), VX279 made a 30-minute maiden flight in the hands of 'Wimpy' Wade. After a road move from the Hawker facility it

was again flown from Boscombe Down. A marked longitudinal change of trim was noted above 150 knots (278km/h) IAS and there was a progressively increasing yaw to starboard with speed when the rudder tab was neutral.

Six days later VX279 took part in the Brussels Aero Show and on 22 July it entered the SBAC Challenge Cup Race in the National Air Races held at Sherburn-in-Elmet. On 19 July the P.1081 was displayed to the press at Blackbushe, with an opportunity for air-to-air photography, but after the starboard undercarriage leg failed to come down the aircraft had to make an emergency landing at Odiham, suffering damage to the fairing door and the starboard oleo leg.

During July and August flight testing was carried out to assess various modifications made to the jet pipe fairing, nozzle angle and to the tail unit, Wade and Hawker's Sqn Ldr Neville Duke DSO AFC DFC sharing the flying. These alterations had been made to eliminate directional oscillation, but on 7 July Duke

VX279 at Heathrow Airport on 22 June 1950, where it had landed for refuelling prior to flying on to Maelsbruck the next day and then to Antwerp for the Brussels Aero Show on the 25th. This was the first occasion that the "Secret Swept Wing Fighter", as the press described it, had been shown publicly.

found a tendency to tighten in turns. He also discovered that the rudder was excessively heavy (almost inoperative at high airspeeds) and well out of harmony with the other controls. By mid-August this buffet had been reduced, but tail vibration still developed into buffet at Mach 0.88 to 0.90 at 30,000ft (9,144m).

During this period preparations were being made for production. It was intended that reheat be introduced on production aircraft, but full performance testing with VX279 in the non-reheat condition was also carried out for the Australian version.

Flying during early September was devoted to the SBAC Farnborough Show. The aircraft was then grounded to permit an electric tailplane actuator, a larger tailplane of increased span, and increased-chord rudder to be fitted, the adjustable tailplane having a range of −½° to +2°. Flying resumed on 6 October with these new features and during that month testing covered an investigation into high Mach numbers.

On the 14th it became known that Australia had ended its interest in the P.1081. The RAAF had completed Specification AC.85 on 29 March 1950 to cover the project and on 8 February, having acquired the necessary production licenses, had placed a contract for 72 P.1081s with the Commonwealth Aircraft Corporation. However, further assessment of the type brought the decision to cancel the order and in November the Tay engine was also abandoned.

During November VX279 was grounded once more so that an extended rear fuselage fairing of finer form and additional supports to the jet pipe could be fitted. The fin trailing edge beneath the rudder was extended to increase the area, while the fuselage was stretched rearwards (with a swept end) to fully enclose the jet pipe. In December it was reported that there were still problems with lateral vibration and an increased tendency for rudder buffet. A longitudinal pitching moment was also present in the region of Mach 0.88 and particularly apparent above 30,000ft. Response to the elevator was 'spongy' at high speeds and particularly at high altitudes, and pilots reported that the modifications had not resulted in any improvement to the handling characteristics.

Through December 1950 to February 1951 P.1081's development flying continued. The extended rear fuselage fairing resulted in an improvement in the aircraft's handling and increased top speed by 6 knots (11km/h). Further modifications to the tail unit were performed with a view to solving the problem of buffeting and vibration, culminating in a marked improvement being obtained with a distributed mass balance rudder, which also had reduced trailing edge sweep.

The aerodynamic balance of the elevator was improved by reducing the gap between its leading edge and the tailplane. This had a marked effect on the elevator forces, the stick force per 'g' being more than halved, although above 450 knots (834km/h) and Mach 0.84 it rose steeply and was still undesirably heavy. The overall reduction in elevator forces made the P.1081 much more pleasant to fly and generally improved its manoeuvre potential. The new rudder also had a marked effect on the severity of the lateral Mach number vibration and overall the level of buffet and vibration was now much smaller and no longer placed any restriction on the aircraft's performance. At 40,000ft (12,192m) the vibration was scarcely detectable up to the maximum Mach reached of 0.94, a speed attained on several occasions.

Latterly, tests were made using the landing flaps in conjunction with the dive recovery flap to provide an airbrake effect, in connection with the forthcoming Hawker F.3/48 fighter project (the Hunter). The results were encouraging. Using the dive recovery flaps and landing flaps (down to 40°) as an airbrake at high Mach number showed satisfactory handling characteristics up to an indicated Mach of 0.90, the maximum tested. However, a dive from 37,000ft (11,278m) with landing flaps down 40° showed that Mach 0.90 could be reached easily and there was insufficient drag at this setting to enable a steep descent to be made without exceeding the Mach number at which rapid trim changes occurred (Mach 0.88 to 0.90).

Manufacturer's flight testing was concluded in February 1951 and the covering report showed that Duke was delighted with the aircraft at Mach numbers even as high as 0.94. Wade had just completed a trip to the United States where he had flown the North American F-86A and F-86E Sabre fighters and he concluded that the P.1081 was, certainly at altitude, a better all round fighter than the F-86 (it also carried a far superior armament to the American aircraft). To date the maximum speed flown had been 563 knots (1,043km/h) IAS at low altitude, 569 knots (1,054km/h) true airspeed, where the handling characteristics

The sole P.1081 before wing fences had been fitted to its leading edges.

had been satisfactory, although air conditions gave a moderately rough ride. However, the performance of the P.1081 at altitude had been severely limited by high engine jet pipe temperatures, which had been in evidence since an engine change and after the jet pipe had been lengthened.

In summary, Hawker declared that the P.1081 had now reached a most satisfactory stage of development. At its fully loaded fighter weight it had exceptional performance, virtually viceless handling characteristics, good manoeuvrability and a controllable Mach number range up to at least 0.94. In these fields it was considered superior to any other British aircraft and its potential as a service fighter would be excellent. It was now time to hand the aircraft over to Farnborough for further trials, but on 3 April VX279 was totally destroyed in a flying accident.

About nineteen minutes after it took off from Farnborough, witnesses near Lewes in

Sussex saw the P.1081 at high speed in a near vertical dive. Close to the ground the aircraft appeared to be recovering and starting to climb slightly when an object, later identified as the ML Aviation ejection seat, was seen to fall away. The seat still had the pilot (Wade) strapped in when it struck the ground and he was killed. Losing the canopy made VX279 'recover', and in fact it flew on in a wide right-hand circuit performing various uncontrolled manoeuvres before finally crashing at Ringmer. Fire broke out on impact and most of the aircraft was destroyed. The last flight prior to the accident had been made on 26 February, after which various modifications had been carried out, including the inter-connection of the dive recovery and landing flaps and the replacement of the tailplane actuator. The cause of the loss has never been fully established, but witnesses were first drawn to the diving aircraft by a noise "like a roll of thunder".

VX279 primarily flew high-speed research and both the P.1052 and P.1081 contributed much to the development of the highly successful Hunter, an accomplishment that should not be forgotten after the tragic loss of VX279.

By 8 December 1950 VX279 sported wing fences, added to curb airflow turbulence over the outer wing. *BAE Systems Heritage*

This Rolls-Royce advertisement for the Nene engine shows VX272 and appeared on the front cover of *The Aeroplane* for 6 January 1950.

Airframe

The P.1052 was a mid-wing monoplane with sweepback incorporated on the wings only. The wing used a two-spar structure (main, plus auxiliary rear spar). The ailerons fitted to the trailing edge had spring trim tabs (plus a ground-adjustable aerodynamic tab on the right aileron only); each trailing edge split flap came in three sections and there were dive recovery flaps under the stub wings. The forward fuselage had a semi-monocoque structure reinforced by a box-section keel member and four longerons. The gun ports in the nose were permanently faired over. The P.1052's rear fuselage and its fin and tailplane were the same as those on the P.1040, and its fuel capacity was 395 Imp gals (1,796 litres) in three fuselage tanks.

Besides the straight-through jet pipe, the modifications that turned the P.1052 into the P.1081 embraced a new fuselage of pure monocoque aft of the rear wing spar, a swept-back, variable incidence tailplane and a new fin and rudder, while the original bifurcated jet outlets gave way to a single jet pipe that necessitated the introduction of wing root fillets. The swept tail had a multi-spar/rib structure, and the wing had to be strengthened by fitting additional stringers. The front fuselage, wing and undercarriage were essentially the same as those of the P.1052. The P.1081's adjustable tailplane provided control in the transonic region and trimming throughout the speed range. 'Brake flaps' were provided as an aid to combat manoeuvring and rapid descent from high altitudes, and provision was made for carrying drop tanks under the wings. The original 'pen-nib' style fairing above the jet pipe had to be modified early on to improve directional stability, the fin trailing edge being extended and faired into the jet pipe to increase surface area.

P.1081 VX279 complete with wing fences.
Copyright Pete West

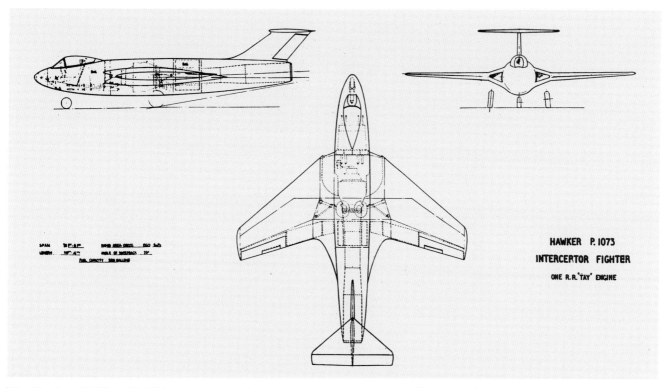

The Hawker P.1052 and P.1081 research aeroplanes prompted a number of studies for single-seat fighter variants, a selection of which are shown here. This is the P.1073 interceptor project of 1949, powered by the Tay engine. Span was 31ft 6in (9.60m), length 36ft 4in (11.07m), sweep wing 35° and gross wing area 260sq ft (24.18sq m). Note the delta tailplane.

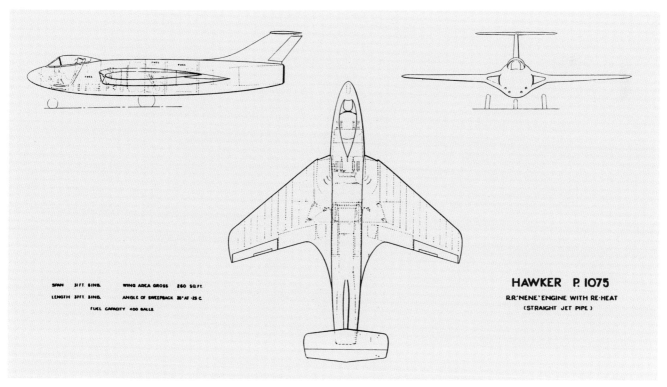

The first Hawker P.1075 interceptor fighter project had a T-tail, reheated Nene and straight jet pipe, plus four guns in the lower nose. Span 31ft 6in (9.60m), length 37ft 3in (11.35m), wing sweep 35° at quarter chord, gross wing area 260sq ft (24.18sq m). Date 16 February 1949.

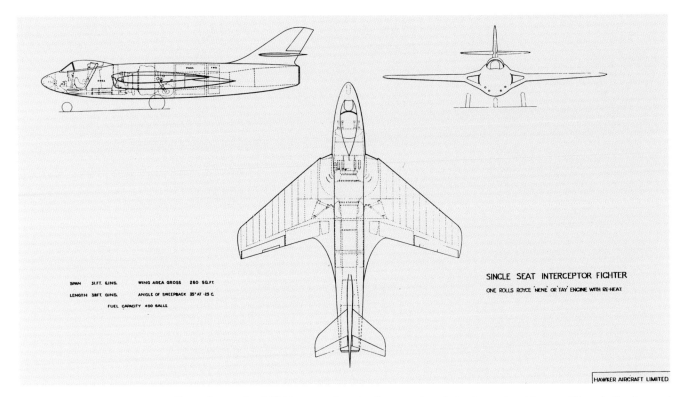

SPAN   31.FT. 6.INS.   WING AREA GROSS   260 SQ.FT.

LENGTH   38FT. 0.INS.   ANGLE OF SWEEPBACK 35° AT .25 C.

FUEL CAPACITY 400 GALLS.

SINGLE SEAT INTERCEPTOR FIGHTER
ONE ROLLS ROYCE 'NENE' OR 'TAY' ENGINE WITH RE-HEAT

HAWKER AIRCRAFT LIMITED.

The P.1075/2 had the same configuration as the P.1075 except that the fin was placed at a lower level in a position similar to that of the company's P.1067 fighter, which became the hugely successful Hunter. The only dimensional change was a length of 39ft (11.89m), and either a reheated Nene or Tay could be fitted. Both P.1075s had a fuel capacity of 400 Imp gals (1,819 litres).

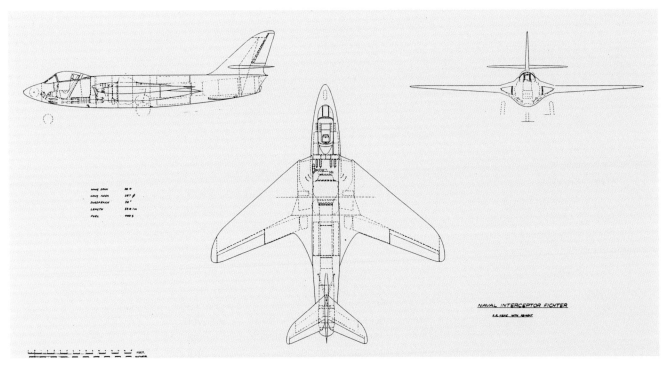

NAVAL INTERCEPTOR FIGHTER

The sleek-looking P.1087 Naval Interceptor would have employed a reheated Nene. Span 36ft (10.97m), length 39ft 1in (11.91m), wing sweep 35°, gross wing area 287sq ft (26.69sq m), four cannon, fuel 400 Imp gals (1,819 litres). Date 22 March 1951.

8 Supermarine Types 510 and 535 (1948 and 1950)

Type 510

Type: single-seat research aircraft

Span: 31ft 8.5in (9.66m)

Length: 38ft 1in (11.61m)

Gross wing area: 273sq ft (25.39sq m)

Wing t/c ratio: 10%

Max weight: 12,177lb (5,523kg), with RATO 12,790lb (5,802kg)

Powerplant: 1 x Rolls-Royce Nene RN.2 5,000lb (22.2kN)

Max speed (source uncertain): 570 knots (1,056km/h) IAS

Max Mach number: 0.93 in level flight

Ceiling: In excess of 40,000ft (12,192m)

Climb rate: Time to 30,000ft (9,144m) 9.3 minutes

Type 535

Type: single-seat research aircraft

Span: 31ft 8.5in (9.66m)

Length: Type 528 38ft 1in (11.61m), Type 535 41ft 1in (12.52m)

Gross wing area: 297.4sq ft (27.66sq m)

Max weight: 14,390lb (6,527kg), overload 15,000lb (6,804kg)

Powerplant: 1 x Rolls-Royce B.41 Nene III 5,100lb (22.7kN)

Max speed (source uncertain): 570 knots (1,056km/h)

Max Mach number: 0.94 at 30,000ft (9,144m)

Ceiling: In excess of 40,000ft (12,192m)

Armament: 4 x fixed 20mm cannon planned but not fitted

The rather pedestrian, straight-wing Supermarine Attacker of 1946 was the Royal Navy's first jet fighter into service. Two Attacker airframes were fitted with swept wings as an experiment, the new version becoming the Supermarine Type 510. Later the second was rebuilt with a tricycle undercarriage as the Type 535, becoming the lead-in aircraft for the firm's Swift jet fighter for the RAF.

Type 510

Supermarine's original proposal brochure for the Type 510 was completed in January 1946 and outlined a version of the firm's E.10/44 jet fighter (which became the Attacker), fitted with swept-back wings and tail. The objective was to obtain full scale experience of high-speed flight and the wing, arranged to pick up the existing root attachments on the fuselage, had 40° of sweepback on the quarter-chord line. This angle had been selected to provide a considerable increase in the critical Mach number without making the aircraft's lateral and longitudinal stability and control excessively difficult. Supermarine added that the time factor was vital since, nationally, Britain was some two to three years behind the USA in the development of such aircraft.

A decision to procure two Type 510 research prototypes was accompanied by the release of Specification E.41/46 on 14 April 1947, which acknowledged that these aircraft were required "so that further knowledge of sweepback and its associated control and stability problems may be acquired". Chief designer for the project was Joe Smith and in many official documents the new type was called the Swift, but this is not to be confused with the later Type 541, which entered service with the official name 'Swift'.

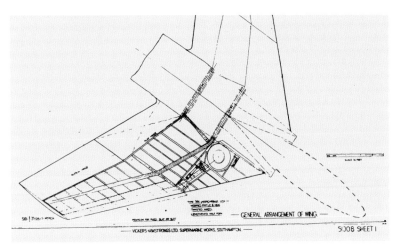

Wing spar detail of the Supermarine 510.

VV106 showing what it is thought to be its original configuration.

VV119 in Type 535 form.

The two 510s, ordered against Contract 6/Acft/1031/CB.7(b), were built at Hursley Park and fitted with Rolls-Royce Nene II engines. However, when the first example, serial VV106, was being inspected prior to its first flight, serious hollows were found in the wings and officials recommended that they be scrapped. Nevertheless, after Supermarine had experimented with fillers it was agreed that the 510 could be accepted for preliminary flights up to a speed of 350 knots (648km/h) with these depressions made good with Araldite. In practice the filling proved very satisfactory, and withstood successfully the highest speeds at which the aircraft was flown.

VV106 became airborne for the first time on 29 December 1948, flying from Boscombe Down and piloted by Supermarine chief test pilot Lt Cdr Michael J. 'Mike' Lithgow, becoming the very first British aeroplane to fly with all flying surfaces swept. Soon afterwards, VV106 moved to Supermarine's own airfield at Chilbolton to begin a programme of low-speed flight trials.

For its initial test flying VV106's nose had taken the rounded form of the Attacker's, but the 510 airframe was soon modified to have a more pointed nose, helping it reach higher speeds and increasing the airframe length by 1ft 9in (53.3cm) – at the same time the aircraft was painted. However, by the time carrier trials began, a return had been made to the blunt nosecone; a strengthened cockpit canopy with heavy framing and smaller windows was fitted at the same time.

Lithgow wrote a report covering the 16 sorties made between the first flight and 21 January 1949, during which the aircraft had fixed leading edge slats extending over rather more than the outboard half of the wings. It was thought that the presence of these slats might cause a longitudinal trim change as speed increased, but no appreciable change was recorded up to the initial limit of 300 knots (555km/h) IAS, while sufficient flying had been done to show that the extent of the slats could safely be reduced (at the time of the report's writing VV106 was grounded so that their size could be halved, the wing leading edge being built up where part of the slat was removed).

Ground handling proved very similar to that of the Attacker, and take-offs were made using 30° flap. In flight the ailerons were on the heavy side by Attacker standards, but just as effective, and the initial approach to land was made at 140 knots (259km/h) with touchdown at about 110 knots (204km/h).

VV106 en echelon with the camera aircraft.

Above and left: VV106 in its original form, during a photographic sortie off the south coast of England on 10 August 1949. *Terry Panopalis*

The test programme came to a halt on 16 March 1949 when Lithgow made a wheels-up landing in VV106 after what was described as 'motor-boating' of the Servodyne actuation of the ailerons. Flying resumed on 10 May and moved up to higher speeds. Lithgow reported in *RAF Flying Review* how: "Within a few flights I was taking it up to Mach 0.9 without any trouble, which at that time was quite phenomenal." A further report from Lithgow covered the sorties made between 11 March and 24 June and noted that the flaps had been modified to introduce a slot between the top of the flap and the wing when they were

| The 510's original air intake shape is well shown in this view.

lowered. They had also been reduced in span by taking 10.5in (26.7cm) from their outboard ends, and while repairs were being affected after the crash, the remaining portions of the slats were also removed.

Buffet previously experienced from the flaps onto the ailerons on the approach was greatly improved by the alterations made to the flaps. In addition, the stalling speed at a weight of around 11,500lb (5,216kg) was 109 knots and 100 knots (203km/h and 185km/h) IAS 'all-up' and 'all-down', respectively, flying characteristics being similar in both cases, with a sharp drop of either wing (but usually the port), preceded by a small amount of aileron snatching.

It had also been found that the 510 became progressively more right-wing-low as speed increased, which required several different approaches to cure. The highest recorded speed in dives was Mach 0.93, but at this speed one wing dropped so far that it required full aileron to correct it (lateral control in fact was lost at Mach 0.93, which made this the limiting Mach number). The wing drop became noticeable at about Mach 0.9 and Supermarine felt that it was caused by asymmetry of the irregularities in the upper wing surfaces, possibly coupled with the loss of aileron effectiveness at high speed. Performance tests suggested a true maximum air speed of 630mph (1,014km/h) at 12,000ft (3,658m).

Early problems had in fact appeared at both the high and low ends of the speed range; at minimum speeds tip stalling was apparent, causing pitch-up. Despite having swept wings, the 510 remained a taildragger, so that on landing pilots had to ensure they kept the aircraft on the level because the wingtips and deployed flaps came very close to the ground.

In October 1949 Supermarine summarised the work done with VV106 over 62 flights, stating that the introduction of swept wings had not only increased maximum speed by 50mph (80km/h), but that the effects of compressibility had been considerably delayed and reduced. Reaching Mach 0.93 also meant that VV106 was at least 100mph (161km/h) faster than the maximum permitted speed of any British fighter type in service. Exceptional rates of roll had been obtained (of the order of 160-180°/sec) after the application of Automotive Products Servodyne power-assistance to the large ailerons via spring tabs, a system that had been perfected after two-and-a-half years of research and development.

VV106 had also made six very successful flights at the Farnborough show in the first half of September, where it flew at speeds up to an estimated 670mph (1,078km/h), making it the fastest aeroplane at the show. In its report, *Flight* magazine declared that this "was probably the fastest flying yet seen in Great Britain," and "almost equally amazing was the rate of roll at very high speeds."

Manufacturer's photo of VV106, still with its Attacker nose and canopy. The fairing to the rear of the tailplane contains an anti-spin parachute.

VV106 with the pointed nose fitted. *Air-Britain via Phil Butler*

A similar view of the Type 535. The 'lipped' jet pipe, introduced to provide a download on the tail and thus reduce take-off run, is seen clearly here.

Above: Two pictures of VV106 taken by an A&AEE photographer. Note the 'P' in a circle marking, identifying the aircraft as a prototype. *Air-Britain via Phil Butler*

Right: Few images appear to exist showing VV106's undersides. *Air-Britain via Phil Butler*

VV106 had been delivered to A&AEE on 19 September 1949 to begin handling trials, where opinions on its performance somewhat at odds to those of its manufacturer emerged. Severe vibration and flicking at high airspeeds was discovered, along with intermittent yawing, the latter of a sufficient amplitude that there were concerns about the airframe's structural strength. It was cured by raising the louvres on the boundary layer bleed plates proud of the aircraft's skin, and increasing plenum chamber ventilation.

A Fairey Firefly and a late mark Supermarine Seafire stand behind VV106 while the research aircraft is prepared for another flight.

There was also a tendency to tighten in turns, crosswind landings were reported as "horrid", and the combination of swept wings and a tailwheel was roundly condemned by A&AEE. However, it was also confirmed that, although there was a limit to the maximum useable lift-coefficient in the transonic region, the introduction of sweepback had so improved the high Mach number drag characteristics that there was considerable improvement in lift at high speeds. But sweepback had also brought longitudinal instability prior to the stall, which limited VV106's manoeuvrability at high altitude to about 2g, while the aircraft's level turn performance suffered from a lack of engine power; in fact at 40,000ft (12,192m) the 510 was almost confined to straight flight.

Despite these points the aeroplane was fairly easy and pleasant to fly, and seemed free of the troubles that had been forecast for aircraft having a large amount of sweepback. Boscombe Down's pilots added: "With a tricycle undercarriage and improved elevator control the aircraft should have the makings of a good fighter."

In the meantime RAE Farnborough had made comparative flights between the 510 and an F-86A Sabre, finding that the 510's performance at low level was inferior, with a maximum speed of 520 knots (964km/h) against the Sabre's 580 knots (1,076km/h), but at 25,000ft (7,620m) the types showed near identical speeds – 536 knots (993km/h) for the 510 and 538 knots (997km/h) for the Sabre.

A deck landing assessment was made by A&AEE in March 1950, after which VV106 was declared suitable for carrier landings, despite the tendency for wing drop when flying at speeds slightly above the stall. It was reported that at low speeds the controls were light, well harmonised and moderately effective, but appreciably better than those of the straight-wing Attacker. After modifications from late July onwards to adapt the aeroplane for carrier operations it was flown again (by Lithgow) on 20 September 1950. The first carrier landings by any swept-wing aircraft were performed on 8 November aboard *HMS Illustrious*, a new 'sinking' approach being used at a speed of around 130 knots (209km/h); the pilot was Lt J Elliot RN.

The first Type 510 about to land aboard *HMS Illustrious* on 8 November 1950. A rocket is just visible beneath each wing root and the aircraft appears to have a landing light in its nose. The undercarriage doors were removed for the trials and an A-frame arrestor hook fitted.

A rare snapshot of VV106 departing the carrier. Note the deployed flaps and ailerons.

Take-offs could only be performed and measured using rocket assistance, however, and on one take-off the next day a rocket failed to fire. The asymmetric power caused VV106's port wingtip to clip one of the carrier's gun turrets and the subsequent landing ashore by Lt Cdr D. G. Parker required a considerable level of skill. Fitting a four-rocket installation, one above and below each wing, permitted VV106's loaded weight to rise to 12,790lb (5,802kg). With the trials over, all of the naval equipment was removed.

General trials at high Mach numbers continued into 1952. When the 510 was first proposed it was hoped that the swept wings would confer the ability to make dives at speeds in the region of Mach 1.0 and it was acknowledged that maintaining full control at such speeds made it desirable, if not essential, that the tailplane could be adjusted in flight. Now VV106 was fitted with a new and unusual rear fuselage, the whole of which was hinged to rotate in the vertical plane by 4° up or down.

With the aircraft redesignated as the Type 517, work began on the installation in February 1952 and VV106's flight test with this variable incidence empennage proved that the arrangement was a powerful and effective trimming device under all conditions up to the limiting speed of Mach 0.95. A&AEE's pilots also liked the new configuration's improved handling characteristics, but one of them had to make a wheels-up landing at Farnborough on 14 November 1952 after the undercarriage failed. Following repairs, Supermarine pilot Sqn Ldr David Morgan took VV106 aloft again on 2 September 1953.

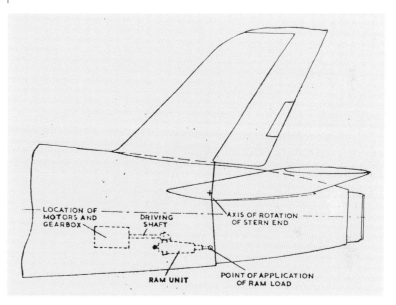

LOCATION OF MOTORS AND GEARBOX — DRIVING SHAFT — AXIS OF ROTATION OF STERN END

RAM UNIT — POINT OF APPLICATION OF RAM LOAD

The variable incidence tail and rear fuselage fitted to VV106 later in its flying career.

While VV106 was serving as ground instruction airframe 7175M it was painted in this now well-worn camouflage scheme. This photo was taken at Cardington on 9 September 1961 and the aircraft appears to have the variable incidence tailcone still in place. *Adrian Balch*

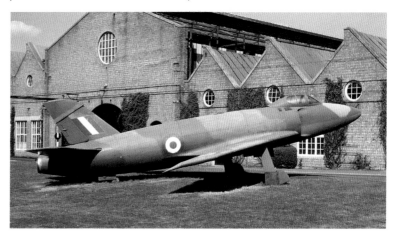

The aircraft continued flying until 14 January 1955 when it was Struck Off Charge, after which it was allotted to ground instruction duties at RAF Halton as 7175M. For a period VV106 was displayed at Cosford, but today it resides at the Fleet Air Arm Museum at Yeovilton. Flight logs from 1954 continued to call VV106 the Swift.

Type 535

The second aircraft, serial VV119, was first flown on 27 March 1950 in Type 510 configuration with a pointed nose. In fact it was known as the Type 528, since it introduced larger air intakes of a different 'elephant-ear' shape, plus a modified rear fuselage in readiness for reheat, although it began its flying career with a Nene II. The aircraft's delivery had been delayed because the original fuselage was used to replace an Attacker fuselage after one of the prototypes crashed and was written off. VV119's manufacture then continued slowly, while approval was given to make provision in the wings for four 20mm Hispano guns, requiring shorter-span ailerons (this facility was later removed after a decision to install guns in any production aeroplanes in the fuselage).

Supermarine's report covering flight trials between 27 March and 6 May showed that much of the flying was devoted to an investigation of buffet on the elevator experienced between 0.72 and 0.74 Mach. Mach 0.92 was obtained on Flight 6 and it was not found necessary to touch either aileron or rudder trimmers, unlike VV106, which required the full range of trimmer at this speed. Aileron buffet was severe at Mach 0.92, however, and the aircraft's IAS was accordingly limited to a maximum of 520 knots (964km/h).

On 4 May, less than six weeks after first flight, VV119 was flown back to the Supermarine Experimental Shop for rebuilding with a tricycle undercarriage and a completely redesigned nose with space for a nosewheel, making the airframe 36in (91cm) longer. The modifications required considerable alteration to the wing shape at the root extension, resulting in a 24sq ft (2.23sq m) increase in wing area compared to VV106, the root being extended forwards and backwards, thereby increasing and decreasing the inboard sweep angles on the leading and trailing edges, respectively. In addition, the air intakes were moved forward by 6in (15.2cm) and the main undercarriage repositioned aft of the rear spar.

The aircraft flew for the first time in this form as the Type 535 from Boscombe on 23 August, again with Mike Lithgow in the cockpit. The longer nose brought a loss in directional stability and the vertical fin had to be extended by means of a long, tapered dorsal fairing, while at the same time the one-piece bubble canopy was replaced by a more conventional framed format.

VV119, photographed prior to the 1950 Farnborough show and highlighting the enlarged intakes. Note the dummy guns in the wings, just outboard of the main undercarriage. The venue is thought to be Chilbolton.

Reheat had also been fitted to what was now a Nene III installation (the only example of the engine to have this feature) and VV119 first flew with it on 1 September 1950; the arrangement proved unsuccessful and the standard Nene was restored. The reheated Nene required a larger diameter, lengthened fuselage to accommodate the installation and fair in the Nene exhaust pipe (in 528 form the jet pipe protruded aft by more than 12in/30.5cm); there was also a special tailcone to reduce diameter at the rear end and preserve the aircraft's aerodynamic shape. Only the one flight was made with reheat operative, but since there was some doubt concerning stresses in engine components the amount of reheat thrust provided was small. Reheat was switched on at all speeds from 250 knots (463km/h) to 500 knots (927km/h) IAS and no abnormal behaviours were noticed.

Lithgow reported that the modified stern had been successful in completely eliminating the elevator buffet experienced in VV119's original configuration. The aircraft was flown at a maximum weight of 14,070lb (6,382kg) and ground handling with the new tricycle undercarriage was described as "excellent". Take-off was straightforward, but the unstick distance was excessive, almost certainly because of an inability to raise the nosewheel off the runway until a speed of about 120 knots (222km/h) had been attained. It was subsequently found that a 'lipped' jet pipe, which gave a download on the tail of about 200lb (907kg), enabled the pilot to raise the nosewheel at just over 100 knots (185km/h) and thus reduce the unstick distance by 300-350 yards (275-320m).

Supermarine Type 535 VV119.

This photo of VV119 was released for publication on 4 September 1950, just prior to Farnborough. The 535 had a heavily-framed canopy from the start, and the tailwheel is also worthy of note. The 'lipped' jet pipe is not yet fitted. *Peter Green*

The aircraft was flown to an indicated Mach number of 0.93 (probably 0.94 true) and, contrary to the Type 510, no lateral trim change was present at this speed. The Mach number characteristics of the aircraft included a gradual nose-down trim change from at about 0.86, which could be held or trimmed out (the latter method was thought preferable). These tests were made at maximum power, but even so, a fairly steep dive was necessary. There appeared to be a large drag increase at about 0.92, and consequently the altitude at which the maximum speed quoted was reached was 30,000ft (9,144m) or below. However, altitude did not appear to be a very critical factor and, since in the dive from 30,000ft, 0.92 was reached at 10,000ft (3,048m) without difficulty. VV119 was dived several times to 575 knots (1,065km/h) and on one occasion, in very still air, to 590 knots (1,093km/h) IAS.

At high altitude the elevator had a 'spongy' feel and the response to stick movement was sluggish. Aileron control and rate-of-roll was of a very high order, as on the 510, but with the Servodyne disengaged the ailerons were extremely heavy and regarded as acceptable only in an emergency. Over 200 knots (370km/h) the rudder became very heavy and over 300 knots (555km/h) not more than a quarter rudder could be applied.

Flight tests with the 535 were encouraging enough for production of a developed version, broadly meeting the same requirements as the Hawker Hunter, to be considered. In October 1950 two Type 541 prototypes were therefore ordered with serials WJ960 and WJ965, and the new type was officially named Swift. The first was virtually a 535 with a Rolls-Royce Avon RA.7 axial jet (a version of the Hunter powerplant) replacing the centrifugal Nene, but the second aircraft came much closer to the intended production standard. In due course the Type 541 would resemble the 535 only superficially.

VV119 took part in the Farnborough show in September 1950 and afterwards, while the Swift prototypes were being built, the sole 535 was subjected to a complete handling test between October 1950 and August 1951. The object behind this effort was to find indications of possible trouble and to develop the airbrakes; the trials revealed longitudinal instability and tightening in turns at high altitude. The high Mach number wing-dropping tendency was already known, but it was shown that by removing "mechanical faults" in the aileron circuit the wing drop could be held. A forward movement of the centre of gravity cured the longitudinal instability, while the airbrake trials revealed that landing flap alone was an excellent and very efficient airbrake, producing no change in trim, but a 3.5° change in incidence. VV119 completed its contribution to the Swift development programme by successfully undergoing spinning trials. A Ministry document from June 1954 stated: "There is no doubt that had the Type 535 not been available, Swift development would have been slowed down."

On 28 December 1950 VV119 was flown with wing fences to ascertain the effect these might have on its aerodynamics. During July 1951, Supermarine performed a speed check on VV119 with all its modifications and recorded level flight figures of 622mph (1,001km/h) at 15,000ft (4,572m), 609mph (980km/h) at 26,000ft (7,925m) and 583mph (938km/h) at 35,000ft (10,668m).

Later, "drag-inducing upper surface flaps" were tried, but they created substantial buffet at high speed. With only landing flaps used for aerodynamic braking the 535 could be slowed from its maximum speed down to 160 knots (296km/h) at low altitude in 58 seconds, or it could glide down from 40,000ft (12,192m) at a rate of 25,000ft/min (7,620m/min) without going above Mach 0.79.

Mike Lithgow displayed the 535 at the September 1951 Farnborough show, *The Aeroplane* reporting that it was very fast indeed, even without the extra power of the Avon used by the Swift, and the demonstration included "the use of partial flap to tighten the radius of turn at high speeds".

From 28 May 1953, VV119 flew with wings altered to accept various combinations of dummy Fairey Blue Sky missiles (the weapon became the Fireflash, carried by the production Swift F.Mk 7). The object was to permit RAE Farnborough to assess the effect the weapons might have on drag, manoeuvrability and handling, and to find a configuration that gave negligible changes to handling in level flight, rolls and dives.

Sqn Ldr Ron Harvey AFC noted that when VV119 was loaded with missiles and dived to the maximum possible speed, the maximum Mach number remained constant, regardless of his efforts to push the aircraft faster. In fact the drag rise from compressibility was so severe at this point that the aircraft could never fly any faster.

This photograph of VV119 was released for publication on 19 March 1951. The dummy guns have now been removed.

Underside detail of VV119 in an undated photograph.

A variable incidence tailplane with a movement range of –9° to +4° was fitted to VV119 during its later life. On 6 September 1954 the Type 535 flew to join the Central Fighter Establishment (CFE) at West Raynham for around a year of tests on arrestor barriers, work that brought the aircraft's flying career to a close. VV119 was retired in 1955 and passed to RAF Halton in September to serve as ground instruction airframe 7285M. Several years later it was broken up for scrap.

The Type 535's major claim to fame must be the role it played in the David Lean feature film *The Sound Barrier* where, during the autumn of 1951, it was filmed as the fictitious supersonic Ridgefield Prometheus. VV119's pilot during filming was Supermarine's Sqn Ldr David Morgan and it proved an unusual use of a prototype that at the time was undergoing its own thorough flight test programme.

Overall the 535 flew well with few or no vices, but the Nene's limited power meant that it lacked performance, particularly at high altitude, which blocked any chance it had of becoming a service fighter. Nevertheless, it provided the base for the Swift that followed.

Airframe

The Supermarine 510's tailwheel-type fuselage was adopted from the Attacker, but introduced wings and tailplanes swept to an angle of 40° (44° at the wing leading edge). The stressed-skin light alloy wings were of laminar flow section and built around a main spar and auxiliary rear spar with plate ribs. The

VV119 banks away from the camera to show its planform, with extended wing roots compared to the Type 510.

main spar was cranked, the inner portions set at a 14° angle and the outer parts, from just outboard of the main undercarriage, at 28°. The wings were furnished with trailing edge flaps and slotted ailerons, and there was no centre section, the wings being attached to the fuselage itself.

The fuselage was also all-metal with stressed skinning, the rear portion of which was semi-monocoque. It used four main longerons and a series of mostly circular frames with intercostals to stiffen the skin, all in light alloy, as were the fin and tailplanes, the latter each having main and auxiliary spars. The engine was mounted centrally midway along the fuselage and fed by a large bifurcated air intake, while the cockpit nacelle was unusual in that it used a form of construction known in the industry as 'lobster-claw'. The undercarriage came from Attacker spares, the main legs retracting inwards. VV106's internal fuel capacity was 312 Imp gals (1,419 litres), all of which was in fuselage tanks.

The Type 517 modification introduced a split at Frame 24, with the rear fuselage hinged around this point and with the tailplane now attached rigidly to the rear body. Apart from the changes outlined in the text the Type 535's structure remained as the 510. Its internal fuel capacity was given as 600 Imp gals (2,728 litres) and it too sported a natural metal finish.

By the time VV119 became a film star in *The Sound Barrier* it had acquired a dorsal fairing on its fin. Note the name *PROMETHEUS* on the nose.

Unbuilt Developments

A more capable proposed development was the Type 532 shown here, a supersonic 510 (Swift) presented in a brochure drawn up in early February 1950. It introduced increased sweepback (50°) for the wings to reduce drag at high Mach numbers and, using a 6,500lb (28.9kN) thrust Rolls-Royce Tay reheated to 1,700K (1,427°C), it was expected to reach Mach 1.0 in level flight at about 35,000ft (10,668m). One again an Attacker fuselage would be diverted from the production line and modified to accommodate the Tay, while a set of wings would be constructed in jigs, but the swept fin and tail would be the same as on the original 510. This previously little known variant of the 510 was not ordered. Its data was as follows:

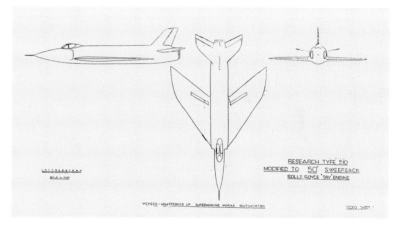

Internal detail drawing showing the Rolls-Royce Tay engine installation planned for the Type 532.

Span: 27ft 4in (8.35m)

Overall length: 44ft (13.41m)

Gross wing area: 287sq ft (26.69sq m)

Wing t/c ratio: 8.3%

All-up-weight: 14,100lb (6,396kg)

Max speed: 739mph (1,189km/h) at sea level; 650mph (1,046km/h) at 40,000ft (12,192m)

Fuel capacity: 400 Imp gals (1,819 litres)

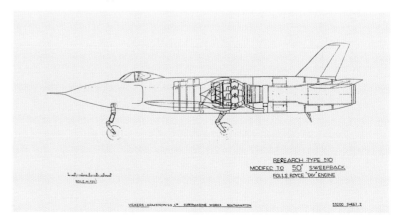

9   Sud-Ouest SO 8000 Narval (1949)

Sud-Ouest SO 8000 Narval

Type: single-seat, long-range carrier strike fighter

Span: 38ft 7.5in (11.77m)

Length: 38ft 10in (11.83m)

Gross wing area: 282.8sq ft (26.30sq m)

Estimated normal loaded weight: fighter 14,563lb (6,606kg), strike 16,007lb (7,261kg)

Powerplant: 1 x Arsenal 12H-02 piston engine (modified Junkers Jumo 213) 2,250hp (1,678kW)

Estimated max level speed (not reached): 454mph (730km/h) at 27,887ft (8,500m)

Ceiling: 32,808ft (10,000m)

Max range: 2,798 miles (4,500km)

Armament: 6 x 20mm forward firing cannon, up to 2,205lb (1,000kg) of stores

Designed for use from French Navy aircraft carriers, two examples of the Sud-Ouest SO 8000 Narval (Narwhal) long-range heavy fighter and attack aircraft were built, but they turned out to be rather poor aeroplanes and their flying career was relatively short.

The prototypes were ordered on 31 May 1946 under Contract 5161/46 and at that point the plan was to manufacture five pre-series aeroplanes plus 65 production aircraft. In its original form the SO 8000 showed features of what could be described as a piston-pusher version of the de Havilland Venom jet fighter, with a cranked wing leading edge; however, as the design evolved the resulting airframe acquired a rather beefier appearance.

Construction proceeded at Sud-Ouest's Courbevoie facility throughout 1947 and 1948 and it was intended that only prototype 01 should be provided with the six 20mm gun armament. Consequently prototype 02 was completed first, making its initial engine run on 26 November 1948.

Test pilot Daniel Rastel began low-speed taxi runs at a weight of 12,566lb (5,700kg) before Jacques Guignard took over for further tests on 23 December and 5 January 1949. On 13 January, 02 was taken to 124mph (200km/h) but, despite the efforts of the pilot, it would not take off. On 25 January, after modifications, Guignard tried again at the same speed, but the SO 8000 still refused to leave the ground.

Drastic measures were needed to fix the problem, and in particular the booms were cut, allowing the tail unit to be angled upwards so that the aircraft could be trimmed nose up. The new boom angle was 2° 15′ and metal reinforcing sheets covered the points where the structure had been severed. Taxi runs made on 10 and 11 February showed more promise.

Then, on 15 February, Sud-Ouest designer Lucien Servanty decided to take a close look at the SO 8000. He had opposed engineer Dupay, the SO 8000's designer, in the decision to place the tailplane as high as possible, away from the turbulence produced by the pusher propellers. Servanty advocated the opposite, but in the end it was decided to lengthen the elevator to improve its effectiveness, so that it now stretched beyond the fins for an increase in surface area from 18.82 to 27.96sq ft (1.75 to 2.6sq m).

Two further taxi runs were performed on 10 and 12 March before finally, on 1 April 1949, Guignard took 02 (F-WFKV) into the air for a 15-minute first flight; for the occasion the

SO 8000 carried 110 Imp gals (498 litres) of fuel and weighed 13,261lb (6,015kg) at take-off. In the air the pilot did not take the machine above 149mph (240km/h) and it was considered rather "delicate" to handle. This first flight was more than a year behind schedule but, after modifications to the spoilers, elevator and undercarriage doors, the second and third flights followed on 21 and 28 April, respectively. On the 21st Guignard retracted the undercarriage without trouble and after retracting the flaps took the aeroplane up to 249mph (400km/h).

On 12 May he flew the aircraft to Orly so that it could be exhibited at the Salon de l'Aéronautique, and it was around this time that the SO 8000 was officially named Narval. It returned to Bricy four days later and on 24 May, Guignard took 02 up to 311mph (500km/h), where he experienced pitching oscillations and required some physical effort to keep the aeroplane under control. The first 14 flights had compiled 30 hours of flying time.

Two days later Guignard had a surprise when he landed at the end of another sortie. By mistake he had left the flaps closed and on landing found that it was now quite easy to

Sud-Ouest SO 8000 prototype 01. The first SO 8000 had its pitot tube located on an outrigger on the port side of the cockpit, whereas the second machine had the pitot in the port wing leading edge.

put the machine onto the ground. On 28 July, Flight 17 was spent assessing the aircraft's longitudinal stability and its behaviour on approach, while most of August was occupied by modifications to the airframe and engine, so there was no further flying until the 30th.

In Flight 25 on 7 September it was planned to perform tests at heights of 4,000m, 5,000m, 6,000m and 7,000m (13,123ft, 16,404ft, 19,685ft and 22,966ft), but at 6,500m (21,325ft) the propeller gave problems and the engine began to run away. During the subsequent descent Guignard experienced a violent vibration at 4,000m (13,123ft) and an airspeed of 236mph (380km/h), while oil fumes entered the cabin. The engine had suffered a broken crankshaft and had to be replaced. On 11 October Guignard took the aircraft up to 7,500m (24,606ft), and on 3 November he attempted speed trials with the engine set at 3,000rpm, but the maximum recorded was only 348mph (560km/h) at 9,186ft (5,800m).

The elevator of the second SO 8000 was extended past the tail fins. Registered F-WFKV, this aircraft was the first Narval to fly. Note the open cockpit, flap arrangement and just how close the lower parts of the fins are to the ground.

F-WFKV's radio mast was located on its back, behind the cockpit – also note the pitot tube on the outer wing. The nose gear door had been attached when this picture was taken, but the main gear doors appear not to be in place. *Wolfgang Muehlbauer*

On 10 November, SO 8000-02 was flown from Bricy to Brétigny for its CEV evaluation as a fighter, bomber and anti-submarine aircraft. For these trials, take-off weight was provisionally limited to 13,999lb (6,350kg), when the theoretical maximum weight was 15,873lb (7,200kg), and landing weight was not to exceed 13,779lb (6,250kg). CEV needed only three flights to complete its tests and the results released in January 1950 were damning.

The SO 8000 featured neat air intakes aft of its cockpit. *Alain Pelletier*

The report stated that performance was inadequate, with a maximum speed well below estimates, the flying controls needed to be redesigned (currently they made the SO 8000 tiring to fly) and the aircraft reacted poorly to changes in engine output. Indeed there was a tendency to go into a dive when power was reduced, an attribute that was considered dangerous and that would make deck landings difficult (CEV's pilots noted that the Narval's landing needed a great deal of pilot input). Overall, CEV considered the SO 8000 poor – other weaknesses included lateral instability at low speed, a marked longitudinal instability (the airframe's instability in the air would prevent it from being a good gun platform), and poor flying characteristics when the flaps were retracted or extended.

All along there had also been problems with the engine and attempts made to cure some of the flaws had brought changes to the air intakes and to the control surfaces. In the meantime, the French government had instructed Sud-Ouest to have the first SO 8000 flying by no later than 31 December 1949. Capitaine Roger Carpentier finally took 01 on its maiden flight on 9 December when, being new to the type, he was surprised by the effort needed to keep the wings level in flight. Two days later the aircraft was weighed and with a

full fuel tank (311 Imp gals/1,413 litres) plus water, oil, armament and the pilot, the figure came to 15,254lb (6,919kg).

Also on the 9th, a Mr Juillian from the Service technique de l'Aéronautique chargé de la partie technique, industrielle et administrative des marchés d'État (STAé) contacted a Mr Cavin at CEV to inform the Establishment that the Narval had been officially grounded, primarily, it is understood, because of its poor handling characteristics. However, the ban on flying was not implemented and on 16 December Carpentier flew 02 for a second time.

During the 45-minute flight he tried to put together the most comprehensive analysis possible of the Narval. He confirmed some of

the problems listed above, but added that another major weakness was a lack of harmony between the control surfaces. He also confirmed that 02's speed performance was much lower than it should be for an aircraft of this class, and when flying at an indicated maximum speed of 286mph (460km/h) it proved impossible to operate the ailerons to take 02 into a roll, even when Carpentier had both hands on the stick.

SO 8000-02 returned to SNCASO at Brétigny on 30 December, Guignard making his first flight in SO 8000-01 that same day –

SO 8000 prototype 02. *Michel Cristescu*

A Narval receives close attention from engineers and what appears to be visiting officials. Note how 'Narval' is marked on the forward fuselage, compared to the 'freehand' version shown earlier. *Michel Cristescu*

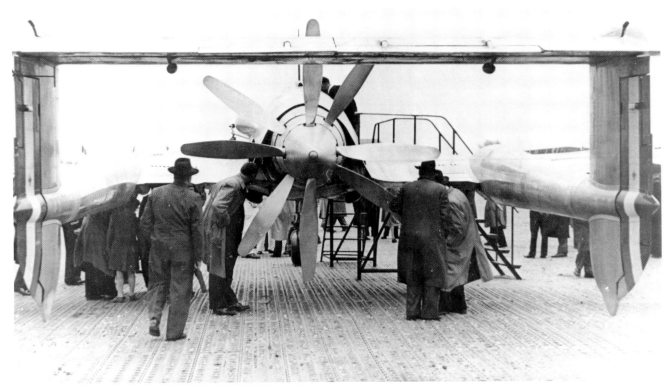

Above and left: The SO 8000 under inspection in the static display at Orly in May 1949. *Collection Jacques Moulin and Alain Pelletier*

it turned out to be the aircraft's final flight. In the air he found the machine behaved contradictory to 02 in that as soon as the flaps were retracted it banked to the right. On 7 January he took 02 up for its forty-fourth and last sortie. The flying programme was halted after prototype 02 had completed a total of 25 hours and 50 minutes in the air. The SO 8000 Narval programme was terminated in April 1950 and both examples were stored in a corner of the airfield before later being scrapped.

Flight magazine for 16 October 1947 had reported how the engine part of the Arsenal organisation was working on a more powerful version of the German Junkers Jumo 213 piston engine, describing it as "an outstandingly fine unit", and how an "Arsenalised 213 with water injection and contra-props is to be installed in the SO 8000 deck-landing fighter." The original plan had been to fit a British Rolls-Royce Griffon in the Narval, but this never materialised.

Instead, Arsenal turned to the Jumo 213A, reworking it into the 12H inverted V-12 engine. Initially the new unit offered around 2,100hp (1,566kW), but this was insufficient

| Rear angle on the SO 8000. *Alain Pelletier*

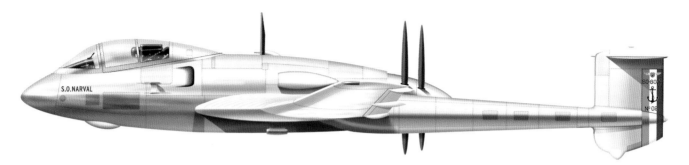

SO 8000 Narval
prototype 02.
*Copyright
Pete West*

for the SO 8000 and Arsenal further developed its engine to raise output to 2,250hp (1,678kW). This increase in power brought caused worries regarding the engine's reliability and resulted in rpm for the Narval being limited to 3,000. In the air it was found that when power was increased the aircraft's nose would rise. (In 1948 Arsenal's aircraft engine branch was absorbed by the Société Nationale d'Études et de Construction de Moteurs d'Aviation or SNECMA.)

Another element to the SO 8000 saga, but not directly related to it, was what French publications described as "bad business practice on the part of Sud-Ouest". Plans made in October 1948 to fit a British Nene jet engine instead of the piston unit (as the SO 8010) also came to nothing, while a further contributory factor behind the Narval's cancellation was the allocation to France of US Grumman F6F Hellcat and Vought F4U Corsair piston-powered naval fighters. At the same time, other contemporary French fighter projects employed jet power and as a consequence the SO 8000 became the last new propeller fighter designed and built in France.

Airframe

The Sud-Ouest SO 8000 had a twin-boom configuration with a relatively short fuselage and tricycle undercarriage. The wings were all-metal

and fitted with double slotted, retractable Fowler-type flaps, lateral control being supplied by a combination of small ailerons placed at the wingtips, and spoilers. The cranked, swept leading edge was set at an angle of 24° inboard and (with dihedral) 13.5° outboard, and the wing could fold upwards for carrier stowage.

The fuselage, booms and tail surfaces were also in metal, the booms springing out from the extremities of the wing centre section to carry the raised tailplane, which connected the tops of the fins. The fins extended above and below the boom ends.

Fuel was housed in the fuselage between the cockpit and pusher engine, which drove contra-rotating 8ft 10in (2.70m) diameter Chauvière lightweight propellers. These proved such a disappointment that they were to have been replaced by Rotol propellers, but the flying programme came to an end before this took place. (The Chauvière company had designed a braking propeller that would have been of great assistance to the SO 8000 in maintaining speed and control on the approach to land, but it was not fitted.) The SO 8000 had a moulded sliding cockpit canopy and was intended to carry full naval radar – production Narvals were to have introduced fairings beneath the booms to house the radar and radio equipment.

The six-blade contra-rotating propellers, twin booms and dihedral on the outer wings are evident in this rear view of the first prototype. *Wolfgang Muehlbauer*

10 Aérocentre NC 1080 (1949)

Aérocentre NC 1080

Type: single-seat navy fighter

Span: 39ft 4.5in (12m); folded 19ft 8in (6.00m)

Length: 42ft 3in (12.87m)

Gross wing area: 305sq ft (28.40sq m)

Wing t/c ratio: 10%

Max weight: 17,196lb (7,800kg)

Powerplant: 1 x Rolls-Royce Nene 102 5,000lb (22.2kN)

Max speed: 607mph (977km/h) at 16,405ft (5,000m); 578mph (930km/h) at 29,527ft (9,000m)

Limiting Mach number: 0.85

Service ceiling (estimated): 41,665ft (12,700m)

Rate of climb: 5,500ft/min (1,676m/min) at sea level; time to 29,530ft (9,000m) 11 minutes 20 seconds

Range: 807 miles (1,300km)

Armament: provision for 3 x Hispano-Suiza 30mm guns, plus bombs and rocket pods under the wings (armament not fitted)

The Aérocentre NC 1080 was one of three single-seat, single-jet fighter designs built as prototypes against a competition launched to find the first jet fighter for the French Navy's air arm (l'Aéronavale). The new fighter was to equip the country's proposed new aircraft carrier, being studied under the designation PA28 and which had been authorised in 1947 but was cancelled in 1950. The NC 1080 joined the Arsenal VG 90 and Nord 2200 in the competition, none of them

entering service. In fact they proved to be tragic group of aeroplanes, with three of the four produced lost in fatal crashes.

The NC 1080 was ordered under contract 5272/46, but cancelled in 1948 to save money on the military budget; however, Aérocentre elected to complete the prototype as a private venture in the hope that it might yet generate a production order. In July 1949 Aérocentre was declared bankrupt and merged with Nord, the latter continuing with the naval fighter project under a new contract, 4269/49. Aérocentre's liquidation resulted from a decision made by Minister of Defence Paul Ramadier and at one stage the idea of storing the NC 1080 after just one flight was considered, but Nord took the project on despite having its own competitor for the requirement.

The successful design was expected to deliver a maximum speed in excess of 559mph (900km/h) between sea level and 29,530ft (9,000m), and a rate of climb of at least 4,920ft/min (1,500m/min). Its span was not to exceed 41ft 4in (12.6m) or, when folded, 15ft 9in (4.8m), and loaded weight was given as 17,637lb (8,000kg). The missions outlined for the aircraft were interception (with two 30mm cannon), strike (with the guns, plus one 1,000kg or two 500kg bombs), rocket attack (three guns and 90 rocket projectiles), or a 'strategic' role, which called for three 30mm guns.

The three rivals all made use of the Rolls-Royce Nene 102 engine, as required by the official specification, and none carried armament. The NC 1080 was registered F-WFZK and constructed at Issy-les-Moulineaux. An innovative feature of the design, which represented a sharp divergence from common practice, was the use of special "compensators" or "lift flaps" in the wings, these having been designed by Pierre Lemoigne to provide lateral control. There were no ailerons in the normal sense, Comb-type spoilers being fitted instead. The idea was that when raised on the upper wing they would reduce lift, which would help with deck landings, and when deployed under the wing they would serve as airbrakes.

The NC 1080 itself was designed by Aérocentre's chief engineer Charles Pillon and on its completion in March 1949 the aircraft was moved to the airfield at Toussous-le-Noble. However, taxi trials did not begin until 23 June, in the hands of Aérocentre's chief test pilot Fernand Lasne, who on the 25th also made the first short hops in the machine. These uncovered weaknesses in lateral stability, which required modifications to remedy – it appears that the height of the fin and rudder were increased and wingtip plates added before the aircraft flew. In early May 1949 a model of the NC 1080 was shown at the Paris Salon, publicly confirming the aircraft's existence. Following the failure of Aérocentre, the NC 1080 was moved to the Réau-Villaroche test airfield from where it made its maiden flight on 29 July, piloted by Lasne.

This first flight was very unpleasant for the pilot. The take-off was satisfactory but once in the air, Lasne found the NC 1080's spoilers were useless and he could not get the aircraft to turn. It was difficult to keep the NC 1080 level, and light turbulence was enough to roll the aircraft to left or right. It was fortunate that the CEV field at Brétigny lay in Lasne's path; after 8 minutes in the air and having somehow managed to make a pair of 20° turns, he landed safely. The prototype was grounded and remained at the CEV base until conventional ailerons had been fitted.

Aérocentre NC 1080 as first built, with the original fin and no plates on its wingtips. Note the long, split nose undercarriage doors and that the registration F-WFZK has not yet been painted on the rear fuselage.

Only the NC 1080's rudder appears to have been painted in national colours.

Note that the nose pitot has been removed in this image. The registration lettering on the underside of the wing is just visible. The photo was taken at CEV Brétigny. *Wolfgang Muehlbauer*

In its final configuration the NC 1080 had vertical endplates fixed to its tailplanes.

Insufficient wind tunnel testing on the new aircraft's sophisticated controls meant these problems had not been picked up prior to flight testing. Nord's engineers attempted to make the original system work without success, and small ailerons had to be introduced outboard of the Lemoigne flaps. The wingtip plates were also removed and replaced by small fins on the tips of the tailplane, while the aircraft's original laminar flow air intake system was also deleted.

Lasne took the aircraft back to Réau-Villaroche on 16 December, and from January to March 1950 a further 19 flights were completed. Additional modifications were made between flights, including the

introduction of servo controls that allowed the ailerons to perform satisfactorily. On 31 March Lasne flew the NC 1080 to Brétigny again, so that official evaluation could begin. For this task CEV used a Junkers Ju 88 and a SIPA S-11 as chase aircraft. The first two CEV flights were made on 6 April, with Jean Sarrail as pilot. The aircraft was taken to a maximum speed of 447mph (720km/h) and Mach 0.64 in a dive, while the landing presented no difficulties, although there were minor problems, for example lateral instability in cruising flight.

Nord test pilot Pierre Gallay took the NC 1080 aloft again on the evening of the 7th, but at an altitude around 9,840ft (3,000m) the aircraft entered a spin, the anti-spin parachute failed and was torn away, and F-WFZK crashed in Sablière forest, Ballancourt, about 6 miles (10km) to the south-east of Brétigny. Gallay was killed. Witness reports indicated that pieces had broken away from the aeroplane while it was in the air, but the reasons why control was lost have never been determined.

F-WFZK had completed around 14 hours of flying and with no second aircraft available the project was abandoned. The competition itself was ultimately abandoned in favour of ordering the British de Havilland Sea Venom, which was built under licence by Sud-Est as the Aquilon.

Details of the air intake are revealed in this picture. *Michel Cristescu*

Airframe

The NC 1080's wing was moderately swept at 22° 30' at quarter chord. The wing used a single spar and was split into three sections (a centre, plus two outer wings). Folding was available for carrier stowage and there were hardpoints for stores. The Lemoigne 'three-layer' flap system originally filled the wing trailing edge, but in due course conventional ailerons replaced the spoilers just inboard of the wingtips.

The fuselage was of circular cross section, built using conventional all-metal construction and formed in forward and rear sections. The nose housed a radar antenna, while the cockpit and a large tank for 429 Imp gals (1,950 litres) of fuel were accommodated in the forward fuselage. The rear portion included the engine and empennage. The single spar tailplane was swept to the same angle as the wing, but the fin had 40° of sweep. Side intakes were placed ahead of the wing and to begin with used laminar flow control through suction. A pitot was fitted in the nose and the aircraft appears always to have flown in natural metal finish with little in the way of national markings (which possibly indicates the private venture status it had at one stage).

With its raked wings and tail the NC 1080 resembled the Supermarine Type 510, the primary differentiators being the French machine's fin-mounted tailplane, less highly swept horizontal surfaces and tricycle undercarriage.

An NC 1080 walkaround after the aircraft's arrival at CEV. *Michel Cristescu*

The NC 1080 stands on the flightline alongside its Nord rival for the carrier fighter requirement – the 2200. Although in many respects similar designs, the contrast of side or nose air inlet designs is notable. *Michel Cristescu*

11 British Anti-Submarine Aircraft (Blackburn Series + Short S.B.3) (1949 and 1950)

Blackburn B.54/B.88

Type: two-seat (later three-seat) anti-submarine aircraft

Span: 44ft 2in (13.46m); folded 19ft 6in (5.94m)

Length: B.54 42ft 5in (12.93m); B.88 42ft 8in (13.01m)

Loaded weight: B.54 13,729lb (6,227kg); B.88 13,091lb (8,891kg)

Powerplant: B.54 2 x Rolls-Royce Griffon 57 piston engines each 2,000hp (1,491kW); B.88 1 x Armstrong-Siddeley Double Mamba 100 turboprop 2,950ehp (2,200kW)

Max level speed: B.54 251mph (404km/h); B.88 320mph (515km/h)

Armament: 6 x depth charges, 1 x anti-submarine torpedo and bombs in bomb bay; bombs and rocket projectiles under wings

Short S.B.3

Type: three-seat anti-submarine aircraft

Span: 59ft 9in (18.21m)

Length: 44ft 9in (13.64m)

Gross wing area: 560.4sq ft (52.12sq m)

Max weight: 23,600lb (10,705kg)

Powerplant: 2 x Armstrong Siddeley Mamba ASM.3 turboprops each 1,475shp (1,100kW)

Max level speed: approximately 320mph (515km/h)

Armament: 2,620lb (1,188kg) of stores

In the years following the Second World War and into the 1950s, a number of programmes were opened to find new anti-submarine aircraft for the RAF and Royal Navy, and these resulted in the Avro Shackleton and Fairey Gannet entering service. There was also the Royal Navy's lightweight Short Seamew, which reached the production stage with some joining No. 700 Squadron for just a few months in 1956/57. In addition a direct rival to the Fairey 17 (Gannet), the B.54 design came from Blackburn, while Short Brothers produced the S.B.3, which also came under serious consideration.

Blackburn B.54 (Y.A.5/7/8) and B.88 (Y.B.1)

By 1945 it was clear that countering submarines had become a much more important task than dealing with surface vessels, a situation reflected in the release of new requirements. In that year Specification GR.17/45 was issued to find a replacement anti-submarine aircraft for the wartime Fairey Swordfish and Barracuda naval torpedo bombers and in April 1946 prototypes were ordered from Blackburn and Fairey. The latter's concept became the well-known Gannet, although it faced stiff competition from its rival which, in the event, did not progress beyond the three prototypes built under Contract 6/Acft/822 – WB781, WB788 and WB797.

When the RAF or Royal Navy issued a requirement for an important military aircraft it was established practice at this time to order at least two quite different prototypes from the designs tendered against the covering specification. In some quarters this was regarded as an extravagant practice, but others considered it to be a valuable and

WB781 banks away from the photographic aircraft on 3 October 1949. "Not for press release before 15 October" is marked on the back of this Blackburn publicity photograph. *Peter Green*

necessary form of insurance, while at the same time giving Britain's aircraft industry additional work and experience.

When the original Naval Staff requirements for an anti-submarine aircraft were received by Blackburn it became immediately obvious to the design team that take-off was the most important single factor influencing the design. GR.17/45 would in due course be amended to having an unassisted take-off run, at full normal load from the deck against a 17 knot (31km/h) wind, that was not to exceed 450ft (137m); originally the figure had been only 400ft (122m), which Blackburn had pointed out would be impossible to meet. Consequently the team, led by chief designer George E. Petty, opted for high engine power and accepted a fairly high wing loading when, on the other hand, Fairey proposed using a lower-powered engine (the Twin or Double Mamba) and a lower wing loading.

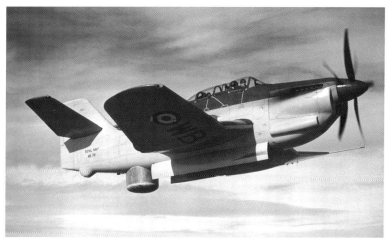

Further Blackburn pictures, believed also to have been taken on 3 October, firstly show the aircraft in clean condition and then with the ASV radar deployed and bomb-bay doors open. *Peter Green*

WB781 photographed in September 1949. The contra-rotating propellers, gull wing and considerable dihedral on the aircraft's tailplane to clear the jet exhaust, are all noteworthy.

WB781 showing the side fuselage exhaust position and the extension made to the height of the fin.

Blackburn's original proposal was designated B.54 (and Y.A.5 under the SBAC numbering system) and its designers opted to use a coupled Napier Naiad turboprop powerplant. However, by mid-1947 it had become clear that the coupled, or Double Naiad, would not be available until much later than previously estimated, and it was agreed to provisionally fit a Rolls-Royce Griffon piston engine in the first prototype to ensure that testing of the airframe's aerodynamics and flight characteristics could at least be kept on schedule.

By May 1948 the estimated first flight of the Naiad-powered aircraft had slipped to December 1949 at the earliest and Blackburn then proposed fitting an Armstrong Siddeley Double Mamba in the second machine to ensure the company would have a turboprop aircraft in the air at the same time as Fairey. In the end both the first and second B.54 prototypes took Griffons (as the Y.A.7 and Y.A.8) while the third had the Double Mamba. As such, the latter was designated B.88 (Y.B.1) and in the end the Double Naiad was never installed.

Y.A.7 WB781 made its maiden flight on 20 September 1949 from its Brough birthplace, crewed by company test pilot Peter G Lawrence. Delivery to A&AEE Boscombe Down for handling trials took place on 15 December, after which WB781 joined a naval trails unit to undergo initial carrier proving trials, the first deck landing being achieved aboard *HMS Illustrious* on 8 February 1950. The landing characteristics at an approach speed of 85 knots (157km/h) were described as good.

By the time the second Griffon-powered machine (WB788) flew on 3 May 1950 it had acquired a third crew member, in fact a second observer, who now sat behind the pilot face to face with the first. The original requirement called for just two crew, but during 1948 the Naval Staff stated a requirement that the new aircraft should be a three-seater, and the design had to be re-examined. The second prototype also introduced revised outer wing sections with an increase in sweep angle on the leading edge (the original was essentially straight, the change moving the CofG rearwards), while its rudder had been cut away at the bottom to accommodate an extended rear fuselage (to compensate, the fin was made taller). The changes to fin and rudder were in due course also made to WB781. Moving the CofG rearwards meant that the nose could be raised at a lower speed, thus reducing the take-off run.

The second aircraft also had water injection for its Griffons and it was these alterations to airframe and crew that brought the new designation Y.A.8. WB788 was flown to Boscombe Down on 6 June. It achieved its first landing aboard *Illustrious* on 19 June and during the trials it completed 23 landings aboard the carrier. With the piston engines in place the B.54 was able to complete its initial deck trials, the two Griffon airframes essentially serving as aerodynamic test beds.

All seemed good at this point, but full handling trials made in October (after the

| WB781 aboard *Illustrious* during deck trials.

carrier trials had ended) revealed several shortcomings. It was found that the ailerons became excessively heavy if there was no boost and there was rudder tramping (the latter was later considerably improved upon by the addition of a "fitting" under the tailplane). In addition, the elevator suffered from hunting and there was also no prior warning of the arrival of the stall, while inside the cockpit the noise from the engines was considered "excessive".

The Double Mamba B.88/Y.B.1 WB797 achieved its maiden flight on 19 July 1950, again from Brough with Peter Lawrence at the controls. In September 1950 it attended the Farnborough show after having made its public debut at Lee-on-Solent on 26 August. The Farnborough performance included high-speed rolls, followed by flying with one engine shut down and its airscrew stopped.

| Blackburn B.54/Y.A.7 prototype WB781. *Peter Green*

The turboprop-powered B.88/Y.B.1 WB797 trailed, almost certainly, by the second Griffon-powered machine, B.54/Y.A.8 WB788. The piston aircraft has a dummy jet exhaust on the side of its fuselage, a fitting over the pilot's canopy (possibly a periscope) and no spinner over the propeller hub. *Peter Green*

Back at Brough, the aircraft's wingtips were extended and made to fold down as the main section of the wing folded up for stowage. Flight trials showed the Y.B.1's take-off performance with flaps down was quite poor (with flaps up the performance came close to predictions) and this counted against it during the official assessment against its rival from Fairey (extending the wingtips apparently exacerbated the flaps-down take-off behaviour). However, in regard to maintenance and accessibility the Blackburn machine was considered the better.

Official trials were held aboard *Illustrious* in October 1950 and the Y.B.1 retained the piston-powered version's good landing characteristics (the approach speed had now gone up a

Left and below: WB797 in July 1950, around the time of its first flight. The diameter of the propeller disc is smaller than that of the Griffon-powered versions, but to compensate WB797 had eight blades rather than the six used previously.

fraction to 90 knots/167km/h), although dummy approaches made using just one engine proved awkward in that the pilot could not hold an accurate speed. Full handling trials uncovered further problems, including instability at low speeds, while heavy rudder forces were required when flying on one engine.

In the end Fairey was declared the winner and a hundred production Gannets were ordered in March 1951. The Blackburn prototypes continued flying however. During 1951, WB781 and WB788 went to RAE Farnborough where they found employment lasting several years, the latter receiving modifications after being allotted to 'bomber trials' in August 1952. The two airframes appeared in the Establishment's scrap yard in 1957 and 1956, respectively.

WB797 during a flypast over Farnborough on 5 September 1950 with, as part of its display, one engine stopped and the forward airscrew feathered.

W8797 with calibration markings on its fuselage side.

The turboprop-powered Y.B.1, pictured on 12 September 1950. The photograph's angle nicely demonstrates the moderate wing sweep introduced on the second and third prototypes. *Peter Green*

WB797 during an engine run with its quite substantial arrestor hook tied to the ground. No safety protection for the ears in those days!

WB797 on approach with everything down, probably at the Farnborough show.

Also in 1951, the Y.B.1 joined Armstrong Siddeley Motors at Bitteswell as a test bed for the Double Mamba. This was after the aircraft had been tested by A&AEE at weights up to 20,000lb (9,072kg) in order to clear it for the role, and it was at Bitteswell that the machine was scrapped in July 1955. By the end of their careers the trio had completed over 1,000 landings in more than 300 hours of test flying, while the Gannet went on to be the backbone of the Navy's anti-submarine forces for many years.

Airframe

The B.54 and its derivatives had a semi-monocoque, all-metal structure with a folding inverted-gull wing. The latter had high-lift flaps with fixed and trim tabs to ensure control at low speeds, while the tricycle undercarriage was designed to cope with high rates of descent. The fuselage contained a substantial bomb bay for a large mix of weaponry, but further stores, including depth charges and rocket projectiles, or external fuel tanks, could also go under the wings. Tandem seating was provided for the original two crewmembers, an additional observer later going behind the pilot.

The elevators and rudder had balance and trim tabs (the rudder also had a horn balance), and the Griffons drove a six-blade, 13ft (3.96m) diameter contra-rotating airscrew. It is understood that the piston-powered variants at least used a chain drive to connect the engines to the propellers and this made a distinct and extraordinary noise during flight. A long arrestor hook was stowed in the tail bumper and a retractable radar scanner (thought to be ASV.Mk 19) was accommodated in the lower rear fuselage. All three prototypes were

The winning design in the Navy's anti-submarine carrier aircraft competition was the Fairey Gannet. This view shows AS.Mk 1 WN348, which was lost in August 1954 when it ditched in the sea during carrier trials, an engine compressor having failed during a catapult launch.

painted Dark Sea Grey on their upper sides and "duck egg green" (probably Sky) on their undersurfaces.

The Double Mamba installation comprised two units placed side-by-side and coupled to drive the contra-rotating propeller; the port unit drove the front propeller, the starboard the rear, and when the Double Mamba was first proposed the propeller had a diameter of 11ft (3.35m). Either unit could be shut down for cruising flight to save fuel and extend the aircraft's range.

WB797 at Farnborough. The Armstrong Whitworth Apollo airliner prototype stands alongside. *Terry Panopalis*

Short Brothers S.B.3

By the late 1940s it was apparent that the Soviet navy was being enlarged to such an extent that it would soon be classed as an ocean-going 'bluewater' fleet. This would need to be countered and one outcome was the May 1949 issue of Specification M.6/49 covering a proposed naval anti-submarine and reconnaissance aircraft design from Short Brothers, designated S.B.3. It had been offered as a potential interim aeroplane to help fill the gap while the Navy waited for a successful dedicated anti-submarine type to emerge from the Blackburn and Fairey competition.

The S.B.3's airframe was based on the company's Sturgeon target tug and M.6/49 called for a maximum speed of at least 265 knots (491km/h), but also with the ability to fly comfortably at a speed as far below 175mph (282km/h) as was possible (these figures were common with GR.17/45); the best performance had to be in the altitude band between sea level and 5,000ft (1,524m). Stores included six depth charges, a 2,000lb (907kg) anti-submarine torpedo, anti-submarine bombs, mines or rocket projectiles, plus sonobuoys, markers and flares. The S.B.3's radar was to be an ASV.Mk XV.

By December 1948 the design was no longer being considered as an interim type, but with its high all-up weight its use would be restricted to the Navy's larger aircraft carriers, which prevented the S.B.3 from competing directly with Blackburn and Fairey. However, during the month it was officially agreed that the prototypes would act as anti-submarine research and development aeroplanes – as yet there were no plans for production.

Major changes from the Sturgeon were a new powerplant of two Armstrong Siddeley Mamba turboprops and the forward fuselage was redesigned and bulged to take the large search radar scanner under the floor, plus two radar operators in a cabin beneath and ahead of the pilot. The original rear fuselage was unchanged and weapons were to be carried in a bomb bay and on underwing hardpoints. The project was in the hands of designer CPT Lipscombe (the chief designer at Short was David Keith-Lucas).

One production Sturgeon airframe was rebuilt against Contract 6/Acft/3955 as the first S.B.3 prototype, WF632, but a second example, WF636, was to be built from scratch. There were delays, in part because of an ongoing effort to move Short's home from Rochester to Belfast, but on 12 August 1950 company test pilot Tom Brooke-Smith was able to take WF632 on its first flight.

Early trials revealed a deficiency in longitudinal and directional stability at slow speeds, and it was also discovered that the Mamba, which exhausted through downward-directed pipes, introduced a separate and quite severe stability problem. Since the Mamba was

Short S.B.3 WF632 during its maiden flight on 12 August 1950. The aircraft was assembled using a Sturgeon target-tug airframe and the new sections have not yet been painted.

The S.B.3 after painting in Fleet Air Arm colours.

a turbine, its thrust and efflux varied with changes in power, making WF632 difficult to trim. Overall the handling characteristics were found inferior to those of the Sturgeon.

In September 1950 WF632 was displayed at the Farnborough show, while the resumption of flight testing resulted in a plan to extend the jet pipes during the early months of 1951. However, on 11 April the decision was made to stop work on the S.B.3, although further flight testing was undertaken using WF632 fitted with modified leading edges to its outer wings and with the aft-ward extensions made to the jet pipes.

It was found that neither feature affected the aircraft's stability characteristics. WF632 last flew on 23 April to complete a total of almost 40 hours' flying time, and the airframe was stripped for spares and broken up for scrap from 30 November onwards. WF636 was 90% complete when the programme was abandoned and soon scrapped.

Detail of the S.B.3's powerplant, undercarriage, radar housing and operator's accommodation. Note the short jet exhaust exit under the nacelle.

WF632 in April 1951 with its wings folded and after the exhaust pipes had been extended downwards and rearwards.

Airframe

The S.B.3 used the Short Sturgeon's two-spar cantilever wing, made using heavy-gauge light alloy booms and plate webs. Stressed skin construction was employed and the fuselage also had an all-metal monocoque structure with a stressed light alloy skin riveted to a skeleton of longerons and stringers. Both the tailplane and fin used two-spar construction with spanwise stringers and were built integrally with the rear fuselage. The aircraft retained a tailwheel undercarriage and was eventually painted in naval colours.

WF632 during its only display at a Farnborough show, in September 1950.

12 Arsenal VG 90 (1949)

Arsenal VG 90

Recorded performance data was well down on expected figures, although neither VG 90 was tested to its fullest potential

Type: single-seat naval fighter

Span: 41ft 4in (12.60m); folded 22ft 11.5in (7m)

Length: 44ft 1in (13.44m)

Gross wing area: 330.11sq ft (30.70sq m)

Max weight: 18,078lb (8,200kg) to 19,222lb (8,719kg) depending on mission

Powerplant: 1 x Hispano-built Rolls-Royce Nene 102 5,000lb (22.2kN)

Max speed: specified max speed 569mph (915km/h) at sea level; 584mph (940km/h) at 19,685ft (6,000m); max speed achieved 531mph (855km/h) at sea level; Mach 0.845 at altitude

Service ceiling: 39,370ft (12,000m)

Climb rate: specified sea level rate of climb 4,331ft/min (1,320m/min) (one source gives 6,300ft/min/1,920m/min at a light weight of 11,508lb (5,220kg)); sea level rate of climb achieved 2,953ft/min (900m/min)

Armament: 3 x Hispano-Suiza 30mm guns to go in nose (possibly with 4 or 6 x 20mm cannon as an alternative); bombs and rocket pods under wings (no armament fitted)

The second of the three naval jet strike fighter prototypes produced for the competition to equip the Aéronavale's new PA28 aircraft carrier was Arsenal's VG 90. The aircraft was fighter follow-on developed from the VG 70 jet-powered research aeroplane described in the first volume of *X-Planes of Europe*. It was similar in general configuration to the VG 70, the most obvious external change being the positioning of the air intakes – whereas the earlier aircraft had used a novel form of intake scoop beneath the fuselage (which proved to be inefficient) the VG 90 employed more orthodox intakes built into the sides of the fuselage under the wing leading edge.

Some experts had been sceptical of the VG 70, and their doubts had perhaps been well founded since it flew just five times, but nevertheless laid the groundwork and provided experience for the Vernisse and Galtier design team at Arsenal, known for their originality of design, to get to work on the striking-looking VG 90 naval fighter.

Arsenal de l'Aéronautique had been founded in 1936 and came under the direct control of the French Air Ministry. Its objective was the study, design and development of prototypes and new equipment that in due course could be put into production in one of the state-controlled factories – that is, it would work in areas and on projects in which private industry could not be or was not allowed to be involved. Until 1940 the facility was located at Villacoublay, but following the liberation, the former Brandt armaments factory at Châtillon-sous-Bagneux became Arsenal's new home for design and prototype developments, this facility being capable of the production of either wood or metal aircraft, and of engines. By 1947 flight tests were being carried out at Villacoublay, although the VG 90 would do much of its testing at Melun-Villaroche.

The VG 70 and VG 90 were linked by the VG 80 swept-wing fighter project, designed for a Rolls-Royce Nene and fitted with five

Arsenal's earlier VG 70 prototype, first flown on 23 June 1948, provided useful data for development of the follow-on VG 90. Comparison with the previous photo reveals the differences between the VG 70 and VG 90, shown here.

0.5in (12.7mm) machine guns in each inner wing. The original VG 90 study was launched in October 1946 and construction of the first example got under way in January 1948; it was completed in May 1949.

Prototype 01 was registered F-WFOE and on 20 June it was transported to Melun-Villaroche airfield. It was 27 September, however, before chief test pilot Modeste Vonner could take VG 90-01 on a 15-minute maiden flight up to a speed of 186mph (300km/h) and an altitude of 2,295ft (700m), without retracting the undercarriage or flaps.

The first sortie revealed the necessity to improve aileron efficiency and modify the air intake ducting. With these changes in place, three more flights were made in December, but during Flight 3, the airbrakes extended without Vonner's input and Arsenal was obliged to alter their shape to prevent a recurrence. Further flights through January 1950 saw Vonner increase maximum speed gradually, until 497mph (800km/h) was

reached on the 26th, but he was then injured in a flying accident in a Junkers Ju 88.

Vonner's replacement was to be Nord test pilot Pierre Decroo, but he had not yet completed his jet training and in the short term CEV test pilot Major Paul Boudier was seconded to Arsenal. Between 13 March and 5 April Boudier completed six flights in 01. On 10 May, the aircraft's 26th flight was a ferry sortie to CEV Brétigny to begin an official assessment.

Jacques Sarrail flew the VG 90 at CEV and on 12 May performed an official display in which he made three rolls at 435mph (700km/h), although the aircraft's roll rate proved quite slow. Soon afterwards Sarrail pushed the maximum speed up to Mach 0.845 at between 16,405ft and 19,685ft (5,000m and 6,000m), the highest so far recorded by a French-designed aeroplane.

The early flights suggested that the VG 90 possessed reasonable flying characteristics. Indeed, the pilot's subsequent report noted

Above: Rare rear angle photo of the VG 70.
Right: A similar angle on the first VG 90. Note the extended fin. *Fabrice Cario (Camosine)*

that the prototype presented no hazards during take-off, but at times it could be unwieldy because of inertia – during the climb and acceleration to 311mph (500km/h), turbulence would make the aircraft roll lightly. However, the control surfaces responded well and the machine was stable in flight. Landing was also reasonable, although forward visibility was very poor and it proved difficult to avoid touching the ground with the rear fuselage. Plans were now under way to present the VG 90 at the 'Festival of the Air', the Paris Air Show, which was due to take place at Orly on 11 June.

Prototype 01 never made it, because on 25 May 1950 it crashed, killing its pilot, Pierre Decroo. Now qualified, Decroo had begun working towards finishing Arsenal's flight test programme. Returning to base at the end of a test sortie during which the flight envelope had been expanded (it was the prototype's

48th flight), Decroo made a pass at high speed. At around 4,920ft (1,500m) altitude, pieces of the airframe were seen to break away, the aircraft then spun before ploughing into the ground at Marolles-en-Hurepoix, south-west of Brétigny. The subsequent crash investigation suggested that the airbrakes had again spontaneously actuated; they were ripped away and struck the tailplane, causing the loss of control.

The first Arsenal VG 90 prototype in an image dated 13 April 1950. Note the nose-mounted pitot.

Up to this point the VG 90 had generally been successful and 01/F-WFOE had put together 35 hours' flying time, the test results having been described as very promising. On 29 July 1950 the Secretary of State for the Navy wrote a memorandum stating that his interest in the VG 90 would continue, and it was his wish that work on a pre-series of five improved VG 90s begin immediately. However, the Navy's General Staff were not so keen and began looking for possible alternative foreign fighter aircraft that could be built in France under license.

Nevertheless, work continued on the second prototype VG 90 which, unlike its wood and metal predecessor, was now all-metal. Other changes included a larger tailfin with the rudder split into two sections, enlarged air intakes, modified undercarriage and a Fairey Hydro-Booster power-control system for the ailerons; new airbrakes were installed between the trailing edge flaps and ailerons.

Like so many French prototypes of the period, VG 90-01 was not painted (apart from its national markings).

Prototype 02 was sent to Orléans-Bricy in the middle of May 1951 and in June made its maiden flight (published sources do not give the exact date of the first trip). Once again the fighter showed promise, recording 559mph (900km/h) on the level, but problems with

equipment prevented further flying until July. After completing its preliminary tests, 02 went to Villaroche from where pilot Claude Dellys performed 15 flights in 45 days, the tests including measuring speed at the stall. During November, while a 9,185ft (2,800m) long runway was being completed at Villaroche, the airframe was used for ground vibration assessment before resuming its flying in early December. At the end of the year 02 was employed in servo-control development, but then came more tragedy.

On 21 February 1952, Dellys was flying the VG 90 from Melun-Villaroche to CEV's Istres airfield in readiness for the next phase of its test programme. With a Ju 88 as escort, all seemed well. After crossing the Loire, Dellys increased the VG 90's airspeed and reported turbulence (which the Ju 88 did not experience), before all contact was lost. The VG 90 hit the ground at Gipcy near Bourbon l'Archambault, about 15 miles (24km) to the west of Moulins. Dellys had apparently tried to eject but his Martin-Baker seat had failed to work and he was killed.

The accident had apparently occurred at moderate speed, caused by flutter that had resulted in tailplane failure. The vibrations were attributed to removal of some of the tailplane balancing when the servo-controls were installed.

This second disaster brought the end for the VG 90. The proposed five pre-production aeroplanes were never ordered and in June 1952, in line with a Direction Technique et Industrielle du ministère de la Défense (DTI) decision, the project was abandoned. The third prototype, fitted with a SNECMA Atar engine was not completed, and on 1 January 1953 Arsenal became a private enterprise with the new name Société Française d'Etudes et de Construction de Matériels Aéronautiques Spéciaux (SFECMAS).

The first VG 90 prototype.
Copyright Pete West

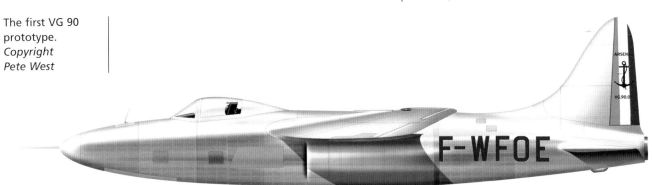

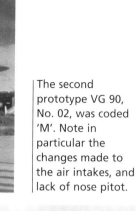

The second prototype VG 90, No. 02, was coded 'M'. Note in particular the changes made to the air intakes, and lack of nose pitot.

The first VG 90 at CEV. *Alain Pelletier*

VG 91

The VG 90s had been underpowered and production aeroplanes (designated VG 91) would have featured the 6,300lb (28kN) thrust SNECMA Atar 101C turbojet. The VG 91 would also have had a thinner wing and in readiness the third VG 90 prototype was to have been produced to this standard. Its first flight was apparently scheduled for March 1953, but all work was halted after the second VG 90 accident.

The incomplete airframe was subsequently used for vibration testing and then for aerodynamic trials as a full-scale model in the wind tunnel at Modane, the objective being to understand the reasons for the appearance of flutter on the VG 90. Many years later the remains of the VG 91 were discovered in the scrap yard at Cazaux in badly corroded condition. It proved impossible to save them and prototype 03 was scrapped in July 1978.

Airframe

The VG 90 was a clean, sleek cantilever shoulder-wing monoplane equipped with a wide-track nosewheel undercarriage. The wing, built up from two spars, had a sweep angle of 25°, with 4° of dihedral. On the first prototype the wing and tailplane skins were of birch plywood and the remainder of the airframe in metal; however, 02 was all metal. The outer wing surfaces could, in theory, be

Photographs of the VG 90's starboard side appear to be quite rare. *Fabrice Cario (Camosine)*

Prototype 02 is prepared for a test flight. *M Augendre via Fabrice Cario (Camosine)*

manually folded and the wing was built in three sections, the centre section complete with the main undercarriage and fuel tanks. Conventional ailerons were used (an idea to use spoilers was rejected), together with airbrakes on the wing upper and lower surfaces, split flaps and rearward-moving slotted flaps – the upper airbrakes could be operated alone for dive recovery.

The Nene received its air via shallow crescent-shaped air intakes on the fuselage sides beneath the wing. Guns and a radar were to be housed in the nose (the guns were originally intended to go in the wings). The fuselage was a semi-monocoque built around four longerons and the tail surfaces were built in a similar form to the wing, again with two spars. Fuel was stored in three fuselage tanks (457 Imp gals/2,080 litres in all) while three tanks in each wing contributed a further 158 Imp gals (720 litres), although it is understood that these capacities would have been reduced had the VG 90 carried external weapons. There were plans to make the fighter capable of carrying four drop tanks.

The first VG 90. *Collection Jacques Moulin*

13 Nord 2200 (1949)

Nord 2200

Type: single-seat naval fighter

Span: 39ft 4.5in (12m)

Length: with original tail 42ft 8in (13m); subsequently 44ft 3.5in (13.50m)

Gross wing area: 339.78sq ft (31.60sq m)

Max weight: 15,344lb (6,960kg)

Powerplant: 1 x Hispano-built Rolls-Royce Nene 102 5,000lb (22.2kN)

Max speed: planned 567mph (913km/h) at sea level; 582mph (936km/h) at 16,405ft (5,000m); max speed achieved 507mph (815km/h), or Mach 0.83

Climb rate: specified sea level rate of climb 4,530ft/min (1,380m/min); sea level rate of climb achieved 2,953ft/min (900m/min)

Armament: 3 x Hispano Suiza 30mm cannon planned (possible alternative of 4 x 20mm), plus bombs (up to a maximum size of 500kg) and rocket pods under wings. No armament was fitted and there appears to be some doubt as to where the guns would have been installed

The third design in the search for a French naval fighter jet was the Nord 2200. Of the three competitors it was the only one to survive a complete flight test programme. Later in its career, after the competition had passed, the Nord 2200 was used for take-off trials with auxiliary rockets.

Louis Coroller and Alain Buret designed the Nord 2200, beginning their studies in early 1946. The final proposal was made on 16 October, and on 27 December order number 5250/46 was placed for a single prototype to be registered F-WFRD. Nord built the aircraft at its Issy-les-Moulineaux plant (previously the Caudron factory) and there were delays in its completion.

A model of the fighter was shown at the May 1949 Paris Salon and, after having been taken to Melun-Villaroche, the 2200 was given its first static engine run on 29 October. Pierre Gallay began taxi trials on 10 November and the prototype finally made its maiden flight on 16 December 1949, in the hands of Nord chief test pilot Claude Chautemps. In order to gain preliminary experience in the techniques of jet flight, Chautemps had previously flown a de Havilland Vampire. The 2200 was the 32nd French prototype of all classes of aircraft to make its appearance during 1949, highlighting the growing momentum of the revitalised French aircraft industry following the end of the Second World War.

The first flight lasted 25 minutes, during which the landing gear was not retracted, while neither wing folding equipment nor armament were fitted. A further flight was made on 21 December with the aircraft still configured for landing, the flaps being extended to 45°. The third sortie followed on 6 January 1950, when the undercarriage was retracted and the aircraft taken to 373mph (600km/h). On Flight 4, on the 17th, 423mph (680km/h) was recorded, while on 6 February the aircraft was presented and displayed to French and British officials and officers. Pierre Gallay flew the 2200 on 15 March but after the next flight, on the 21st, the aircraft went back into the shop to have its rear fuselage modified for the fitting of servo controls.

F-WFRD was ferried from Villaroche to CEV Brétigny on 3 April for official trials, during

This view of the 2200 prototype was taken shortly after the aircraft's completion. It was a very neat and clean design apart from the rudder, which one observer described (with its balances and tabs) as "very bitty".

which test pilots Roger Carpentier and Jean Sarrail made a dozen flights each. Carpentier completed the first CEV flight on 7 April and the programme lasted through April and May. Overall, the CEV pilots found that the Nord 2200 possessed generally very good flying and handling qualities (the latter quoted as superior to the VG 90), especially in landing configuration. The aircraft reached 507mph (815km/h) and Mach 0.83 on the level without any trouble from the effects associated with transonic speeds, although this was rather less than the estimated speed given previously by the manufacturer.

The aircraft was actually underpowered for its size and its best climb rate was just 2,953ft/min (900m/min). In addition, due to the complete ineffectiveness of the airbrakes, it proved impossible to look at potentially higher performance figures. The airbrake arrangement produced no deceleration, the CEV report stating that the 2200 should be considered "as having no airbrakes". Finally, the stall at a particular weight was preceded by severe yaw oscillations and this, coupled with other rolling characteristics, made for an unpleasant ride when passing through turbulence. The stall occurred at 118mph (190km/h) clean and 103mph (165km/h) with everything down.

F-WFRD went back to Villaroche on 5 June, and six days later Chautemps displayed it at the Paris Air Show. Then, on 24 June 1950, when Chautemps had the 2200 rolling down the runway to begin Flight 56, he heard a loud explosion. This was followed by smoke entering the cockpit and, after making an emergency stop, Chautemps jumped from the aircraft as firefighters moved in to extinguish the flames that were now coming from the rear fuselage.

The Nord 2200, before its markings had been applied. At this stage some of the main undercarriage doors had still to be fitted.

Opposite top: Early photograph of the Nord 2200 registered F-WFRD. The aircraft first visited CEV in this form.

Middle and bottom: Walkaround of the 2200 during its first visit to the CEV. *Michel Cristescu, Alain Pelletier*

The subsequent official enquiry found that a filler cap had been left open after the 2200 had been refuelled and kerosene was able to spill into the plenum, where it ignited. As a result Nord was found guilty of "gross negligence" and fined financially, while any chance that the 2200 might win a production order had now gone. It is understood that Arsenal VG 90 was the preferred competitor, although it seem that at one stage a batch of five pre-series machines could have been ordered for both it and the Nord 2200.

The Navy and CEV requested that F-WFRD be repaired so that its trials could continue and the CAMS (Chantiers Aéro-Maritimes de la Seine) factory at Sartrouville on the River Seine carried out the work. At the same time, several modifications were made to the airframe, including the introduction of Jacottet Leduc servo controls, fuselage-mounted dive brakes, a fin extension and, the most visible change, a lip fairing over the nose intake as a potential radar housing. The work took almost a year and ground testing began again at Villaroche on 24 April 1951. The 2200, its fuselage now marked with the letter 'G' (from its new registration F-ZWRG), finally achieved its 56th flight on 24 May.

Preparations for another test flight. Note that all of the undercarriage doors are now in place. *Michel Cristescu*

With its rounded fuselage the Nord 2200 was a classic late 1940s'/early 1950s' jet fighter in appearance, especially after the lip had been introduced to the upper part of the nose air intake. The aircraft retains its F-WFRD registration but the extended dorsal fin is not in place.

The 2200 in later form, with 'G' and a roundel painted on the rear fuselage. The enlarged fin and modified rudder are well shown. *Michel Cristescu*

After Flight 72 on 11 July, the 2200 went into store. Its next flight did not occur until 20 December, while further flights were made during January and March 1952. On 25 February 1953, the CEV's Marcel Perrin took the aircraft on its 100th flight, but it was Claude Chautemps who returned to the cockpit for the next phase of the aircraft's flying career, rocket-assisted take-offs.

Chautemps performed the first take off with rockets fitted (both inert) on 21 June 1953 and the next day saw take-off for Flight 107 with one of the rockets lit; the next flight had both rockets running. Two rocket-assisted take-off gear (RATOG) bottles were housed in permanent fairings underneath the fuselage. Back in the public eye at the Paris Air Show on 4 July, Chautemps made dramatic short take-offs using the rockets, the British aviation press describing how the 2200 ascended from a vast column of smoke. The reports added: "Although now growing obsolete, the 2200 evidently handles well at low speeds and has an exceptionally short landing-run," with the Fowler flaps conferring "a remarkable slow-speed performance."

By the early months of 1951 it was clear that none of the three naval fighter contestants, NC 1080, VG 90 or Nord 2200,

The Nord taxiing at the Paris show. Note the anchors in the French Navy roundels and fin markings.

could ever be successful as an operational aircraft. Instead the French Navy ordered a license-built de Havilland Sea Venom as the Aquilon. Nonetheless, during 1951 Nord managed to garner official interest in a Nord 2200 featuring the more powerful 6,300lb (28kN) Rolls-Royce Tay engine, the size of the aircraft's fuselage ensuring that such an installation would require few alterations. The project remained only a paper study.

Nord 2200 prototype in final form. *Copyright Pete West*

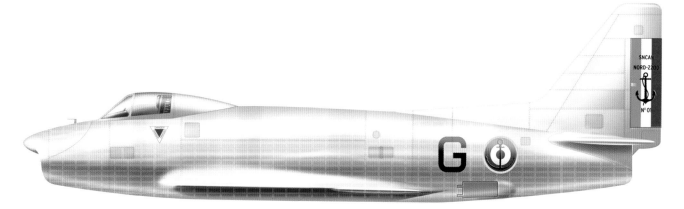

The 2200 flew in natural metal finish. From certain angles the intake lip appeared very small, but this view indicates that it could have housed a radar scanner of reasonable size. *Wolfgang Muehlbauer*

After Paris, the sole Nord 2200 went back into store at Villaroche on 7 July 1953, although it still flew occasionally. Another CEV pilot to sample it was Michel Marias, on 6 May 1954, after the 2200 had returned once more to the establishment. The 121st and last sortie of the aircraft's career took place on 16 June 1954, with Chautemps in the cockpit.

Like so many prototype aeroplanes, the condemned Nord 2200 ended its life serving as a target, in this case on the range at Bourges, with the engine and much of its equipment removed. However, the remains of the fuselage and wing sections have survived. Recovered in the 1980s, they were preserved at the Musée Aéronautique Vannes-Monterblanc ('Brittany Old Wings Flying Museum'), but during 2014 the facility was dissolved and its collection was to be distributed across other French museums. The Nord 2200's future is currently uncertain, although its condition suggests that anything like a full restoration would be an extremely difficult objective.

Airframe

The Nord 2200 naval fighter had a low cantilever wing of generous area, while its flattened nose air intake was a distinct and characteristic feature. Both wing and tail surfaces had moderate sweep back, the undihedraled wing being swept 24° at quarter chord and built around two spars, with ribbing and a thick skin. Slotted deep-chord Fowler flaps occupied most of each wing's trailing edge. Outboard of these were very short span ailerons which, for lateral control, operated in conjunction with upper surface spoilers. Dive brakes were fitted to the lower wing surfaces, but by the time of the RATOG trials airbrakes had been mounted on the sides of the rear fuselage.

Nord's 2200 on approach, with everything down. Note the metal sections at the rear of the open cockpit canopy.

The ovoid fuselage was formed as a shell using transverse frames and built in three sections. The centre portion contained the 2200's entire fuel load, 475 Imp gals (2,160 litres), while the rear section could easily be removed to access the Nene. The variable incidence tailplane used a similar structure to the wing and all control surfaces had trim tabs. Provision was made for naval equipment (for catapult attachments and a tailhook, etc, had testing progressed that far) and the aircraft had a tricycle undercarriage. A radar would have been installed above the air intake and a 209-Imp gal (950-litre) long-range drop tank was planned for beneath the fuselage.

The sole 2200 about to touch down. The large area of slotted Fowler flap is well shown.

Detail of the 2200's nose, nose gear and air intake, revealing the subtle curves and shaping around its fuselage and wing-fuselage junction.

14 Sud-Ouest SO 4000 (1951)

Sud-Ouest SO 4000

Performance figures are estimates for a take-off weight of 55,115lb (25,000kg)

Type: two-seat medium bomber

Span: 58ft 7in (17.86m)

Length: 66ft (20.11m)

Gross wing area: 806.45sq ft (75sq m)

Wing t/c ratio: 10%

Max weight: 55,908lb (25,360kg)

Powerplant: 2 x Hispano-built Rolls-Royce Nene 102 turbojets each 5,000lb (22.2kN)

Max speed: 534mph (860km/h) at sea level; 497mph (800km/h) at 29,530ft (9,000m)

Limiting Mach number: 0.88

Ceiling: 32,810ft (10,000m)

Climb rate: 2,165ft/min (660m/min) at sea level

Range: 1,180 miles (1,900km) at 26,245ft (8,000m)

Armament: 4 x 15mm defensive cannon and up to 11,023lb (5,000kg) of bombs planned

The Société Nationale de Constructions Aéronautiques du Sud-Ouest SO 4000, France's first medium/heavy jet bomber, was designed in competition with the Aérocentre NC 270. The SO 4000's flying career was very short indeed, however, although it was preceded by two research aircraft, the SO M.1 and M.2, described in the original volume. For completeness they are briefly reviewed again here.

SO M.1 and M.2

An order for two scale model test aircraft (5117/46), a full-size SO 4000 and parts for a second was placed on 25 May 1946, with Jean-Charles Parot as chief designer. Having been under construction since the previous March, the SO M.1 was first displayed to the public at the November 1946 Paris show (where some disappointment was expressed that no model was present of the projected full-size SO 4000). Although intended to fly, at least initially, as a glider, the M.1 was shown at Paris with exhaust for a bi-fuel rocket system.

It was also the first undercarriageless, high-speed aircraft shown outside Germany (a skid was to installed, retracting to lie flush with the fuselage underside). The wing was swept at an angle of about 38°, a figure, according to press reports, based exclusively on French theories. Orthodox two-spar construction was employed on the 10% thick wing. The flaps were made in three pieces, linked together and extended from the ailerons right to the fuselage, while the ailerons themselves were tiny. The tailplane had conventional elevators, but with four trimmers, two on each side, locked together.

The M.1 was expected to fly soon after the Paris show had ended, at a weight of less than 7,000lb (3,175kg), but in fact its first captive flight, aboard a Languedoc carrier aircraft, did not take place until 6 April 1948. The first free flight following release from its carrier had to wait until 26 September 1949. The M.1 never became a rocket-powered aircraft and ended its career as a target on a gunnery range, the airframe providing experience in firing the latest weapons at modern aircraft structures.

The Rolls-Royce Derwent-powered, half-scale M.2 appeared at the May 1949 show, having made its maiden flight on 13 April, well

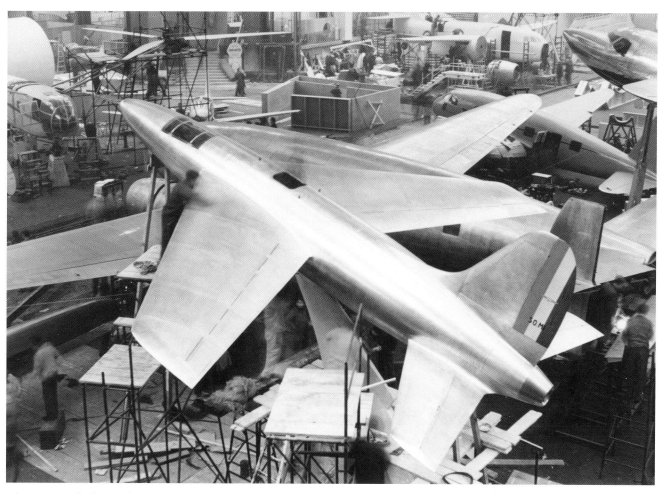

The M.1 on display at the 1946 Paris Salon. It is fitted with an exhaust pipe. *Alain Pelletier*

Here the M.1 is mounted above a Heinkel He 274 launch aircraft, its exhaust pipe having been closed off. During its flight tests the M.1 carried the registration letters F-WFDJ.

The M.2 at the Paris show in 1949, complete with flush cockpit canopy (the windscreen was retractable). Not visible in this image are the registration letters F-WFDK on the rear fuselage sides.

The M.2's air intakes are clearly shown here, along with plenty of undercarriage detail. A new canopy is in place and the registration letters have been applied.

ahead of the M.1's first free flight. At the June 1950 Paris show the M.2 looked impressive, flying level speed runs that *Flight* recorded as a genuine 600mph (965km/h), although the journal added that in the air its "demonstration generally was disappointing".

However, this single-Derwent aircraft was able to investigate at least some of the forthcoming SO 4000's flight characteristics and also proved valuable in building up knowledge of flight with swept wings and control through the use of spoilers. After the full-size bomber had been abandoned, the manufacturer continued to use the M.2 in high-speed experiments until October 1952, gathering data for the company's new SO 4050 fighter-bomber. It subsequently became a fire-training hulk at Cazaux, before being scrapped.

The M.2 fitted with wingtip nacelles. It has French roundels and national colours painted on the rudder. By now a new registration, F-ZWRD, had been applied, signified by the letter 'D' at the rear. The M.2 completed the last of its 73 flights on 8 October 1952. *Alain Pelletier*

Few photographs of the SO 4000 were taken, which is hardly surprising when the machine flew just once.

SO 4000

Design work on the SO 4000 began in 1946 and during 1947-48 the team arrived at a definitive configuration. The completed prototype SO 4000-01 (registered F-WBBL) was taken to Orléans-Bricy airfield on 4 March 1950 to be prepared for its flight trials, but on 23 April the undercarriage collapsed during a taxi run. In the meantime, government officials had expressed doubts about the project (and also about the rival NC 270, which was never completed) and in due course plans for a second SO 4000 were dropped. From this point onwards, the first machine was considered as an experimental aircraft only – no production orders would be forthcoming and 01 would not carry weapons or operational equipment.

The programme was officially cancelled in May 1950 because of financial constraints and the first flight was made at Sud-Ouest's expense (the contract was finally closed in December 1951). Even before the aircraft had flown it was likely clear to the Sud-Ouest design team that the SO 4000 would be of little use and was near obsolete. Proposals had been made to fit more powerful British axial jet engines, along with the development of a reconnaissance version, but these had been rejected.

Repairs to SO 4000-01 combined with other work and considerable time, so that engine ground running did not begin until the end of 1950. On 14 February 1951 test pilot Daniel Rastel made the aircraft's first 'hop' – beginning his run at a weight of 37,324lb (16,930kg) he took 01 off the ground for a distance of about 655ft (200m).

The first (and only) full flight was recorded on 15 March, from Orléans-Bricy, with Daniel Rastel and flight engineer Paul Pistrak onboard. The jet was loaded with 440 Imp gals (2,000 litres) of kerosene and took off at 39,914lb (18,105kg), the crew noticing a roll oscillation almost immediately after lift off. At an airspeed of 155mph (250km/h) the elevator seemed oversensitive, and as the aeroplane climbed at a rate of about 787ft/min (240m/min) this sensitivity increased with speed. The SO 4000 became very difficult to control and Rastel decided to end the flight prematurely. A maximum speed of 182mph (293km/h) was recorded and by the time this speed had been reached a pitching oscillation had also begun.

Despite the arduous task of controlling the machine (the rudder also proved heavy), Rastel made a safe landing at a touchdown speed of 140mph (225km/h). During the flight the undercarriage had been left extended and a Sud-Ouest Corse chaseplane had been in attendance. With its poor controls and stability the bomber would clearly never fly again. The SO 4000's flying career had ended after just 15 minutes in the air, and the airframe would also finish its career on the gunnery range at Bourges.

Rear angle view of the SO 4000 bomber prototype.

SO 4000-01, on the ground at Orléans-Bricy. The complex undercarriage and cigar shape of the fuselage are well illustrated.

Despite the failure of its first major bomber programme, Sud-Ouest's design experience with the SO 4000 was valuable in the development of its next type, the SO 4050 Vautour fighter-bomber, which first flew in October 1952 and entered service with l'Armée de l'Air in 1958. In all, 149 Vautours were built.

Airframe

The Sud-Ouest SO 4000 bomber was very streamlined, but appeared rather awkward sitting on the ground, perhaps because of its fragile undercarriage, the nose leg of which was very long while the main gears used individual legs for each of the tandem wheels. Each of these four legs retracted outwards into the underside of the wings, excluding wing fuel tanks. The wing was swept 31° at quarter chord and small ailerons were fitted to its outer surfaces to provide roll control in conjunction with powered spoilers; the remainder of the trailing edge was occupied by substantial slotted flaps. The wing used conventional twin-spar construction with thick, smooth skinning over a torsion box, and was built in three sections. The empennage also had a conventional metal structure, here with a single spar, although at one point during the design process a butterfly shape had been considered.

Like so many early French jet prototypes, the SO 4000 was powered by the license-built Rolls-Royce Nene, in this case two of the engines were positioned side-by-side in the rear fuselage and fed by fuselage side inlets placed well ahead of the wing. They exhausted through separate pipes either side of the fin. Only 1,430 Imp gals (6,502 litres) of fuel was carried, all in shallow tanks in the upper centre fuselage. Provision was made for a large bomb bay under the centre wing and twin automatic 15mm machine gun turrets were to go on each wingtip. These would provide defensive fire to the rear and were to be radar controlled. The pilot and observer were seated far forwards over the nose.

The SO 4000 during its one and only test flight. Note the deployed flaps. *Michel Cristescu*

| The large trailing edge wing flaps are also deployed in this nose view.

15 Breguet Br 960 Vultur (1951)

Breguet Br 960 Vultur

Type: two-seat carrierborne attack aircraft

Span: 52ft (15.85m) without tip tanks; 54ft 10in (16.70m) with tip tanks

Length: 43ft 10in (13.35m)

Gross wing area: 390.32sq ft (36.30sq m)

Wing t/c ratio: 15% at root, 10% at tip

Max weight: Br 960 21,362lb to 21,604lb (9,690kg to 9,800kg); Br 965 16,733lb (7,590kg), or 17,526lb (7,950kg) with 6 rockets

Powerplant: Br 960-01 1 x Armstrong Siddeley Mamba I turboprop 970hp (725kW) and 1 x Rolls-Royce Nene 101 turbojet 4,850lb (21.6kN) thrust; Br 960-02 1 x Mamba III 1,320hp (984kW) and 405lb (1.80kN) of residual thrust, and 1 x Nene 104 5,000lb (22.2kN); Br 965 1 x Armstrong Siddeley Mamba IV turboprop

Max speed: Br 960 249mph (400km/h) turboprop only; 559mph (900km/h) on both engines; Br 965 277mph (445km/h)

Absolute ceiling: Br 960-02 42,000ft (12,800m)

Armament: 1 x 1,000kg (2,205lb) bomb and up to 8 x 5in (12.7cm) rockets

The Breguet Br 960 Vultur was a mixed-power strike aircraft for the French Navy, ordered in prototype form against official requirements but not put into production in its original configuration. At the time its powerplant was considered unconventional, and was simplified in a modified design designated Br 1050 Alizé (Tradewind), which entered into production and served as an anti-submarine aircraft.

In November 1947 the Marine Nationale issued a call for proposals for a new carrier-based anti-shipping and anti-submarine aircraft, and Breguet was among the companies that responded. Its chief designer for the project, Mr Allain, had a reputation for enterprising and novel solutions to the problems of aircraft design and considered jet engines essential to provide the new strike aircraft with good performance. However, such types also required long endurance and frequently flew in situations where high performance was not required, so Allain's solution was to place a small turboprop in the nose and a large turbojet in the rear fuselage for use on take-off and in combat.

Once again the licence-built Hispano-Suiza (Rolls-Royce) Nene was selected, along with another British engine, the Armstrong Siddeley Mamba axial turboprop, which would be fitted with a special four-blade Rotol airscrew.

The first Br 960 design had twin fins, but a central fin soon replaced them. There was a widely-spaced undercarriage to permit carriage of an anti-ship missile, a weapon to be designed along the lines of the wartime German Henschel Hs 293 and which would be guided to its target by the 960's crew.

Two Br 960 prototypes were ordered on 23 April 1948 and test pilot Yves Brunaud performed the maiden flights of both, on 4 August 1951 and 15 September 1952, respectively. Both airframes were built at Toulouse and it was from here that the first sorties and their initial flight trials were made. During the remainder of 1951, Vultur 01 flew general handling tests and problems with the Mamba I arose since it did not provide sufficient power, to the point where the aircraft could not fly on the turboprop alone at maximum weight.

The second prototype's more powerful Mamba III eliminated the problem, but the first machine had to rely on the Nene to fly at such weights, although the heavy turbojet penalised the Vultur during cruising flight on the turboprop alone. The Vultur's flying qualities were also quite poor, except in the low-speed region for landing, which was satisfactory. Nevertheless, 960-01 performed a great deal of work with CEV, for example looking at the general aspects of the operation of naval aircraft aboard carriers, including procedures used in aircraft and ships as an aeroplane approached to land.

Vultur 02 was used a good deal on mass-balancing tests, which resulted in various excrescences being fitted to the elevator. In late January 1953 it joined the Naval Flight at RAE Farnborough, England to undergo

| The Br 960 as built. *Michel Cristescu*

catapulting and arresting trials since no French establishment had the required equipment available. *Flight* for 15 May described the trials in some detail, noting how RAE's equipment worked. "The aircraft is aligned on the runway about half a mile behind the arrester wires and is run up to full power against the brakes; then the brakes are released and the machine accelerates towards the wires at full throttle; finally the hook is dropped and the throttles cut and the aircraft brought to rest, usually on the first wire. Full readings of weight, impact velocity and deceleration are recorded." This procedure saved so much time when the alternative was to make complete circuits, and it was fully representative in proving the aeroplane's arresting gear.

| The Br 960 carrying weapons – firstly with just a bomb beneath the fuselage and then together with underwing rockets. *Michel Cristescu*

One of the compound-powerplant Breguet Br 960 Vultur prototypes at the Paris show in 1953. The first Sud-Ouest SO 9000 Trident interceptor fighter prototype is parked alongside. *David Hedge*

The French officer in charge on the Br 960's English trip was Ingenieur Principal René Perineau. His pilot for most of the trials was Breguet chief test pilot Yves Brunaud, while Lt de Vaisseau (First Lieutenant) Georges Picci served as second pilot. The article noted: "starting up the Mamba appeared effortless and the airscrew was soon running smoothly. The Nene followed and its roar completely drowned the noise of the tiny turboprop. The steerable nosewheels showed their worth in getting out of confined spaces, take-off was rapid and the wheels were up 10 seconds from the start of the run." The overwhelming impression given to the author, however, was that: "...the airscrew was being pushed through the air by the Nene and was a hindrance to progress, [though] the Rotol

four-blader was constant-speeding even at 460 knots (853km/h) at which speed the pitch angle was over 60°." A very steep approach to land was made at about 100 knots (185km/h) and a large part of the run-in took place with the Vultur's nose raised high in the air. The landing tests performed at Farnborough between February and April 1953 were a success.

The trials performed with 02 during 1952 and 1953 showed that overall the aircraft met the Navy's requirements. In particular, a maximum speed of around 528mph (850km/h) had been recorded, and when cruising at around 249mph (400km/h) on the turboprop an endurance of up to four hours was possible. The stall occurred at 93mph (150km/h), but came sharply and with little warning. Simulated landings were also performed at Istres, but the Br 960 had originally been designed for the now abandoned PA28 aircraft carrier and was too heavy for the lightweight vessels then in Navy service.

Moreover, submarines were increasingly becoming the target for new naval attack aircraft and the Br 960 was generally unsuited to the anti-submarine role, since it was too heavy and carried the quite unnecessary Nene (apart from a possible 'dash' to the target area, anti-submarine work was generally performed at low speeds and low altitudes). Following a long period of discussion it was decided to adapt the Vultur as an anti-submarine warfare aircraft, a move that would require major modifications, including deleting the pure turbojet part of the powerplant.

The second prototype revised as the Br 965, with a revised canopy and no wingtip nacelles. The new underfuselage radar scanner can be seen, while the bulged housing for the strike radar remains forward on the port wing. *Michel Cristescu*

Vultur 02 was modified as such in 1955, in the process being redesignated Br 965. The Nene was taken out and its exhaust pipe blocked, while the turboprop was upgraded to a more powerful Mamba IV. New wing fences were installed and the canopy enlarged over the third crewman, who operated a search radar and was located in the rear fuselage where the Nene had previously been installed (the radome could be retracted). Still a heavy aircraft, the 965's type's characteristics limited its value as a demonstrator airframe – it took a long time to reach any sort of altitude, for example.

The wing fences improved the 965's behaviour at the stall, however, and the aircraft proved the general concept so that Breguet's three-seat Br 1050 anti-submarine design was ordered as the Alize. The Br 965 continued flying until 2 May 1956 when an accident damaged the undercarriage. By then the aircraft's test programme was well advanced and it was not repaired, being used instead as a source of spares for the first prototype.

In the meantime, in 1954 Br 960-01 had been fitted with a blown canopy as the Br 963, though this designation was rarely used and

The Br 965 with covers over its fuselage radar and erstwhile jet pipe. *Michel Cristescu*

the aircraft always retained its Br 960 No. 01 label. As such, and also with the civil registration F-WEVU, it was used to research improvements in lift by bleeding air from the Nene and blowing it through a set of slots placed in the wing uppersurfaces, a concept at the time known as 'hyper-circulation'. A first series of trials proved successful in that wing lift was increased, but a second series was halted through budget restrictions. It is thought the first Br 960 did not fly beyond 1957.

Breguet Br 1050 Alize prototype 01, at Paris Le Bourget on 29 May 1957.

| Breguet Br 960. *Copyright Pete West*

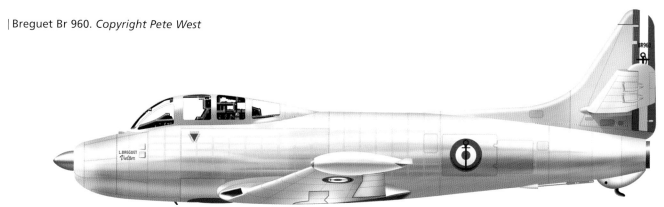

A production Alize pictured aboard the French carrier *Clemenceau* in July 1970.

Detail of the Br 960, including the twin wheels on the nose leg, the complex cockpit canopy and considerable tailplane dihedral. *Michel Cristescu*

Proposed versions of the Vultur were the Br 960 F1 and F2 'hunter/killer' types where different versions of the same airframe were intended to work together against submarines, while a land-based ground attack version, the Br 961, was offered to the Air Force; the Br 962 was a revised anti-submarine aircraft.

The initial Br 1050 Alize prototype, powered by a Rolls-Royce Dart turboprop, first flew on 5 October 1956, piloted again by Yves Brunaud. The premier production machine was delivered in March 1959 and altogether 87 aircraft were delivered on top of two prototypes. The success of the Alize was in no small measure due to the work performed with the two Br 960 Vulturs.

Airframe

The Br 960's airframe used straightforward all-metal, stressed-skin construction. Its wing was built in three parts, a centre section plus two outer portions that could fold, and had a moderate 16° 10' of sweep on the leading edge. The tailplane was also given moderate sweep, along with pronounced dihedral and it had a quite complex elevator balance system.

The elliptical-section fuselage was a conventional monocoque and the *Flight* report noted how the skinning and general finish on 02 was "first-class" and showed "an extremely high standard of workmanship". The piece added: "The tiny Mamba is quite lost in the Vultur's nose." Air for the turboprop entered around the spinner, with gases exhausting through an orifice immediately beneath the port wing root leading edge. There were speed brakes on the sides of the rear fuselage. The Nene's air supply came from intakes in the wing leading edges and the jet pipe was in the aft end of the fuselage. A large cockpit seated the two crew side-by-side. The main gear was placed in the wings just inboard of the wing fold and retracted towards the fuselage, while the nose gear retracted rearwards.

Wingtip nacelles housed an overload fuel tank on the port side, balanced by a strike radar in the starboard side, and a large search radar could be carried in a container beneath the fuselage. An underfuselage hardpoint could take a 1,000kg (2,205lb) bomb, while eight rocket projectiles could go under the outer wings, two launchers per wing, with two rockets on each. No guns were carried and there was no internal bomb bay.

The main tank contained 242 Imp gals (1,100 litres) of fuel and the first prototype had a variable-speed Mamba I turboprop, but Vultur 02 received the more powerful Mamba III, which was a constant-speed engine. The constant-speed characteristic was a most valuable property for a carrierborne aircraft in that it permitted rapid 'opening up' during an aborted landing when the aircraft was required to go round again. While it was at RAE Farnborough, 02 had provision for RATOG, but this was not used.

France also built several light ground attack/counter insurgency (COIN) aircraft prototypes.

Powered by a 483hp (360kW) Potez 8D-32 piston engine, the Potez 75 first flew on 10 June 1953. The only prototype was scrapped after suffering a crash landing on 16 September 1958. The first view here shows it carrying a Nord SS10 anti-tank missile and a single nose gun, the second eight rocket projectiles and four guns in the nose. Span 30ft 0.5in (9.16m), length 43ft (13.10m), gross weight 5,291lb (2,400kg), max speed 174mph (280km/h).

A series of light COIN prototypes was also built in consideration of operations during the war in Algeria, including the Morane-Saulnier MS 1500 Epervier, SIPA S 1100, Sud Aviation SE 116 Voltigeur and, a little later, the Dassault MD.410 Spirale (the latter based on a light transport known as the Communauté).

The SIPA S 1100 was powered by two 603hp (450kW) Pratt & Whitney R-1340 radial piston engines and armed with two 20mm guns. Only one was built and it first flew on 24 April 1958. It suffered a fatal crash on 2 July, an event that brought work on a second machine to a close. Span 48ft 6in (14.78m), length 37ft 0.5in (11.29m), gross weight 11,243lb (5,100kg), max speed 236mph (380km/h). *Alain Pelletier*

Left: Two examples of the Turbomeca turboprop-powered Morane-Saulnier MS 1500 Epervier (Sparrowhawk) were built, the first flying on 12 May 1958. Span 34ft 8.5in (10.58m), length 42ft 10.5in (13.06m), gross weight 6,063lb (2,750kg), max speed 216mph (348km/h). The Epervier carried rocket pods or 50kg (110lb) bombs.

Below: The first of three Sud Aviation SE 116 Voltigeur prototypes flew on 5 June 1958, powered by piston engines. This view shows the second, turboprop-powered machine. One aircraft was lost with its crew in a crash and no more were built beyond the first SE 117 pre-production aeroplane. Span 58ft 11.5in (17.97m), length 40ft 1in (12.22m), gross weight 12,537lb (5,687kg), max speed 277mph (445km/h). The aircraft had two 30mm guns and could take bombs or rockets under the wings. *Alain Pelletier*

16 Short Sperrin (1951)

Short Sperrin

Type: five-seat medium bomber prototype

Span: 109ft 1in (33.25m)

Length: 102ft 2.5in (31.15m), with modified nose 103ft 6in (31.55m)

Gross wing area: 1,897sq ft (176.42sq m)

Wing t/c ratio: 12%

Max weight: 115,000lb (52,164kg)

Powerplant: 4 x Rolls-Royce Avon RA.2 each 6,000lb (26.7kN) or RA.3 each 6,500lb (28.9kN)

Max speed: VX158 with RA.2 engines 494 knots (915km/h) at sea level, 443 knots (821km/h) at 40,000ft (12,192m)

Design max Mach number: 0.85 (aileron flutter limited the aircraft to 0.78 IMN)

Max cruising speed: 501mph (806km/h) at 40,000ft

Ceiling: 42,000ft (12,802m)

Climb rate: VX161 with RA.3 engines at 100,000lb (45,360kg) 3,500ft/min (1,067m/min) at sea level

Range: 3,350nm (6,208km) with 10,000lb (4,536kg) load

Armament: Up to 20,000lb (9,072kg) bombs, including nuclear stores, housed in central bomb bay

The Short Sperrin was a medium bomber design at one stage intended for production, but the arrival of Britain's three V-Bombers halted such plans. The Avro Vulcan, Handley Page Victor and Vickers Valiant all fell within the medium-bomber class and featured more advanced wing shapes that made the Sperrin seem rather out of date. Thus only the two Sperrin prototypes were flown, but both fulfilled successful careers in research flying.

Plans were laid down soon after the end of the war to replace the main portion of the RAF's World War II piston bomber fleet with new jet-powered aircraft. In late 1946 Specification B.35/46 was prepared for a new medium-size jet bomber featuring advanced wing shapes and this was the starting point for what became the V-Force. However, by then the programme that led to the Sperrin was already up and running.

Back in February 1945, the Air Ministry had asked Short Brothers at Rochester to make a study to see if a jet-propelled high-speed bomber could achieve a range of 5,000 miles (8,045km). The firm's resulting S.A.4 proposal was completed in November and showed a huge machine powered by six Rolls-Royce AJ.65 (Avon) engines. Shortly afterwards, Short was asked to revise the S.A.4 and make it smaller using perhaps four AJ.65s instead of six and the firm's second investigation was completed on 26 April 1946.

In due course work began on the acquisition of the new medium bomber against B.35/46 but this project, with as yet untried design features including swept wings, would be difficult to satisfy. Therefore, an Interim Bomber was introduced as a back-up requirement and the four-engine S.A.4 was chosen, with Specification B.14/46 and Operational Requirement OR.239 prepared to cover it. The aircraft's cruise speed was to be 450mph (724km/h) at altitudes between 35,000ft and 45,000ft (10,668m and 13,716m), its maximum bomb load would be 20,000lb (9,072kg) and with a 10,000lb (4,536kg) load the radius of action should be 1,500nm (2,780km). The S.A.4's chief designer was David Keith-Lucas.

Photos of VX158 taken as new and prior to painting. The venue is Aldergrove and the images were made soon after the aircraft's first flight.

In late February 1947 agreement was reached to order two S.A.4 prototypes at which point it was planned to house the AJ.65s in single underwing nacelles. However, in mid-February 1949, following extensive tunnel test work at RAE Farnborough that looked at five different engine nacelle positions, Keith-Lucas confirmed that a configuration of two engines in a single vertical 'double-banked' nacelle above and below each wing had now been selected.

The RAE had favoured engines arranged horizontally in a nacelle suspended below the wing by a slim, faired strut, but Keith-Lucas rejected this arrangement because it presented structural problems and would also be difficult to accommodate without redesigning the wing quite extensively (construction of the first prototype having just commenced).

The B.35/46 competition was won by the designs submitted by Avro and Handley Page, featuring a delta wing and crescent wing, respectively, which became the Vulcan and Victor. They were very advanced for their day and a less extreme design with a more straightforward swept wing was also ordered from Vickers, becoming the Valiant, and it was the ordering of production Valiants that put paid to plans to build the straight-wing S.A.4 in quantity.

There remained a desire to complete the two S.A.4 prototypes for test flying, however, as part of the background effort leading to the introduction of the V-bombers into service. In early 1950 there were plans to use both prototypes on 'ballistic trials' because it was essential to obtain information on the behaviour of bombs released from aircraft flying at high

speeds and the necessary trials could not be completed until an S.A.4 or one of the V-types was available. In May it was agreed to complete the second S.A.4 as a flying laboratory for ballistic research and the development of the new H2S/Navigation and Bombing Computer (NBC). It was also confirmed during May 1950 that the S.A.4 would not go into production.

In addition to VX158 and VX161, the two prototypes ordered against Contract 6/Acft/1056, a third airframe was built for exhaustive static testing. Design work for the S.A.4 had begun at Rochester, but the aircraft were built at Sydenham in Belfast. When the company made its move from Rochester to Belfast in 1947 the S.A.4's design effort was in full swing and it was estimated that the move delayed progress by at least four months.

Manufacturers frequently hastened the development of new aircraft designs by flight testing elements of their incomplete new types on existing aircraft. This was the case with the S.A.4 when, in November 1950, the bomber's fin and rudder were assessed on Short Sunderland flying boat PP151, fitted with a special aerodynamic-servo rudder to replicate the S.A.4's arrangement.

On 19 September 1950, Short offered the name Stormont for the S.A.4, but the Ministry of Supply would not accept it and the bomber remained as the S.A.4 and B.14/46 (and S.42 at Short) until the official name Sperrin was confirmed in 1954.

When Short test pilot Tom Brooke-Smith piloted the S.A.4 on its initial test flight from Aldergrove near Belfast on 10 August 1951, he became the first man in Britain to fly a four-jet bomber. Sydenham's runway was not long enough to take this class of aircraft but later, after it had been extended, the S.A.4s flew from there. VX158 was first flown in natural metal finish, but when it was unveiled at that year's Farnborough show in September its paint scheme was a matt-finish of light grey over black undersides, with a red fuselage cheatline.

Flight reported a general criticism of the aircraft because it seemed to follow conventional lines rather than being "more

The first S.A.4 Sperrin prototype was VX158, here in a picture dated 13 September 1951. *Short Brothers*

| Sperrin VX158 in its Farnborough colours. *Copyright Pete West*

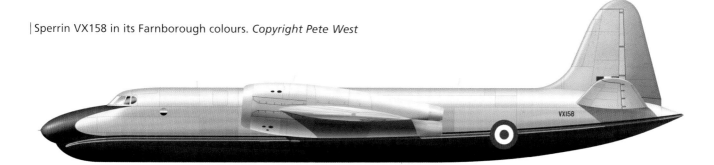

VX158's first paint scheme was an attractive light grey with black undersides and red fuselage cheatline. *Short Brothers*

characteristic of the 'jet era' with sweepback, buried engines and so forth". Nevertheless the aircraft aroused much interest. Tom Brooke-Smith flew it at the show, but the test pilot who performed almost all of the manufacturer's trials flying for the S.A.4 was Sqn Ldr WJ 'Wally' Runciman, who joined the company in 1952 (he was killed in 1956 while demonstrating a Seamew anti-submarine aircraft).

VX161 made its first flight on 12 August 1952, again from Aldergrove with Tom Brooke-Smith piloting, powered by 6,500lb (28.9kN) Rolls-Royce Avon RA.3 engines, whereas VX158 had been fitted with RA.2 Avons (these were later changed for RA.3s). The second prototype, with cleaner, more streamlined nose lines and finished in a silver/grey scheme, attended that year's September SBAC show, where Runciman performed a display that indicated the aircraft had excellent handling qualities. Especially remarkable was the speed at which he brought the big bomber along the enclosures – substantially faster than that shown by VX158 the previous year when, admittedly, the first prototype had been restricted in what it was allowed to do (VX158 also attended the 1952 show).

Two 'official' pilots made handling flights in VX161 on 9 April 1953, with a view to assessing its capabilities as a high-altitude bombing platform for the NBC. The system required accurate flying at high altitude and high Mach numbers and the ability to make rapid changes in course for a bombing run. Back in September 1952 similar handling assessments by RAE's Aerodynamic Flight had found the aircraft unsuitable for the work due to unsatisfactory aileron feel, but since then Short had made several modifications to the aileron circuit, including a new design of aileron screw jack.

Some of the trouble came when the aircraft flew at well over 40,000ft (12,192m) where, naturally enough, problems appeared largely on account of the intense cold at that

VX158 on 21 September 1951. Although its wing was considered old fashioned, there was a limited amount of sweep on its leading edge. This underside view shows that the Sperrin had quite a sleek design. *Peter Green*

VX158 taxis at Farnborough. There seem to be few colour photographs showing this original scheme. The dihedral on the tailplane shows up well here. *Peter Green*

altitude. The screw jack system had worked well in tests at −60°C (-76°F), but on one flight a temperature of −74°C (-101°F) was recorded and the flying-control system virtually froze solid. The problem was traced to the grease used in the system and subsequently found that the system's pulleys worked much better at high altitude without any grease at all.

One of the two pilots, Sqn Ldr HT Murley, wrote the subsequent official report. For the handling flights VX161's weight at take-off was 95,000lb (43,092kg), at landing approximately 78,000lb (35,381kg), and the maximum permissible IAS and indicated Mach number (IMN) were 390 knots (722km/h) and Mach 0.78, respectively (all knots and Mach figures quoted here are IAS and IMN).

By the time of its second Farnborough show in 1952, VX158 had become all-silver. Note 'Shorts SA4' written beneath the cockpit windows, because at this stage the aircraft had still not been named. *Peter Green*

Murley reported that during taxiing the view out was somewhat restricted – the wingtips were in view but nothing closer than the engine nacelles could be seen. During take-off the nosewheel was eased off the ground at 75 knots (138km/h) and the aircraft flew off at 105 knots (195km/h). On selecting wheels up at 130 knots (209km/h) there was no noticeable trim change, but on raising the take-off flap there was a slight nose down trim change. Accelerating to a climbing speed of 250 knots (463km/h) gave no noticeable change in longitudinal trim and all controls felt light and effective with good response. On reaching 10,000ft (3,048m) the speed was further increased to the limiting 390 knots (722km/h) at less than full power and again no change in trim was necessary; in fact it was not necessary to retrim the aircraft longitudinally throughout the speed range. At 390 knots (722km/h) an intermittent rear fuselage tremor was felt in the cockpit, caused by an asymmetric breakaway somewhere near the tail, but otherwise flight at the limiting IAS was smooth and uneventful. (Earlier tests had shown that losing an engine at take-off presented no real difficulties, even at a weight of

The date of this view of silver-painted VX158 is uncertain. *Peter Green*

115,000lb/52,164kg the directional change was slight and the three-engine climb-out described as adequate.)

Approaching the stall all controls were light and effective with good response down to 140 knots (259km/h), but below this speed the ailerons, although effective, suffered from the usual lag in response experienced in most large aeroplanes. The clean stall showed a slight tail buffet commencing at 110 knots (204km/h) and becoming quite a severe shake as speed reduced to 105 knots (195km/h). The stall with flaps and wheels down had a slight buffet commencing at 100 knots (185km/h), increasing as speed was lowered to 90 knots (167km/h). Here the nose dropped gently and recovery was affected quickly by easing the stick forward. There was no tendency for either wing to drop at the stall.

As regards the individual controls, from approach speed to limiting speed the elevator maintained an adequate effectiveness and good response, and at 390 knots this, coupled with the light stick forces, made it feel "decidedly touchy". However, the elevator's general behaviour was considered most pleasant.

Fewer images of VX161, the second prototype, appear to exist. Here the aircraft is shown fairly early in its flying career. *Short Brothers*

Rare picture showing the two Sperrins flying together, XV161 leading VX158. *Terry Panopalis*

VX161 at the Royal Aircraft Establishment's Golden Jubilee celebrations at Farnborough in early July 1955. The aircraft was parked on the compass-base near 'A' Shed and, with bomb bay doors open, shown ready to receive a 10,000lb (4,536kg) folding-fin bomb lying on the ground underneath. *Peter Berry*

Control with the ailerons was carefully assessed and found to be an obvious improvement from the situation that had existed prior to the modifications. There was, however, a lack of self-centring and the general feel of the control was not ideal, but there was no longer a residual force remaining in the opposite direction when coming out of a turn, and the wheel could be placed in the centre and the aircraft straightened onto a heading without any difficulty. The ailerons remained very effective throughout the speed range, with good response except at the approach speed, where there was some lag.

On the whole it was thought the rudder was too light for comfort, particularly at high speed, although it remained very powerful for even small deflections and had immediate response at even the lowest speed tested. A sharp rudder application would send the bomber's tail end round with a considerable jar that the pilots considered to be "most unpleasant".

The S.A.4's manoeuvrability at low altitude was generally good for an aircraft of its size. The maximum rate of roll at full deflection of 30° per second was considered to be "quite satisfactory", and the times quoted to pass through 90° when flying at 10,000ft (3,048m) at 150 knots (278km/h) was 5.0-5.2 seconds and at 240 knots (444km/h) 3.0 seconds; at 390 knots and quarter deflection the time was 7.2 seconds.

The effectiveness of the split trailing edge airbrakes was considered "quite good" – in operation they produced a moderate degree of airframe buffet but no trim change. Selecting brakes out and closing the throttles at the same time at 390 knots reduced the speed to 250 knots (463km/h) in 75 seconds.

In a climb to 40,000ft (12,192m) starting at 2,000ft (610m), and at a climbing speed of 250 knots changing to 0.65 IMN in the climb, 5,000ft (1,524m) was reached in 43 seconds, 10,000ft in 2 minutes 7 seconds, 30,000ft (9,144m) in 11 minutes dead and 40,000ft in 19 minutes 7 seconds. On reaching approximately 25,000ft (7,620m) a slight snaking began and remained above that altitude.

VX161 generated a great deal of noise and interest at Farnborough. The aircraft had a slightly different nose to VX158.
Terry Panopalis

Part of the Sperrin support team in a picture taken at Aldergrove on 10 April 1953, immediately before VX161's departure to RAF Woodbridge for a programme of bombing trials. Flight Shed Superintendent Bill Day is fourth from left, next is test pilot 'Jock' Eassie, then flight test engineers Malcolm Wild (sixth from left) and Ian King (seventh), and on the far right is Doug Scard, head of the Short Flight Test Department.

Flying the aircraft at 40,000ft presented the usual effect of decreased stability and increased sensitiveness when displaced from trim, but the effectiveness of all three controls and the response to them appeared to remain unaltered and the aircraft was pleasant to fly. On reaching this altitude an immediate check of control forces showed no appreciable change from those encountered at low level, but as time passed and because of the low temperature, these increased with control circuit stiffening.

The aircraft's performance at 40,000ft was described as "quite commendable" and the IMN limit of 0.78 was reached in almost level flight. Between 0.755 and 0.76 IMN there was faint tail buffet, at 0.76 a slight nose down trim change occurred with smoothing out of the buffet, and at 0.78 the S.A.4 was in trim with no noticeable effects.

The application of 0.2 or 0.3g at 0.78 IMN produced some moderate to severe buffeting that worsened with an increase in applied 'g'. The aircraft was also flown at 0.815 IMN, where a similar buffet appeared and it was considered that continuous flight at Mach 0.815 was taxing the aircraft's structure. This strong 'g' buffet restricted manoeuvres at 40,000ft at speeds of Mach 0.78 and above, but VX161 appeared to have a reasonable degree of manoeuvrability up to 0.75 IMN.

The bomb doors were operated quite successfully up to 0.78 IMN at 40,000ft, a set of deflector gills having been provided to help smooth airflow over the open doors. It was not possible to judge by just how much the gills helped, but the resultant airframe buffet was moderate and proportional to speed, and it was not as severe as had been experienced on the English Electric Canberra.

Approach and landing were straightforward. A speed of 150 knots (278km/h) was maintained in the circuit and there was no change of trim with the wheels extended. Full flap was selected on turning into the final approach at 125 knots (232km/h) and on landing, the Maxaret brakes worked well, the landing distance of approximately 1,200 yards (1,100m) not requiring the deployment of the aircraft's braking parachute. The effectiveness of all three controls was satisfactory on the approach and during landing, the elevator feeling light and pleasant with no noticeable lag in response.

By the September 1955 Farnborough show, VX158, now named Sperrin, had a de Havilland Gyron jet in the lower position of its port engine nacelle. The larger diameter and more powerful Gyron required the lower nacelle section to be widened. *Peter Berry*

In conclusion, Murley stated that the S.A.4's "handling qualities and performance were somewhat better than expected and were rather belied by its appearance." It was a simple, generally pleasant and straightforward aircraft to fly at low and high altitudes, and the improvements to the aileron circuit had rendered it satisfactory for the projected work at RAE. There was some criticism concerning the lack of self-centring of the controls (particularly the ailerons) which, although serious, did not render the aircraft unsatisfactory for prolonged accurate flying at high altitude.

Two days after these flights, VX161 joined the Armament & Instrument Experimental Unit at Martlesham Heath to begin bomb-dropping

VX158 shows the difference in the lower nacelle size and shape for the Avon (starboard side) and Gyron (port). The photo was taken during a Farnborough display.

VX158 in August 1955 with just the one Gyron. *de Havilland Engines*

Above: VX158 with both Gyrons in position.
Right: VX158 under tow at Farnborough, possibly prior to a display.

trials, the sorties for this programme being made from nearby Woodbridge, a much larger airfield better equipped for such a heavy aircraft. Stores dropped during the trials included concrete dummies of the Blue Danube and Blue Boar nuclear bombs, the objective being to find out how these behaved on leaving the bomber. In September 1954 VX161 joined RAE Farnborough for more weapon trials. It returned to Sydenham on 16 July 1956 and was sold for scrap there on 2 June 1958.

Returning to VX158, from May 1953 it had operated out of RAE Farnborough on navigation and bombing system research flights using an advanced H2S Mk 9 radar and electro-mechanical computer, forming what was called an Optical Aiming System (VX161 did not have this equipment, but it did have a fully operational weapons bay for its bombing trials). By this time VX158 was painted all silver, apart from the unpainted black radome and it remained with RAE until almost the end of the year. All of these vital trials were directly related to preparations for the V-Force and at least until 1955 the public knew nothing of this work, such was its secrecy.

| VX158 with the two Gyrons installed, most likely in August 1956.

de Havilland Gyron Research

In December 1953 VX158 was allotted to temporary storage, but on 23 January 1954 it was assigned to the 'fitting of special engines' against Contract 6/Acft/10145 – in fact the new de Havilland Gyron, a 15,000lb (66.7kN)-class supersonic fighter engine. The bomber prototype's strong structure and superimposed engine arrangement made it ideal for this work although localised strengthening was needed to accommodate the now bulged lower portion of the nacelle.

The aviation press reported that the aircraft had a maximum permissible Mach number of 0.85, a maximum level speed of 490 knots (908km/h) at 15,000ft (4,572m) and an operation ceiling of 45,000ft (13,716m), making it well suited for the task. A supersonic aeroplane would have been needed to conduct tests at the high end of the speed range, but that point was never reached because the Gyron programme was eventually cancelled. It first ran on the bench

Details of the de Havilland Gyron installation in 1955 and 1956. The views also shows the bomb bay doors. de Havilland Engines

on 5 January 1953 and a 25-hour special category flight-approval test at a rating of 15,200lb (67.6kN) was completed in January 1955.

A Gyron was first fitted in VX158 in the lower port engine position, the conversion being done by Short Brothers and Harland in its hanger at RAF Aldergrove. The first flight with the engine in position took place on 7 July 1955, from Aldergrove, with Short's test pilot 'Jock' Eassie at the controls and accompanied by Chris D Beaumont, chief test pilot for the de Havilland Engine Company; during the flight the Gyron was opened up to its full flight-approved thrust.

The modified aircraft's preliminary handling trials were conducted from Aldergrove before it was ferried to Hatfield on 4 August to begin an intensive engine flight test programme flown by Beaumont, the engine's behaviour being explored fully up to the limits imposed by the airframe. For the trials the Sperrin was normally crewed by the pilot, a flight engineer and two observers, and they described the Gyron's starting, handling and general behaviour as "exemplary". Not once did the unit stall in the air and it could accelerate from flight idle to full thrust in just three seconds.

In this condition VX158 attended Farnborough in September 1955, *Flight* noting how with all three Avons idling "the Sperrin sailed by comfortably on the power of the single Gyron carried asymmetrically in its port nacelle." On 4 December, VX158 returned to Aldergrove to have a second Gyron installed, this time in its lower starboard nacelle. The first ground run took place on 4 June, and with Eassie as pilot again and with Chris Beaumont also in the cockpit, VX158 was taken on its first flight in this form on 26 June. The aircraft's port outer undercarriage door broke away and fell into the sea during the sortie and was replaced by the equivalent door from VX161 – as a result, the second Sperrin never flew again.

On 29 August, test pilot R Plenderleith, who had joined the de Havilland Engine Company in 1947, flew the twin-Gyron Sperrin to Hatfield and in September the de Havilland Engine Company entered it into its fourth Farnborough show and the crowds experienced the incredible noise generated by two Avons and two Gyrons running together on full power. With the two Gyrons in place, control problems were explored at altitudes in the region of 50,000ft (15,240m).

Then in April 1957 a new Defence White Paper cancelled all future manned fighter programmes (except the English Electric Lightning), bringing the termination of some fighter engine development, including the Gyron. Flight trials with VX158 continued until the autumn, the research including measuring the output of infra-red radiation from a large turbojet like the Gyron and the knowledge gained going towards development of de Havilland's new heat-seeking missiles. In September 1959, VX158 was sold to de Havilland and late that year the first and last airworthy Sperrin went for scrap.

By 1955 the two S.A.4 Sperrins had accumulated a large number of hours of test flying and logged probably more trials than any other pair of British research aircraft of their time. After two years' flying in the hands of the Ministry of Supply their serviceability was described as "excellent" and it was confirmed that the prototypes had been singularly free from problems encountered with "other aeroplanes of comparable performance."

Airframe

The Sperrin's structure was a conventional stressed-skin light alloy assembly, although several new manufacturing processes developed by Short had produced a very high standard of external finish. Its mainplane, tapered in plan with a small amount of sweepback (18° 15' at the leading edge), essentially had a torsion-box main spar formed from front and rear girders connected by sheet members, and an aft auxiliary spar. Between the fuselage and nacelles, and the nacelles and ailerons, were four simple flaps, the outboard units incorporating split airbrakes that opened above and below the wing trailing edge.

The fuselage was built as one unit formed from nose, centre and tail sections, the centre fuselage having four heavy booms onto which the mainplanes were fixed, while the tail section had a conventional fin and tailplane; both the dihedral tailplane and fin had two spars.

The engine nacelles housed four Avons mounted in a double-banked form with their jet pipes passing both above and beneath the wing. The Sperrin had twenty-two fuel tanks (eight in the fuselage and seven in each wing), for a total of 6,170 Imp gals (28,054 litres). The full crew comprised pilot, second pilot, wireless operator, navigator and air bomber (the last three facing rearwards and seated behind the pilots). Both prototypes, and the fuselage, mainplane and tail unit constructed for structural testing, were built in production jigs.

Further Research

On 13 March 1950 the Short design team completed an aerodynamic study into the relative merits of delta and high-aspect ratio swept-back wings for a high-speed, long-range bomber. The three layouts considered (they were not official proposals submitted to the Ministry) suggest how bomber design at the company might have proceeded had the Sperrin entered production, or if Short had won a B.35/46 contract.

One, known as 'Design A', was a delta 'S.A.4', the second ('S.A.4 Development') a swept development of the S.A.4 with a tailplane and the third a version of the team's swept wing S.B.1 tailless proposal to B.35/46 (both the second and third showed a form of 'crescent' wing reminiscent of the Handley Page Victor). All three types had four Rolls-Royce Conway engines and for the comparison each was to carry a 10,000lb (4,536kg) bomb load. The results showed that a delta-winged bomber was less efficient aerodynamically than a comparable high-aspect ratio swept-wing type. However, the saving in weight on a delta tended to offset this loss in aerodynamic efficiency, so that the overall performance of the delta was comparable to that of the tailed swept-back aircraft, but fell short of the tailless design.

'Design A', essentially a delta-winged S.A.4 Sperrin. A sweep angle of about 40° at the quarter chord line was necessary to meet the high-speed requirements, while a 10% thick symmetrical section satisfied aerodynamic requirements and gave room to bury the engines in the wings. The chief advantage of a delta-wing type was that it had a more efficient structure than the high-aspect ratio form for a saving in structural weight; 'A's' estimated structure weight was higher than expected, but still below that of the other two.

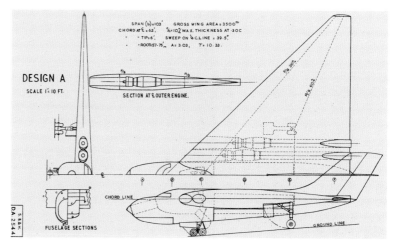

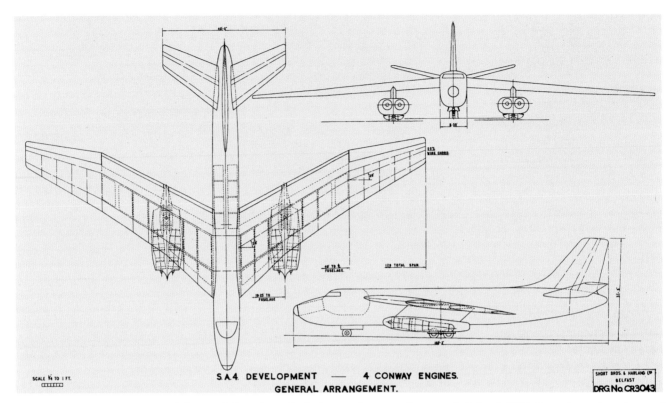

'S.A.4 Development'. Span 129ft (39.32m); length 102ft 2in (31.14m); gross wing area 2,424sq ft (225.43sq m); equipped weight 83,000lb (37,649kg); total fuel 70,930lb (32,174kg); take-off weight 164,400lb (74,572kg); sea level rate of climb 2,820ft/min (860m/min); cruising speed 470 knots (870km/h); cruising Mach number 0.82; initial cruise altitude 40,200ft (12,253m); final cruise altitude 51,150ft (15,591m); still air range 5,005 miles (8,053km).

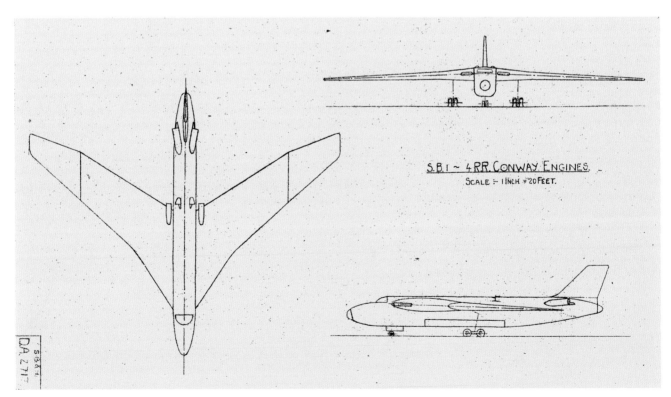

S.B.1 (dimensions uncertain). Gross wing area 2,642sq ft (245.71sq m); equipped weight 79,150lb (35,902kg); total fuel 70,385lb (31,927kg); take-off weight 160,000lb (72,576kg); sea level rate of climb 3,300ft/min (1,006m/min); cruising speed 500 knots (927km/h); cruising Mach number 0.872; initial cruise altitude 43,000ft (13,106m); final cruise altitude 54,000ft (16,459m); still air range 5,975 miles (9,614km).

17 Supermarine Types 508 and 525 (1951 and 1954)

Type 508/529

(Sources vary slightly on speed data)

Type: experimental single-seat, straight-wing day fighter prototypes

Span: 41ft (12.50m); folded 20ft (6.10m)

Length: Type 508 50ft (15.24m)

Gross wing area: 340sq ft (31.62sq m)

Wing t/c ratio: 9%

Normal loaded weight: Type 508 18,850lb (8,550kg); Type 529 21,100lb (9,571kg); overload weight with tanks 25,630lb (11,626kg)

Powerplant: 2 x Rolls-Royce Avon RA.3 turbojets each 6,500lb (28.9kN) thrust

Max level speed: Type 508 603mph (970km/h) or Mach 0.89 at 30,000ft (9,144m); Type 529 607mph (977km/h) or Mach 0.92 at 30,000ft

Service ceiling: Type 508 50,000ft (15,240m)

Climb rate: Type 508 time to 30,000ft 2.5 minutes; time to 45,000ft (13,716m) 5.1 minutes

Armament: 4 x 30mm Aden cannon (installed in Type 529 only – Type 508 carried ballast)

Type 525

Type: experimental single-seat, swept-wing day fighter prototype

Span: 37ft 2in (11.33m); folded (had option been installed): 20ft (6.10m)

Length: 53ft 0.4in (16.16m)

Gross wing area: 450sq ft (41.85sq m)

Wing t/c ratio: 8%

Normal Loaded weight: 19,910lb (9,031kg); max overload weight 28,169lb (12,777kg)

Powerplant: 2 x Rolls-Royce Avon RA.7 turbojets each 7,500lb (33.3kN) thrust

Max speed: 647mph (1,041km/h) or Mach 0.954 at 30,000ft (9,144m) (supersonic in a slight dive)

Service ceiling: 50,000ft (15,240m)

Climb rate: time to 30,000ft (9,144m) 2.5 minutes; time to 45,000ft (13,716m) 5.25 minutes

Armament: none carried but 4 x 20mm Hispano cannon listed in brochure

The Supermarine Types 508 and 525 were ordered purely as prototypes for a new day interceptor fighter for the Royal Navy, which in due course became the Scimitar. However, as these projects matured, the process of design saw the original layout with a straight wing changed to a swept form, while other features were introduced, including flap blowing. In many respects, therefore, these aircraft can be classed as research aircraft or demonstrators.

Type 508/529

This photo was among the first taken of Supermarine Type 508 VX133, most probably prior to its first flight. A horizontal bead sight is fitted to the upper nose cone.

VX133 at the Farnborough Air Show in 1951. The hinge point for the moving tailcone is between the roundel and the tailplane root leading edge.

In 1945 the Ministry of Supply asked Supermarine to put together a scheme for an undercarriageless, high-performance interceptor fighter powered by two jet engines. The outcome was a large design designated Type 505, but soon afterwards Supermarine was asked to revise the project and add an undercarriage. Three prototypes of the resulting Type 508 were ordered to Specification N.9/47 in August 1947, under Contract 6/Acft/1508, and they were given the serials VX133, VX136 and VX138. Joseph 'Joe' Smith led Supermarine's project design team and all three aircraft were built in Supermarine's Experimental Department at Hursley Park.

During March 1948 Smith seriously considered fitting a tailwheel instead of a nosewheel because once the aircraft had engaged the arrestor wire the latter would have to absorb a massive load, but in the end the idea was discarded and the tricycle arrangement retained (it also improved the pilot's forward view).

Construction of the first prototype began in mid-1949 and VX133 performed its maiden flight from A&AEE Boscombe Down on 31 August 1951, piloted by Lt Cdr Mike Lithgow (the first engine runs had been made on 20 June); the following week it attended the Farnborough Air Show. During a low-speed, low-altitude flight on 5 December, VX133 experienced violent vibration that began with a very strong nose-up pitch. This built up to a severe overload that forced open and damaged the undercarriage doors, and also ripped away both wingtip pitot booms. The reason for this remained a mystery until the following 12 July, but during the incident Lithgow lost consciousness when VX133 began a vertical roll to a height of 11,000ft (3,353m). A peak of 11g was recorded.

By mid-January 1952 measurements of stalling speeds had been made with the aircraft in a number of configurations of leading edge and trailing edge flap settings. It

VX133 about to touch down at Farnborough.

The Type 508 at Farnborough in September 1951.

VX133 shows off its flap and spoiler arrangement as it lands on the Farnborough runway, again in September 1951. *Peter Green*

VX133 in May 1952, during its trials aboard *HMS Eagle*.

was established that with the two sets of flaps interconnected, the optimum leading edge flap position was 10° and the full 50° of trailing edge flap could be used with advantage. In the optimum configuration and at a weight of 20,000lb (9,072kg), VX133's stalling speed was 97 knots (180km/h) equivalent airspeed (EAS) with the undercarriage and flaps down, compared to 129 knots (239km/h) EAS with the flaps and undercarriage raised. In this arrangement the ailerons were also drooped by 3.75°. Also, sealing the gaps between the inboard ends of the leading edge flaps and fuselage had produced only a small reduction in stalling speed, but a very large reduction in the violent pre-stall buffeting that had occurred at intermediate leading edge flap settings with the gaps unsealed.

The first Type 508 completed arresting proofing trials at RAE Bedford on 1 May 1952 and was thus cleared for preliminary deck landing trials. Operating from RNAS Ford, Mike Lithgow made the aircraft's first deck landing aboard the carrier *HMS Eagle* on 28 May 1952, and next day he made six more landings at weights between 18,670lb and 19,000lb (8,469kg and 8,618kg).

He found the light and effective ailerons and elevator, excellent throttle response and tricycle landing gear meant that the big

prototype presented few difficulties. Because of this he added that pilots used to Supermarine's lighter, straight-wing Attacker naval jet fighter would find the 508 a much easier proposition (the Attacker had a tailwheel undercarriage). Between 30 June and 4 July VX133 took part in the Central Fighter Establishment's Annual Convention at West Raynham, and on 12 July it joined Supermarine's Type 535 fighter prototype for the Lee-on-Solent air show, where severe vibration during a low-level demonstration damaged the airframe. The cause was aileron flutter (as it had been on 5 December), but this time it was seen from the ground. Critically, on both occasions the flutter had not been recognised as such by the pilot and one observer noted how the degree of oscillation made the ailerons appear to be 'a foot thick' at their trailing edges.

The second N.9/47 prototype, VX136 first flew from Chilbolton on 29 August 1952 and compared to the first machine it featured a white nose cap for a ranging radar and a larger tailcone for a tail-warning radar. These additions had extended the fuselage by 6in (15.2cm) and the aircraft also carried guns (the radars were never fitted). In this form VX136 was redesignated Type 529 and shortly after its first flight presented at the annual Farnborough show.

Type 508 VX133.
*Copyright
Pete West*

Underside detail of the type 508, probably at the SBAC show. Although gun ports are visible, the aircraft never carried weapons.

Supermarine pilots Mike Lithgow, Dave Morgan and Les Calquhoun documented the 508/529's general handling characteristics in a report compiled on 9 March 1953. VX133 had been flown at weights between 19,750lb (8,959kg) and 21,100lb (9,571kg) and all statements in the report referred to the fighter in its optimum flap condition. The aileron flutter incidents had been responsible for the comparatively small amount of flying completed by the two aeroplanes (remedial measures to the one having delayed the other). Further, on each occasion when aileron flutter occurred it was on the eve of the start of high-speed and high-Mach number testing, and this meant that an investigation into Mach number handling did not begin until November 1952.

VX133 at RAE Bedford in July 1957, where it was employed on arrestor gear development. The aircraft now has strakes ahead of its tailplane.
Peter Berry

The aircraft's acceleration was rapid during and after take-off, the unstick was clean and it was necessary to select wheels up immediately in order to avoid exceeding the maximum permissible IAS for wheels down of 200 knots (371km/h). The landing was extremely straightforward, with 120 knots (222km/h) IAS proving a comfortable approach speed; the aircraft was exceptionally steady on the approach, with lateral and fore-and-aft control excellent. However, in crosswinds, the lack of directional control was an embarrassment – full rudder could be applied with no response other than a small rolling moment, and considerable difficulty was experienced in lining up when the wind was other than straight down the runway.

The stalling speeds quoted earlier related to low-level flight and it was found that there was a large increase in indicated stalling speeds at higher altitudes. At 10,000ft (3,048m) the all-down stall speed rose to 114 knots (211km/h) IAS and at 45,000ft (13,716m) it was 162 knots (300km/h) IAS. The stalling characteristics were in the main docile, but it was particularly noticeable that at the stall the wing appeared to retain lift to a surprising degree and it was virtually impossible to promote a high rate of sink. This feature was surprising in view of the aeroplane's weight. The stalling speed was the speed at which the nose dropped sharply, usually with either wing, preceded by fairly violent buffet. However, on occasion a wing dropped fairly sharply before the nose, which was enough to constitute a minimum practical speed.

The airbrakes were powerful but at times subject to juddering, a phenomenon similar to that experienced on the company's Swift fighters, though not as pronounced. At times the landing flaps were used as airbrakes up to moderately high speeds without difficulty, albeit with little deceleration.

An altitude of 10,000ft (3,048m) was reached 1.4 minutes after brakes off and 40,000ft (12,192m) in 5.56 minutes. The highest speed reached to date was 520 knots (964km/h) (Mach 0.81 indicated) at 1,000ft (305m), recorded at well below maximum permissible cruising power; acceleration to this speed had been extremely rapid.

In bumpy air the lateral and directional control were disliked, and in very bumpy air the aircraft's behaviour was such that attempts for a further increase in speed were abandoned. The reason for this was thought to be a combination of ineffective rudder control, poor lateral damping and a lack of directional

Type 529 VX136 under tow, possibly at Chilbolton. Note the strake ahead of and slightly above the V-tail, which was not an original feature on VX133.

VX136 took part in the September 1952 Farnborough show, the venue for this series of images. Note the flaps deployed for landing, the slightly longer tailcone than had been used on the Type 508, and that 'Royal Navy' has been added beneath the serial number.

stability. Lateral control was heavy and the rate of roll noticeably diminished over 350 knots (649km/h) IAS, while at over 400 knots (741km/h) noise and vibration were excessive (some of this problem was subsequently traced to the gun ports). At high altitude, particularly at high Mach numbers, the 508's cockpit was extremely noisy.

The maximum Mach number to which the aircraft had been taken was just under 0.88 IMN at 40,000ft. At Mach 0.82 Indicated there was a nose down trim change (gradual and progressive) with slight to moderate buffet, while at 0.84 there was a high level of buffet and the ailerons were very heavy and becoming ineffective. At 0.86 the buffet level was very high, with a general shaking of the aircraft; large aileron deflections were necessary to roll, the elevator was heavy and manoeuvring was easier using the tailplane. At Mach 0.88 there was violent shaking and buffet, and the aircraft could only be termed under control by virtue of its variable incidence tailplane. The rate of operation of this control was much too fast even for operation at high Mach numbers, however, which usually required the coarsest use of controls likely to be encountered in any flight conditions. In fact the rate of operation of the tailplane incidence was too fast in all flight conditions and dangerously fast at high indicated airspeeds.

In general the feel and response of the elevator control in manoeuvre was excellent up to the order of 400 knots (741km/h) and Mach 0.78 Indicated. Above these speeds a large increase in values of stick force/'g' was apparent, and recourse to tail incidence was preferred for manoeuvring. The limiting factor governing the amount of 'g' that could be applied at high altitude was buffet. At the highest 'g' attained the degree of buffet was remarkable and the general shaking cause for concern. The buffet was accompanied by uncontrollable aileron snatching.

In their original configuration the ailerons (spring tab operated with power boost) were pleasant and crisp, although the resulting rate of roll was not up to the standard of a modern fighter. Later, however, several necessary modifications, including the fitting of dampers to the servodynes and aileron spring tabs, had the cumulative effect of making the ailerons heavy and much over-damped. With a 'flying' start the time taken to roll 360° at 250 knots (463km/h) indicated airspeed (IAS) was 4.6 seconds, and at 400 knots (741km/h) IAS, 5.0 seconds. The rate of roll decreased rapidly at higher indicated speeds and also above an indicated Mach number of 0.76.

The major criticism of the aircraft stemmed from its lateral and directional characteristics, and in bumpy air it was considered extremely unpleasant to fly, due, it was thought, to a combination of factors, some of which appeared to be inherent to the butterfly tail (there was, for example, an inter-relation between lateral and directional characteristics that caused a combined rolling and yawing motion). Full rudder control was applied up to 200 knots (371km/h) IAS, its application causing a small rolling moment on the same side that required only a quarter aileron to hold. The application of rudder caused no change in heading at any speed and various measures had been tried to improve these features. Eventually the directional troubles were improved upon slightly by fitting small dorsal fins forward of each tailplane.

Use of the airbrakes had been discontinued due to the excessive nose-down trim change and excessive buffet. According to contemporary reports, the basic trouble with the system was that the landing flaps produced a negligible longitudinal trim change, whereas the spoilers caused a strong nose-down trim change even at speeds as low as 200 knots (371km/h). The landing flaps were thereafter used as airbrakes within prescribed limits of 20° at 400 knots (741km/h), 30° at 300 knots (556km/h), etc. As noted, however, they were not very effective as airbrakes and in this respect were not in the same class as those of the Swift.

On the credit side, besides its excellent take-off and landing (and deck landing) characteristics, the aircraft possessed a vary satisfactory performance, even on 6,500lb (28.9kN) static thrust engines, and it had a pleasant elevator control with good response up to the speeds at which it started to 'heavy up'. It was agreed to continue the flight test programme using both prototypes against characteristics that would provide useful data for the forthcoming swept-wing version for the Navy. These included the measurement of arrestor hook loads, further deck trials and armament tests.

VX136 performed deck trials aboard *HMS Eagle* in early November 1953.

Upper fuselage and wing detail of the Type 529.

This November 1953 picture of VX136 reveals wing fold, jet pipe and rear fuselage detail, and the aircraft's very distinctive V-tail. The aircraft was being prepared for another launch from the carrier *Eagle* and it appears that the extended tailcone was not in place during the aircraft's visit to the ship.

By 28 April 1953 the best speed attained during contractor's trials had risen to 530 knots (982km/h) IAS. In 1953 VX136 was used in tail-down landing and catapult acceleration trials at RAE Farnborough, and on 3 and 4 November the second prototype completed six landings aboard *Eagle*. Next VX136 went to RAE Bedford to join the Royal Navy's test unit, but during a flight on 6 May it experienced violent vibration, which broke the pitot heads away. Finally, on 2 December, its pilot, Lt Perkins, made an emergency landing at Chilbolton after the starboard undercarriage leg locked up.

VX136 was so badly damaged, with distortion to the starboard wingtip, aileron and flaps that it was clearly not worth repairing. The aircraft was Struck Off Charge on 27 October 1954 having been in store since mid-January, but it was not until 30 July 1956 that most of the airframe (fuselage and wings) was finally despatched to the Proof & Experimental Establishment (P&EE) for use as a target on the range at Shoeburyness. The remains were scrapped there in September 1961 but the nose and cockpit had gone to Farnborough in December 1958. (Many retired aircraft, including unique prototypes, became targets for gunfire at Shoeburyness where work was carried out to assess the ballistics of bullets and shells, and also the resistance of modern airframes to battle damage.)

VX133 continued flying for quite some time. In July 1953, RAE accepted it for measurement of loads on arrested landings and then it joined RAE Bedford in August 1955. During the first half of November 1955 the aircraft performed trials aboard the carrier HMS *Bulwark*, but when it was used to test the hanger deck strength of the carrier *Centaur* at Devonport Dockyard from 24 September 1956, it was taken there by road. Arrestor gear trials continued at Bedford from late November, but its flying days were soon done. At the end of 1963 VX133 was delivered by road to RNAS Culdrose for ground instruction, the outer wings being removed. After being burned out during fire practice at Predannack, the metal carcass was scrapped in the 1970s.

Type 525/555

A leader in *Flight* magazine for 6 February 1953 declared that that the Royal Navy had once been expected to order the RAF's Supermarine Swift as its new fighter. However, the naval correspondent for *The Times* newspaper wrote that neither the Swift nor the Hawker Hunter day fighter was "suitable for conversion into a carrier-borne aircraft." A little later a naval document referred to a production version of the Type 508 and suggested that a swept wing version was not far away. And so it proved. With projected developments in carrier

VX133, without wings, at Culdrose in 1966.
Terry Panopalis

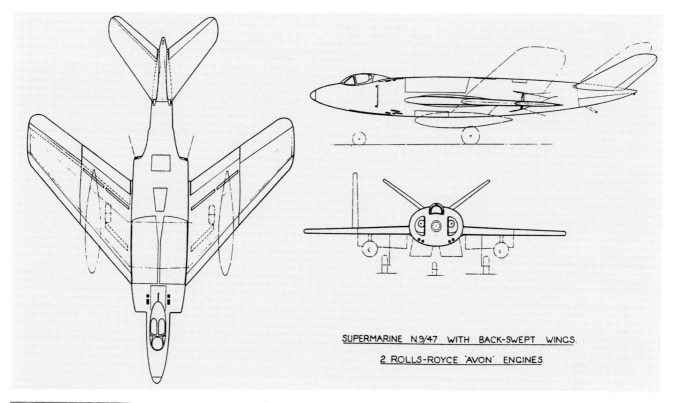

SUPERMARINE N.9/47 WITH BACK-SWEPT WINGS.

2 ROLLS-ROYCE 'AVON' ENGINES.

Above: The original proposal for the Supermarine Type 525, the third N.9/47 prototype, with a swept butterfly, or 'V' tail.

Left: The swept-wing, swept V-tail Type 525.

arresting and catapulting equipment, and the tractability of Supermarine's own swept wing Type 510 at approach speeds, the company's position was distinctly encouraging.

Indeed, well before VX133 had begun its flying programme, the Supermarine design team had investigated fitting the N.9/47 airframe with a swept wing for naval use. Studies showed that the swept version could perform all of the straight-wing N.9/47's duties while offering a rather higher top speed – sea level speed rose to almost 600 knots (1,119km/h) and there was the potential for supersonic performance at altitude. There was also talk of fitting the engines with reheat (which in the end was not adopted) and in due course a go-ahead was given to complete the third N.9/47, VX138, with swept wings.

The new project was designated Type 525 and had been first proposed in June 1949. Initially it featured a 45° swept wing together with a swept butterfly tail, but wind tunnel tests revealed structural problems with this tail arrangement. Stresses in the pivot that held the complete tail to the airframe were found to be excessive and as a consequence a more conventional cruciform tail with all-flying horizontal surfaces was substituted. The V-tail offered the benefit of reduced drag compared to the T-tail, but because the latter was horizontal "it also acted like a wing and prevented the loss of airflow from the fin."

After being moved by road from its Hursley Park birthplace, the one-off Type 525 made its first flight from Boscombe Down on 27 April 1954, piloted by Mike Lithgow. On 6 May it was flown to Chilbolton to begin contractor's trials and from 5 September it was at the Farnborough show. A notable occurrence on the Tuesday at Farnborough came when the 525 provided the first instance of a supersonic boom timed to coincide with the aircraft's appearance within the airfield boundary. *Flight* reported how the form of the shock waves produced "was illuminated fleetingly by sheets of condensation coming from the 525's wings as the aircraft sped soundlessly across the airfield."

The sole Type 525, VX138 photographed at Boscombe Down around the time it made its first flight on 27 April 1954. The tailplane had no anhedral or dihedral, the wing had 1° of anhedral and at this stage the aircraft was in natural metal finish.

In June, however, Lithgow had conducted intense contractor trials and there was criticism of the aircraft's directional characteristics. There was a steady directional oscillation with associated roll, which became more pronounced with increases in speed, and this prevented any flying at high speeds during the first sorties made with VX138. Damping in yaw was poor, but a small increase in fin area, achieved by extending the leading edge, helped with the problem; however, it was the addition of a friction damper that made the largest improvement and subsequently allowed flight at much higher speeds. By November 1954 handling trials had revealed serious problems associated with engine surging and the aircraft's pitch-up characteristics. By 1 November, however, the aircraft had reached Mach 1.08 in a shallow dive (despite the very high level of installed thrust, VX138 proved incapable of reaching supersonic speed on the level).

On 17 May 1954 approval was given for proposed modifications to provide VX138 with supersonic air blowing over its flaps and in early 1955 the aircraft was returned to Hursley Park by road for the system to be installed. It reappeared in June 1955 with the flap blowing in place, together with a new-look wing with the outboard section extended to give a saw-tooth appearance (in this new form it was known as the Type 555).

Air was bled from the engine compressor and projected as a slim, high-pressure jet through a tiny slot along the trailing edge, slightly ahead of the flap. The double slotted flaps had been replaced by plain trailing edge flaps, and the full span leading edge flaps now moved fully down when the trailing edge flaps began to move – the leading edge extensions reduced the tendency for pitch-up.

156

Above: An early photograph of VX138 shows the aircraft on approach to land at Boscombe Down. Note the size of the vertical fin in its original form.

Right: VX138, now painted cream, performing its display at the September 1954 Farnborough show. The flaps, undercarriage and tailskid are deployed.

Below: VX138 touches down at Farnborough with its full-span leading edge flaps deployed. Note the variable incidence tailplane in action.

An investigation into the use of boundary layer control applied to the wing trailing edge flaps to increase lift (known as 'Super Circulation' or Flap Blowing) had begun at Supermarine in October 1953. The idea of blowing very high velocity air over extended flaps was to re-energise the airflow remaining in contact with the wing and flap uppersurfaces, thus preventing it from breaking away – without blowing, the upper surface airflow could break up at low speeds and become turbulent, leading to a loss of lift and increase in drag. Flap blowing dramatically improved lift and in consequence, stalling speed was reduced.

VX138 arrived at Boscombe on 4 July to begin a full flap blowing trial, but on the 5th it crashed into the ground from an altitude of 3,000ft (914m) and caught fire at Idmiston, near Salisbury. The A&AEE pilot (Lt Cdr Anthony Rickell) was making a 'preview' trial flight and was on the approach to land at Boscombe when the aircraft stalled. Despite ejecting he died of his injuries. The aircraft had accumulated 64 hours flying time.

The Type 525 only really proved useful to the later Scimitar in the investigation and development of flap blowing, and its destruction before any in-depth trials had begun pushed the latter's development programme back by a prolonged period. Nevertheless, preliminary trials conducted by Lithgow with VX138 during June had shown that flap blowing reduced the approach speed by about 12mph (19km/h) and considerably improved the aircraft's stability and control at low speeds.

In regard to the production of the swept-wing type for the Navy, the Type 525 had failed to meet the specification in full. Supermarine's answer was the Type 544, a full redesign that in truth resembled the 525 only in its shape. The wingtips had been subtly re-shaped to postpone the onset of compressibility drag rise which, working in tandem with a waisted, but not area-ruled fuselage increased the maximum Mach number by a fraction. The first of three Supermarine Type 544 Scimitar prototypes, WT854 flew on 19 January 1956 and the Scimitar production run stretched to 76 aeroplanes. The Type 525 primarily served as an interim development towards the more advanced Scimitar.

This rare photo of VX138 provides interesting detail, including the cover for the jet pipe and the enormous main undercarriage.

Cream-painted VX138 displays multiple scoop intakes behind its cockpit. The enlarged fin is also evident. *Peter Green*

VX138 at Farnborough in September 1954. *Terry Panopalis & Peter Green*

A possibly unique image of VX138 during wet runway trials at Farnborough. *Terry Panopalis*

The Type 525, after its repaint in naval colours.
Peter Green

Above: VX138 performing landing and approach trials after flap blowing had been installed.
Peter Green

Left: On 8 June 1955 VX138 performed a 'shop window' display that included its first touchdown on a carrier, in this case *HMS Centaur.* Mike Lithgow was the pilot and the main task was to demonstrate the effects of flap blowing.

Airframe

The Type 508 naval fighter prototype had massive airframe, particularly around the centre fuselage, which housed the twin Rolls-Royce Avon powerplant, with light alloy stressed skin structure. The straight, tapered wings were built around a main and auxiliary rear spar. They had a very thin section, plain trailing edge flaps and ailerons, 'droop-snoot' leading edges (full-span leading edge flaps) and 90° folding, just outboard of the main undercarriage. The airbrake arrangement consisted of spoilers on the upper wing surface that operated in conjunction with the normal landing flaps. The pilot was seated well forward in the fuselage, the lateral intakes for the turbojets were mounted to each side and slightly rear of the cockpit, and the tailpipes emerged just aft of the wing trailing edge.

The butterfly tail was the most unorthodox feature of the aircraft's design; it was built around main and auxiliary spars and set at a dihedral of 35°. Types 508 and 529 both had a hinged rear fuselage cone that moved up in its entirety by a maximum of 9° and down by 3° to create an all-flying tail – the tailplanes themselves were fixed and the arrangement proved quite satisfactory in providing longitudinal trim. The trailing edge 'ruddervators' served as combined rudder and elevator surfaces and were hinged to the rear spar – for the role of elevators they moved in the same direction but when acting as rudders they moved in "opposition".

An 'A-frame' arrester hook was positioned under the aft fuselage and there was provision for underwing external tanks, but these were never carried. The guns in the Type 529 were housed in the lower fuselage, two per side to the rear of the air intakes. The aircraft was near identical to the 508 and apart from the strakes fitted ahead of the tailplane root leading edges, other changes introduced on VX136 were minor (and included the position of the radio aerial). Both airframes spent their entire careers in natural metal finish.

The Type 525's fuselage was near identical to that of the 508 from the nose to the tailcone, but aft of this the two-spar fin was built integrally with the modified rear fuselage. The aircraft's swept wing was attached further forwards than the 508's straight wing, requiring localised modifications to the structure. The wing again used a main and auxiliary rear spars, with multiple ribbing. It was swept 50° at the leading edge and 45° at quarter chord.

The tailplane had 50°of sweep on its leading edge, was 'all-flying' and could rotate through angles from +5° to –10°. It was mounted on the lower part of the fin so that the rudder had to be split into two. The 525's twin Avons exhausted below and to either side of the rear fuselage and the swept mainplanes were very thin. The 525 initially had double-slotted flaps inboard of the ailerons. Full span leading edge flaps, set at 30° at the beginning but later reduced to 20°, operated only when the trailing edge flaps moved to their fully down position of 50°. Airbrakes were fitted on the underside of the fuselage and to the upper and lower surfaces of the wings (during early flights the latter were fixed shut) and the 525 did not have wing folding, but this facility could have been installed at the break between the flaps and ailerons.

Contemporary Supermarine advertisement for the 525, published in *The Aeroplane* for 6 August 1954.

There were no guns, the ports on the earlier machines having been faired over for the 525. Having been painted cream for much of its early flying career, for its final flight trials VX138 was repainted with Dark Sea Grey uppersurfaces and duck egg green (possibly Sky) lower surfaces and sides.

Supermarine's prototype series eventually led to the Type 544 Scimitar for the Royal Navy. Scimitar XD229 spent its entire career with the Royal Aircraft Establishment as a weapons development aircraft, for which role it was painted pale blue and white in 1963. This rare colour photo of the newly repainted XD229 was taken at the Biggin Hill show on 14 September 1963. *Alan Trent*

18 de Havilland DH.110 (1951)

de Havilland DH.110

Type (initially): two-seat night-fighter prototype

Span: 51ft (15.54m)

Length: 52ft 1in (15.88m)

Gross wing area: 648sq ft (60.26sq m)

All-up-weight: 32,000lb (14,515kg)

Powerplant: WG236 2 x Rolls-Royce Avon RA.3 turbojets each 6,500lb (28.9kN) thrust; WG240 2 x Rolls-Royce Avon RA.7 each 7,500lb (33.3kN)

Max level speed (WG240): 610 knots (1,130km/h) or Mach 0.924 at sea level; 536 knots (993km/h) or Mach 0.936 at 40,000ft (12,192m)

Service ceiling: 50,000ft (15,240m)

Climb rate (WG240 at 28,700lb/13,018kg): time to 40,000ft (12,192m) 6.8 minutes

Armament: provision for 4 x fixed 30mm Aden cannon, but none carried

The two-seat de Havilland DH.110 was a prototype design subsequently developed into the production Sea Vixen naval fighter. However, in many respects the DH.110 was very different to the resulting service machine, having been schemed as a land-based RAF prototype.

de Havilland first proposed the DH.110 in March 1947 against RAF night-fighter Specification F.44/46; a version was subsequently offered against a Royal Navy requirement for a new twin-jet naval night fighter, Specification N.40/46. The DH.110 and a design from Gloster (which would become the Javelin) were selected as the winners of the RAF requirement and the DH.110 was also accepted for the Navy, along with a design from Fairey.

The covering specifications were subsequently upgraded in 1948 and 1949 as F.4/48 and N.14/49 respectively and three DH.110 night-fighter prototypes were ordered, while plans were made to acquire another ten as prototypes for a wide range of duties for both services, including naval strike. A joint programme for the RAF and Navy was agreed, but in November 1949 the naval DH.110s were cancelled to save money. This left five F.4/48s on order (serials WG236, WG240, WG247, WG248, and WG252 all now as night fighters) under a contract dated 26 May 1950, although the final three were also cancelled in June 1952. J Philip 'Phil' Smith led the DH.110 design team until the programme was moved to de Havilland's Christchurch facility.

WG236 and WG240 were assembled in de Havilland's Hatfield experimental shop and the first aircraft began taxi trials on 16 September 1951. John Cunningham, the firm's chief test pilot, took WG236 on its maiden flight on 26 September, with Tony Fairbrother as observer. Early test flying revealed good flight characteristics, but there was a problem with 'snaking' at high speeds. This was found to be the result of aeroelasticity (flexing) of the twin booms. WG236's fin area was therefore increased by the addition of curved extensions faired onto the line of the rudder trailing edge under the rear of the booms, while the tailbooms themselves were stiffened with steel reinforcing strips riveted onto their inside and outside surfaces. This proved to be an effective, but rather crude stop-gap for the first machine; WG240's modified booms were of thicker gauge aluminium alloy.

On 26 November 1951 WG236 suffered a complete electrical failure at 35,000ft (10,668m). Cunningham (accompanied by Tony Richards) lost the use of both generators, all of the flight and engine instruments bar the airspeed indicator and altimeter, and the electrically-powered tail trim. Fortuitously he spotted Heathrow Airport through a gap in the clouds and decided to go in, where he was able to make a safe but flapless glide landing; the aircraft's arrival, however, was completely unannounced to the airport because WG236 had also lost its radio. After repairs, the DH.110 was flown back to Hatfield.

On 24 March 1952 de Havilland reported on WG236's test flying to date. In terms of handling and control at high Mach numbers, nose down trim changes were experienced from about Mach 0.86 up to Mach 1.01 and the elevator showed signs of loss of effectiveness at Mach 0.95. The trimming tailplane was very effective up to Mach 1.015 and the ailerons were good at low speed on approach and very powerful at all normal speeds, although lost effectiveness at Mach 0.94, a characteristic that became more noticeable as Mach number increased.

WG236, in original configuration, in the first image released of the DH.110 in flight (during October 1951).

WG236 after the booms had been strengthened and rather rough looking curved extensions fitted beneath them.
BAE SYSTEMS Heritage, Farnborough

General handling at high IAS was "very satisfactory" and the presence of 'Dutch Roll', a simultaneous oscillation in both roll and yaw that occurred during certain conditions of flight and was a characteristic accentuated by swept wings, had been cured completely at heights above 20,000ft (6,096m) by a yaw damper. Above Mach 0.9 and also at low speeds and altitudes, there had been little or no Dutch Roll. In general the ailerons and elevators were light and effective at normal speeds and adequate at high Mach numbers. However, during take-off and at the stall the rudders were too heavy.

The DH.110 became supersonic for the first time on 20 February 1952 when de Havilland test pilot John Derry (with Tony Richards) took WG236 through the 'sound barrier' in a dive. This meant that the firm's new fighter was the first operational-type aeroplane, the first two-seater and the first twin-engine aircraft to achieve supersonic speed. The second DH.110, WG240 made its first flight on 25 July 1952 and, although not fitted with reheat, its more powerful engines provided an impressive increase in performance over WD236. In August 1952 de Havilland reported that the

second prototype had reached a maximum level Mach number at heights above 22,000ft (6,707m) of between 0.93 and 0.94, while at 5,000ft (1,524m) the figure was Mach 0.92. WG240 had also been dived to Mach 1.13 and reached 605 knots (1,121km/h) on the level at low altitudes, while WG236 had been dived to a maximum true Mach number of 1.14 to 1.15, but in level flight could only reach 590 knots (1,093km/h) at low altitude and Mach 0.915 at 40,000ft (12,192m); in dives the DH.110s had exceeded Mach 1 "frequently". The ailerons on WG240 were considered good at low speed on the approach and proved very powerful at all normal speeds.

In early September 1952 WG240 flew displays for most of the Farnborough show, but on Saturday 6th it went unserviceable with engine problems. John Derry and Tony Richards therefore collected the older WG236 from Hatfield and flew directly to Farnborough to display. Tragically, while straightening out from a steep turn, WG236 broke up in the air, killing both crew. Even worse, one of its Avon engines broke away and landed in the crowd, killing 27 people and injuring 63.

At the start of its career WG240 also sported a silver colour scheme. This picture was released to the public on 19 August 1952. |

WG240 makes a low pass with everything down.

By the time of the September 1952 SBAC show at Farnborough, WG240 had been painted in a satin black scheme.

Official photo of the second DH.110, WG240, by an A&AEE Boscombe Down photographer.
By the time of its return to flight test in 1953, WG240 had been repainted in naval colours.

Opposite top: de Havilland publicity view of the black WG240 in the run up to Farnborough 1952. The firm made several colour images of its products in the decade following World War II and used the medium rather more than many UK aircraft manufacturer's. *BAE SYSTEMS Heritage, Farnborough*

Bottom: Detail of WG240 in another de Havilland photograph. *BAE SYSTEMS Heritage, Farnborough*

167

A photo taken on 23 September 1954 showing WG240 overshooting HMS *Albion*.

It took some time to identify the cause, but eventually it was established that as WG236 had banked to the left towards the crowd its starboard outer wing had detached, immediately followed by failure of the port outer wing. With just the inner wings remaining, a rapid nose-up change of trim following the wing failures caused other parts (cockpit, engines and tail) to break away in secondary failures brought about by abnormal levels of 'g' (all of this took place in about one second).

It was found that WG236 had succumbed to twisting forces (a joint action of torsion, shear and bending loads), which occurred when the aircraft had performed a manoeuvre combining a turn and a climb. The problem was the DH.110's wing, which had been built with an unusual D-nose leading edge. This arrangement had been used successfully on de Havilland's earlier lightweight Vampire and Venom fighters, but on the larger and heavier DH.110 with its greater performance, the D-nose could not handle the more severe stresses of the manoeuvre.

WG240's wing structure had to be substantially redesigned with the inclusion of a new front spar web, thicker wing ribs and inter spar stringers. The aircraft did not fly

again until 17 June 1953, when Cunningham and Fairbrother formed its crew. However, from this point Lt Cdr Jock Elliot, chief test pilot at Christchurch, Sqn Ldr John Wilson, Chris Capper and observer Ron Ashford did almost all of the aircraft's flying.

There were problems, but overall the aircraft's performance was most impressive and clearly better than had it been prior to its grounding. However, it was also clear that an all-moving tail was required for manoeuvrability and holding changes of trim above Mach 0.97, so WG240 was fitted with an all-moving 'flying' tail instead of the original tailplane with hinged elevator (at the time making it the only British aircraft so equipped). In addition it acquired new powered rudders, cambered 'droop-snoot' outer wing leading edges and improved aileron controls. In this form WG240 flew for the first time on 11 June 1954 and quickly showed large improvements in control and manoeuvre at high Mach numbers.

In the meantime, however, the Farnborough crash had cast a cloud over the DH.110 project as a whole. The Gloster Javelin had been ordered to fill the RAF's night-fighter requirement and so there would be no more land-based DH.110s.

WG240 had the new 'flying tail' in place for its trials on *Albion*. *BAE SYSTEMS Heritage, Farnborough*

Having ordered a navalised de Havilland Venom (the Sea Venom) as a stopgap, the Navy was still seeking a new all-weather fighter, however. A navalised DH.110 proved to be the solution and in July 1953 the type was formally accepted.

Major changes required compared to the existing land-based prototype included a folding wing, arrester gear and other standard Navy fittings, Avon RA.14 engines, the installation of AI.Mk 18 radar, adoption of the all-moving tail and larger flaps. This proved to be some task, not helped by the 1953 transfer of DH.110 design effort to Christchurch. A new specification, N.139D&P (D&P for Development & Production) was written around the aircraft and a third DH.110 was contracted in November 1953, to be assembled from spare components. Production aeroplanes would carry guided missiles and the first order for the new fighter, named Sea Vixen in 1957, covered 75 aircraft. The navalised third DH.110, with serial XF828 and piloted by Elliot, first flew from Christchurch on 20 June 1955. It more closely resembled the Sea Vixen than did the first two DH.110s and can be considered the true prototype of the Navy's new fighter.

A photograph from April or May 1956 showing the more pointed nose radome fitted to WG240 late in its career, along with a nose probe pitot. The tow is a static 'bomb' used to measure airspeeds. *BAE SYSTEMS Heritage, Farnborough*

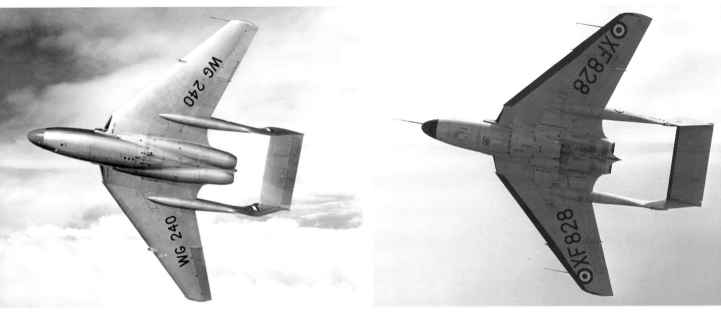

These images of WG240 and the third, 'naval' DH.110 prototype, XF828, allow comparison of planforms, revealing how the latter was much closer in configuration to the production Sea Vixen. The reduction in length of the jet pipes is particularly noticeable.

During preparations for Navy service, on 23 September 1954 WG240 performed a set of preliminary approaches, overshoots and touch-and-go landings on the deck of the carrier HMS *Albion* – the aircraft's behaviour in carrier operations was described as outstanding. On 5 April 1956, XF828 made its first fully arrested deck landing aboard the new carrier HMS *Ark Royal*. By the beginning of 1957, the third DH.110 had acquired a large fixed inflight-refuelling probe with

On 5 April 1956 XF828 made its first deck trials aboard the new carrier HMS *Ark Royal*.

which it made its first successful inflight refuel (at 10,000ft/3,048m) on 10 January.

The second and third aeroplanes were worked hard. WG240's last flight (its 570th) was on 20 May 1957 and it was broken up for scrap in July 1965. XF828 completed 574 flights, the last of them on 14 October 1959, and the burnt remains of the airframe were still at Culdrose in April 1979. The DH.110 will always be most associated with 1952 Farnborough show crash, but that should not hide the fact that all three prototypes proved to be good flying machines and valuable research tools.

Flight Lieutenant David Atherton recalled flying the WG240 to the author, and remembered that at the time it was not really a pilot's aeroplane   you had to get to know it well to be able to fly it successfully. In other words, it was a little heavy to handle and a pilot could not take his hands off the stick – it was not a forgiving aircraft. This was not a criticism, because it must be remembered that all prototypes are development machines. Flt Lt Atherton was involved with testing the DH.110's structure, where various items of measuring equipment recorded stresses and loads on key parts of the airframe and how they changed during violent manoeuvres (of the kind expected in combat), work tied up with 'g' forces. He added that WG240 also required constant attention and maintenance, but overall it was a tremendous aeroplane. With many of the problems ironed out, the Sea Vixen was first class.

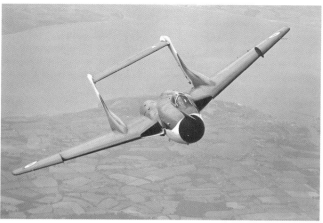

XF828 in its original 'Navy' colour scheme and carrying the a nose pitot used for calibration purposes.
The third DH.110 took part in the 1956 Farnborough show.

Publicity photo of XF828 taken on 23 July 1956. *Peter Green Collection*

| XF828 on 31 August 1956, in a revised Navy colour scheme.

Airframe

For a fighter the DH.110 was a large aeroplane. It had an all-metal structure and a single spar carried the main bending loads at the root of the wing, but these were gradually reduced along the span until the thick skin and stringers took the whole bending load. The wing was swept 40° at quarter chord and had a thickness/chord ratio of 10%. Its main Fowler-type wing flaps came in four sections and had rearward travel that substantially increased wing area in landing configuration.

| Detail of WG240's forward fuselage at the September 1954 Farnborough show.

The first production Sea Vixen fighter was XJ474, seen here in mid-1958.

Two Rolls-Royce Avon engines were fed from wing-root intakes and exhausted through short jet pipes placed well below the tailplane. The tailplane itself was unswept, but of very thin section and in its original form the DH.110 had unassisted rudders, fully-powered ailerons without feedback, an electrically-operated variable-incidence tailplane and a elevator with hydraulic boost, but these features were later updated by the introduction of an all-moving tailplane and powered rudders. "Dive brakes", conforming to the shape of the engine nacelles, were mounted on the central body.

The pilot's cockpit was offset well to port while the radar operator was housed to starboard, in a cabin completely within the contours of the forward fuselage. Unlike the pilot, he had no canopy, but there were windows on the starboard side. Neither WG236 nor WG240 had radar or armament installed, and the total internal fuel capacity for the original DH.110 was 1,120 Imp gals (5,093 litres), with provision for two 150-Imp gal (682-litre) external tanks.

This de Havilland advertisement for the DH.110 was published in *The Aeroplane* during October 1954.

19 Ikarus Projects (1951 onwards)

During the 1950s Yugoslavia's Ikarus produced a string of pioneering jet aircraft designs and prototypes. The three main aircraft manufacturers operating in Yugoslavia before the Second World War were Ikarus (first established in 1923 and with factories at Novi Sad and Zemun in Belgrade), Rogožarski, with a Belgrade factory, and Zmaj at Zemun. During the conflict all these facilities were destroyed or badly damaged by bombing, at first from Axis air arms and later, following the German occupation, by the Allies.

In 1945 the Ikarus plant at Zemun was rebuilt sufficiently for aircraft work to recommence, and in August 1946 the remnants of the three companies and their surviving technical staffs were brought together as a national concern. In 1948 the Yugoslav government established a state enterprise using the Ikarus name and by 1952 the country's aircraft industry essentially comprised a central national research, design, prototype manufacturing and testing establishment, coupled with a number of separate production factories. The Vazduhoplovnotehnički institut Žarkovo (VTI Žarkovo, Aeronautical Technical Institute) was established on 10 August 1946 as a design bureau for aeronautical research and the design of military aircraft.

Ikarus was soon working on several programmes, including the Aero 2 basic trainer, S-49 piston fighter reminiscent of the Soviet Yakovlev Yak-9, and several light aircraft types. Ikarus continued aircraft manufacture until 1961 and since Yugoslavia was not aligned with NATO or the Warsaw Pact, these alliances were considered as possible enemies. In 1954 Ikarus began manufacturing buses and from 1961 SOKO became responsible for aircraft manufacture in Yugoslavia, the aircraft factory section of Ikarus having been relocated to Mostar to form this new organisation.

Test pilot Tugomir Prebeg with the 451 prone-pilot research aircraft. Two 451s were built, one flying until 1953 and the other until 1957, although most of the latter's flying was apparently completed in the first two years of its career. After VOC assessment the 451 did not enter production; among its weaknesses was poor visibility from the cockpit, in particular to the rear. The aircraft also experienced longitudinal instability, oscillation and 'porpoising'. *Yugoslav Official*

During the 1950s Ikarus produced a number of experimental aircraft types, beginning with the small 451 all-metal light attack aircraft prototype, powered by two 161hp (120kW) Walter Minor 6-III piston engines and equipped with a prone pilot cockpit. The first of two built flew on 22 September 1951, piloted by Glavičić Radivoj. The 451M jet research aircraft followed, based on the 451's airframe but with a conventional cockpit and two Turbomeca Palas jet engines in wing nacelles (the 'M' designation stood for mlazni, or jet).

The 451M first flew on 25 October 1952 as Yugoslavia's first domestically designed and built jet aircraft, and was subsequently developed into the 451M Zolja light trainer, flown in 1954. The Ikarus 451, 451M and 452M were all designed by Lieutenant Colonel

Dragoljub Bešlin, while test pilot Captain Tugomir Prebeg performed the first flights of the 451M and 452M, and the second 451, on 26 February 1952.

Ikarus J451MM Stršljen

Next in this line of development, the J451MM Stršljen (Hornet) close-support aircraft was intended for production but failed to progress beyond the prototype stage. Work on the project began in 1954, this larger, beefier-looking aeroplane introducing a tricycle undercarriage, Turbomeca Marboré II engines providing more than twice the power of those used in the earlier aircraft, plus an armament of two HS.404 20mm cannon in fairings under the forward fuselage, and four 57mm or 127mm rocket projectiles on carriers beneath the wings.

The J451MM's official Vazduhoplovni Opitni Centar (VOC, Flight Test Centre) assessment began in 1957 although the aircraft was only about 95% complete. For a small aircraft, on take-off at normal loads the prototype had a heavy wing loading of 51lb/sq ft (250kg/sq m), and as a result much of the flight testing had to be conducted without armament, at a weight of around 4,410lb (2,000kg). Nevertheless, the J451MM reached 503mph (810km/h) in a shallow dive.

Note the cannon fairings under the J451MM's nose. *Yugoslav Official*

A line-up of Ikarus twin-jet prototypes – the J451MM Stršljen nearest, Š451MM Matica and 451M, Yugoslavia's first jet aircraft built to its own design. *Yugoslav Official*

Note the cannon fairings under the J451MM's nose. *Yugoslav Official*

The Š451MM Matica, showing detail of the engine nacelles and undercarriage. *Yugoslav Official*

The J451MM Stršljen employed all-metal construction and had a span of 25ft 3in (7.70m), length 25ft 3in (7.72m) and wing area 112.90sq ft (10.50sq m). Its maximum take-off weight was 6,473lb (2,936kg), maximum level speed 451mph (725km/h) and ceiling 36,255ft (11,050m).

The follow-on Š451MM Matica (Š for školski, or school) was a two-seat trainer version used in 1957 to set a world speed record in its category of 466.24mph (750.34km/h), while the T451MM Stršljen II with more powerful engines was a single-seat aerobatic trainer that flew for the first time on 3 December 1958, piloted by Major Josip Zubek. Two Stršljen IIs were built, but only one of the Matica (which the VOC rated as unsuitable for pilot training). A T451MM Stršljen II is preserved at the Museum of Aviation in Belgrade, while the J451MM Stršljen is understood to have been scrapped after 1960.

Ikarus 452M

An altogether different aircraft was the Ikarus 452M prototype of 1953. This single-seat research aeroplane was the second jet aircraft developed in Yugoslavia and was built in an unnamed "experimental" alloy. Of extremely novel and unconventional configuration it was powered by two 360lb (1.6kN) Turbomeca Palas 056A engines arranged one above the other towards the rear of the fuselage, with the upper unit fed by air inlets on each side of the upper fuselage behind the cockpit and the lower engine by intakes in the wing root leading edges.

The swept cantilever wing mounted two booms with vertical tail surfaces on each, with a swept V-shaped tailplane between them, supported at its centre by a small dorsal fin on the aft end of the fuselage. Wing leading edge slats were fitted outboard of the booms and the 452M had a tricycle undercarriage with the main wheels retracting into the fuselage.

Built at the Ikarus factory at Zemun, the 452M made its first flight on 24 July 1953 and was apparently considered a predesign for a light ground-attack aircraft that would also be used for high-speed reconnaissance. It was officially stated that the 452M's small dimensions were the result of a balance between military requirements and demands for economy. Very little appears to have been made known in regard to the aeroplane's flying career, but two examples were apparently built and, according to the contemporary authorities, the type achieved both speed and altitude world records for its class.

Besides its fin and rudder, this Ikarus 452M photo shows the 'stacked' engine and jet pipe arrangement. This may be the occasion of the aeroplane's roll out. *Angelo Romano*

Tugomir Prebeg and detail of the 452M's starboard side. The aircraft behind the 452M are the 451M, the piston 451 and at the far end one of two examples of the Ikarus 232 Pionir (Pioneer). The latter was a prone-pilot research aeroplane designed by Dragoljub Bešlin and powered by a pair of 66hp (48kW) Walter Mikron III piston engines. It was smaller than the 451 and preceded it, having made its maiden flight on 2 October 1947. In this case the prone position apparently proved difficult for flying. *Yugoslav Official*

The Ikarus 452M prototype had an extremely unusual appearance. *Yugoslav Official*

Extremely rare photo of the Ikarus 453MW experimental glider. *Yugoslav Official*

However, during flying with the VOC at Batajnica, the forward fuselage of the first example was badly damaged in a crash following engine failure. The pilot was injured but survived. It is not known if the second machine was completed. The 452M had a span of 17ft 2.5in (5.25m), length 19ft 7in (5.97m), wing area 120.43sq ft (11.20sq m), loaded weight c.2,425lb (1,100kg), maximum speed 466mph (750km/h) and service ceiling 32,150ft (9,800m). A separate source gives a maximum take-off weight of 3,704lb (1,680kg) and top speed 489mph (786km/h), but no original documents were consulted for any of the performance data.

Ikarus also produced the 453MW, a one-off experimental glider with an M-shaped wing to be followed by a version fitted with Marboré II engines. However, the glider flew just once, in 1952, and the flight ended in a crash after ground effect produced an excessively long landing run. The pilot was unharmed, but the 453MW was destroyed and the project abandoned. The extraordinary aircraft was designed by Bešlin and an engineer named Levachichem, from the General Directorate of Aviation Industry or GDVI.

'Bešlinovog' B-12

Another unusual project, the B-12 was a lightweight, single-seat, supersonic interceptor fighter with a fuselage similar to that of the 452M but more streamlined. Work on the project lasted from 1954 to 1958, again under the leadership of Dragoljub Bešlin, but the prototype was never completed. The name 'Bešlinovog' was applied to the aircraft, but its origin remains unknown.

The Yugoslav Government produced a ten-year development plan to place a light fighter along the lines of the British Folland Gnat into Air Force service and three projects were proposed, the B-12, ML-1 and PL-1. Bešlin's B-12, powered by two 1,765lb (7.8kN) thrust British Armstrong Siddeley Viper turbojets (as the B-12-V) was the only one to progress.

Three prototypes were planned with production to follow, the work being carried out by Ikarus (one source indicates that the production version might have been named 'Falcon'). However, progress was slow. Initial plans had expected to see the manufacture of several airframes well advanced by 1955 or 1956, with the prototype complete by 1 May 1955, but by the end of 1957 the first machine

Wind tunnel model of the B-12 supersonic light fighter and interceptor.

was only about 50% complete. Models were tested in a transonic wind tunnel in Sweden and in a supersonic tunnel in the UK, and it was apparently after the results of tunnel testing had been made available that the Ratno vazduhoplovstvo i protivvazdušna odbrana (RV i PVO, Air Force and Anti-Air Defence) suspended development. Studies of a variant designated B-12-OR continued for a while (OR indicated the Bristol Orpheus turbojet, which might have been the production powerplant) but production plans were abandoned in 1957.

An improvement in Yugoslav-Soviet relations in 1955 also weakened the case for the B-12 (although Yugoslavia would always take an independent course in world politics and shunned the influence of Western and Eastern powers). The real problem, however, was that developing a supersonic fighter was too large a challenge for the country's industry.

In 1992 General Basin Desert, director of the VTI Institute, stated that the B-12 was Yugoslavia's first national project to have a thin swept wing to permit flight at supersonic speeds. But he described the project as unrealistic because, compared to countries having much larger and more developed aircraft industries. aerodynamics and phenomena that surround supersonic flight. The country's experts lagged behind their equivalents elsewhere due to the lack of available laboratory and wind tunnel facilities.

The B-12 had a 45°-sweep wing with a span of 21ft 8in (6.6m) and area of 117.20sq ft (10.9sq m), its thickness/chord ratio was 5% and the estimated take-off weight 4,974lb (2,256kg); the aircraft's length is unknown, but appears to have been around 18-19ft (5.5-5.8m). A bicycle undercarriage was used. The project was replaced by plans to acquire the Folland Gnat and two examples of this aircraft were acquired for evaluation; one was lost in a crash in October 1958. No further orders for the Gnat were placed, however, and in due course Yugoslavian military jet development centred on the SOKO G-2 Galeb trainer, flown on 3 July 1961, and the J-21 Jastreb attack aircraft developed from it, which first flew on 19 July 1965. For the record (quoting former Yugoslavia sources translated), the ML-1 was apparently to be equipped with a jet engine (possibly called the Ardagama) reputedly giving around 5,500lb (24.5kN) of thrust. Its span was 28ft 9in (8.76m), wing sweep angle 43° and t/c ratio 8%, and estimated take-off weight 11,861lb (5,380kg). Design maximum speed at sea level was 665mph (1,070km/h) Mach 0.872, sea level rate of climb 8,595ft/min (2,620m/min) and ceiling with half fuel consumed 47,900ft (14,600m); the armament was four 20mm cannon.

By comparison, the PL-1 was planned with two 3,195lb (14.2kN) thrust Hispano R.800A engines and its estimated take-off weight was 9,634lb (4,370kg). Span was 26ft 2in (7.97m); wing sweep angle and t/c ratio 43° and 8%, respectively; wing area 204.30sq ft (19sq m); internal fuel capacity 2,205lb (1,000kg); and armament three 20mm cannon. Design maximum speed at sea level was 717mph (1,153km/h) or Mach 0.94, maximum sea level rate of climb on full power 15,455ft/min (4,710m/min) and ceiling with half fuel 52,755ft (16,080m).

180

20 English Electric P.1 (1954)

ENGLISH ELECTRIC P.1

Type (initially): single-seat supersonic research aircraft and interceptor prototype

Span: 34ft 10in (10.62m)

Length: 50ft 11in (15.52m)

Gross wing area: 458.52sq ft (42.64sq m)

All-up-weight (WG760 in March 1955): 27,100lb (12,293kg)

Powerplant: initially 2 x Armstrong Siddeley Sapphire Sa.5 turbojets each 7,200lb (32kN); WG760 later 2 x Armstrong Siddeley Sapphire Sa.5R turbojets each 4,200lb (18.7kN) dry and 9,200lb (40.9kN) with reheat

Max level speed: Mach 1.51 (stability limit)

Climb rate: time to 40,000ft (12,192m) without reheat 4 minutes 43 seconds

"Ceiling limitation": 55,000ft (16,764m)

Armament: 2 x 30mm Aden cannon when fitted

The English Electric Lighting was the only purely British-designed service fighter capable of supersonic speed on the level. The firm's P.1 research aircraft, built to Specification F.23/49 and Operational Requirement OR.268, sowed the seeds for what became one of Britain's favourite military aeroplanes. The aircraft then went through a substantial redesign to become the P.1B Lightning prototypes.

After the US had first broken through the sound barrier in October 1947, in early 1948 The Advanced Fighter Project Group committee was established in the UK at RAE Farnborough, to assess the potential research

that could be done into supersonic flight and the development of supersonic fighters. The committee's report was issued in November 1948 and envisaged a level flight Mach number of 1.4, and the outcome of these initial thoughts was a pair of research aircraft – a Fairey design that became the Delta 2 record breaker (see *X-Planes of Europe Volume I*) and the English Electric P.1. On 16 March 1950 the British Minister of Defence Emmanuel Shinwell reduced the programme's secrecy a little by announcing in the House of Commons that work had started on an aircraft capable of supersonic flight, but he did not add that the project was already two years down the line.

Model of the P.1 project, as first proposed in November 1948. *North West Heritage Group*

This original P.1 wind tunnel model has the horizontal tail placed on the sides of the fin.

Wind tunnel testing was critical in the development of the P.1 and Lightning. This model is seen generating transonic shock waves while 'flying' at Mach 0.98 in the manufacturer's wind tunnel.

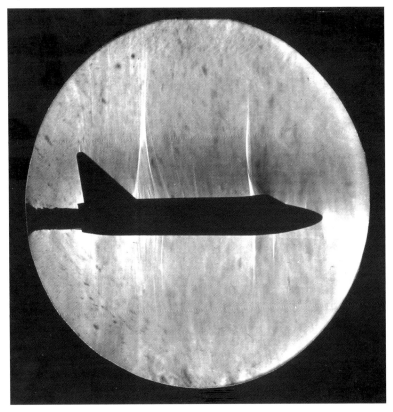

The first English Electric P.1 proposal brochure was completed during November 1948 and a notable feature were the finlets on the tips of its tailplane. Soon afterwards a single central fin was introduced and gradually the tail was lowered until it was positioned low on the rear fuselage. This final arrangement produced a good deal of discussion and controversy, particularly with the experts at RAE Farnborough, who felt that it would not perform satisfactorily at low speeds (English Electric had chosen this position to cure a problem of pitch-up experienced in the wind tunnel).

To check it out, a -scale low-speed model was ordered from Short Brothers. Designated S.B.5 and serialled WG768, it flew on 2 December 1952, initially with a T-tail as favoured by RAE and later with the low tail. The aircraft's trials proved that English Electric was correct in its choice of horizontal tail position (the S.B.5 also features in *X-Planes of Europe Volume I*).

Back in the late 1940s, supersonic fighter design relied on slide rules, mechanical calculators and a limited amount of theoretical fluid mechanics information for wing shapes. There were few wind tunnels and no computers, and when the P.1 was turned into the P.1B in the mid-1950s, it made use of several technological firsts, including a new supersonic tunnel at Warton, the first such tunnel built in Europe and which had been brought into use in July 1950.

The choice of wing for the P.1 was preceded at English Electric by an investigation into the performance of more than 200 planforms using supersonic theory. It was decided that thin, highly swept wings would have the best transonic performance and stability. In addition, using a V-shape would reduce tip stalling, structural problems and aileron ineffectiveness.

Specification F.23/49 covered the P.1 (not ER.103 as so often reported – this 1950 document covered only the Fairey Delta 2). F.23/49 described a twin-engine, single-seat "Interceptor Fighter with Supersonic Performance" and the draft OR.268 was prepared in May 1949, although the full specification was not issued until 10 April 1950. The design requirements at this stage were not too rigid, but covered a day fighter with guns and radar ranging, having a minimum top speed of Mach 1.2, plus the ability to climb from engine start to 50,000ft (15,240m) in no more than six minutes. Rate of climb at 55,000ft (16,764m) was to be at least 1,000ft/min (305m/min) and a minimum of two 30mm Aden cannon were to be carried. Although begun as a potential interceptor, the P.1 would subsequently become a pure research aeroplane.

Apart from its tailplane, the P.1 introduced another major innovation – twin engines mounted one above the other in the fuselage, in an arrangement that proved most successful and reduced the aircraft's frontal area. In fact, apart from the French Sud-Est SE.2410 Grognard prototypes in 1950/51 (see *X-Planes*

From December 1952 the low speed S.B.5 from Short Brothers was used to assess the tail position for the forthcoming P.1. It began trials with a T-tail as shown here, but an alternative tailplane for the P.1's low position could be fitted as an alternative. The photo was taken at the 1953 SBAC Farnborough show and DH.110 WG240 can be seen directly behind the main undercarriage.

of Europe Volume I), this format was never flown on another fighter-size aircraft.

English Electric and Rolls-Royce worked together on the shape of the P.1's fuselage and the stacked twin engine layout was in due course changed from the original upper engine forward/lower aft to upper aft/lower forward. Gas turbines were essential for any practical supersonic endurance, but in 1949 obtaining the best possible thrust per square foot/square metre of frontal area made it necessary to stagger the engines one behind the other in the fuselage to obtain a margin of thrust over drag at supersonic speeds. Also, a simple pitot intake was the only type to have a reasonable predictable efficiency, drag and effect on engine handling at transonic speeds. The length of the fuselage was then dictated by the minimum fairing of the engines, their intake and reheat ducting, together with other essential items in the fuselage.

In the beginning the P.1's engine was to be a supersonic version of the Rolls-Royce Avon designated RA.4 and known for a while as the Tyne. However, compressor problems with the original RA.1 meant that Rolls-Royce was forced to stop work on supersonic engines until its knowledge of compressor design had improved, a decision that killed the Tyne programme. Chief Designer on the P.1 was Edward 'Teddy' Petter who had joined English Electric just after the war and already produced the hugely successful Canberra, Britain's first jet bomber. Abandonment of the Tyne was not well received by Petter and the only other suitable engine available for the P.1 was the Armstrong-Siddeley Sapphire; a pair of Sapphire Sa.5s was chosen for the first aircraft. Petter left English Electric in 1950 for Folland, and Freddie Page took on the job of leading the team that would turn the P.1 into the Lightning.

WG760 with its original straight, notched leading edge. *North West Heritage Group*

The first English Electric P.1, WG760 displays its highly swept wing and controversial low tailplane position. *Patrick Tilley via Phil Butler*

WG760 with the kinked leading edge. *Patrick Tilley via Phil Butler*

Contract 6/Aircraft/5175/CB.7(a) was approved in April 1949 for two P.1 aircraft. Serials WG760 and WG763 were allocated on 27 July 1950 and WG760 made its maiden flight on 4 August 1954 from Boscombe Down, with company chief test pilot Wg Cdr Roland 'Bee' Beamont in the cockpit. On Flight One WG760 reached Mach 0.85 and a week later, on Flight Three, it became the first British aircraft to exceed the speed of sound in level flight (and reheat had not yet been installed).

The P.1 proved a great success although a

| WG760 displays the straight outer wing arrangement. *North West Heritage Group and Patrick Tilley via Phil Butler*

directional stability limit owing to the lack of fin area kept it below Mach 1.51 in level flight. It was nevertheless a lovely aeroplane to fly, but suffered from insufficient fuel capacity, rectified to some extent by an underbelly tank fitted to the second machine, WG763.

Towards the end of 1955 WG760 received rudimentary afterburners, reducing available dry thrust quite badly, but producing a reheated maximum of 9,200lb (40.9kN) per engine. This gave as vast improvement in climb rate and 40,000ft (12,192m) could now be reached in 3.5 minutes. In 1957 WG760's wing was modified with a kinked leading edge and expanded tip chord, a feature used on production Lightnings. However, the P.1 was never going to be a frontline fighter (though the second aircraft did carry guns).

In March 1955, 'A' Squadron pilots from A&AEE performed a preview assessment of WG760, although under severe restrictions appropriate to the stage of flight development: a Mach number of 1.15 or 480 knots (889km/h) IAS, maximum altitude of 48,000ft (14,630m) and no more than 4g acceleration. Within these limits, however, the aircraft gave a very favourable impression, particularly with its high performance potential and docile handling characteristics. The highly swept thin wing and low tail, in conjunction with full power controls with artificial feel, had been successful in providing pleasant, straightforward and conventional handling characteristics, and particularly docile transonic behaviour. WG760 was easy to taxi and for take-off the engines were opened up to 7,500rpm on the brakes and then to full power as the aircraft moved forward. Initial acceleration was good but not startling, but became rapid and the rudder was effective early in the run. The tail became effective at about 100 knots (185km/h).

The climbing attitude was steep and one pilot had trouble in flying at the optimum climbing speed. He found it particularly difficult to prevent the IMN from exceeding Mach 0.91. The P.1's high IMN performance was completely outside this pilot's experience. On his first sortie, while levelling out from a climb at 41,000ft (12,497m) with 8,300revs still on, the aircraft exceeded Mach 1.0 IMN while still in a slight climb. After this he found that with full power, IMNs in excess of 1.1 could be attained in a 10-12° dive from 42,000ft (12,802m).

The aircraft's basic high IMN characteristics were found to be straightforward and, overall, there were no noticeable Mach number effects – the Machmeter needle simply went round the dial. This pilot's control assessment at Mach 1.10 showed that the tailplane was effective but moderately heavy and it exhibited some response lag to stick movements. The ailerons were light and very effective and very responsive, while the rudder (small movements only) was moderately effective and moderately heavy, but responsive. The rate of roll at this speed was very high.

In further "operational" high-speed climbs it was found that the angle of climb at 450 knots (834km/h) was very steep at 30,000ft (9,144m), this altitude appearing to be the aircraft's best performance height band. An IMN of 0.90 was also thought to be a very good cruising condition. However, high-rate descent from altitude was somewhat complicated by the lack of an airbrake and by the fact that the aircraft's limitations would not permit a steep dive so, consequently, on some occasions a descent was made in a 3-4g spiral dive. In conclusion, at this stage the aircraft needed a useable airbrake and more fuel. In addition, a small but sudden pitch-up occurred with applied 'g' when decelerating at high subsonic Mach numbers (0.98 to 0.96) and this required investigation.

When A&AEE flew the machine again in October and November 1955 the Sapphire Sa.5 engines had been uprated and the speed limits had been raised to Mach 1.31 or 600 knots (1,112km/h) IAS. WG760 continued to be a very pleasant aircraft to fly; it could exceed Mach 1.0 straight and level and would accelerate very rapidly in a dive. Pilots from the Air Fighting Development Squadron (part of the Central Fighter Establishment) found that to achieve the maximum permissible Mach 1.3 it was necessary to dive the aircraft from 40,000ft (12,192m) to approximately 20,000ft (6,096m), and the recovery from high speeds was smooth. By now airbrakes had been fitted, but they produced a heavy nose-up trim change, accompanied by considerable buffet, so it was recommended that they were used only in an extreme emergency (the airbrakes were redesigned for the P.1B). The P.1's cockpit was also described as "extremely cramped".

Clearly a considerable amount of development work still lay ahead and there was also criticism of WG760's transonic handling in the Mach 0.90 to 1.00 IMN range. Up to 0.94 IMN the handling was normal, and between 0.94 and 0.97 the lateral control remained satisfactory, but the longitudinal control was described as "somewhat touchy". This characteristic was noticeable when small amounts of 'g' were applied, or when re-trimming to counteract the slight nose-down trim change that occurred during this range of Mach numbers. It was manifest as over-controlling, which was of a mild degree but could make accurate aiming difficult. Above 0.97 IMN the longitudinal sensitivity decreased, control became much more pleasant and accurate flying became easy once more.

Beamont took WG763 up for its first flight on 18 July 1955, this time from English Electric's airfield at Warton. Back in November 1951 the predicted first flight dates had been October 1953 and April 1954 respectively, so there had been a substantial slippage which, at one stage, was a concern to the Air Council.

WG763 was the first P.1 revealed to the general public when it was shown statically at the September 1955 Farnborough. Development work performed by the second P.1 included trials with a 250-Imp gal (1,137-litre) ventral fuel tank to increase range and the installation of two 30mm Aden cannon, high on the sides of the nose. By autumn 1956, WG763 had fired its guns at supersonic speeds and various altitudes.

By December 1955 the Ministry of Supply could report that since the summer of 1954 the P.1As had frequently attained supersonic speed in climbing flight, an entirely new capability for fighter-type aeroplanes. Retrospectively designated P.1A after work began on the P.1B, the aircraft flew on English Electric's test programme for several years and generally gave few problems, although on three occasions the canopy was lost in flight. In each case the pilot (Beamont once and Desmond de Villiers twice) was able, with difficulty, to land, and on one of these occasions de Villiers became the world's first open cockpit supersonic pilot. After completing their English Electric duties both P.1As were used by military establishments for various trials. In May 1957 the first P.1 was used for landing run assessments on wet runways both at Boscombe and Finningley. The unarmed WG760 then went to Farnborough in September 1957 to display the new kinked wing leading edge (neither aircraft had attended the 1956 Show), where P.1B XA847 accompanied it. In fact, for the first few days of the show XA847 was unserviceable and WG760 performed the demonstration flying, which included low-level passes at Mach 0.98.

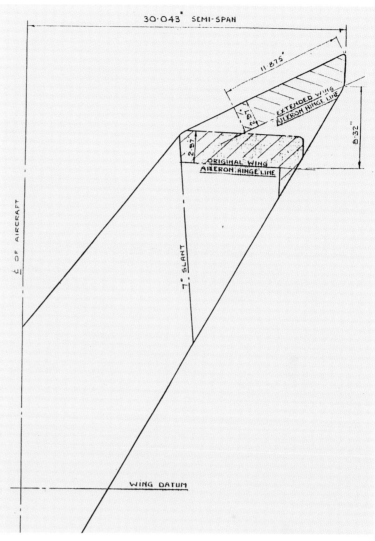

The P.1 and Lightning wing was unusual in having the ailerons at the ends of the wingtips. Later in the P.1/Lightning story, English Electric suggested modifications to the fighter's outer wing. This drawing shows a tip extension with the ailerons still on the outer edge. *National Archives*

WG760 at Farnborough in 1957. *Barry Jones via Terry Panopalis*

An A&AEE cameraman took a series of photos of WG760 with the kinked wing. Here the P.1's massive intake, long, slim, tube-like fuselage and small fin are evident. They have rarely been published before. *Patrick Tilley via Phil Butler*

WG760 was used for Safeland runway barrier trials at RAE Bedford from January to March 1958 and again from June 1958. In 1960 it performed infra-red radiation assessment and trials, and made its last of 703 flights on 18 February 1961. It was allotted for ground instruction in July 1962 as 7755M, first at Weeton and later St Athan. Since 1986 WG760 has resided at Royal Air Force Museum Cosford.

WG763 joined Aero Flight at RAE Bedford in June 1957 and was used on a variety of trials programmes, even after its flying career had ended on 7 December 1959. In 1960 and 1962 for example, it was used for ground resonance tests at Bedford and in February 1962 for parachute streaming tests. WG763 was allotted for ground instruction as 7816M in July 1963, and since 1982 it has been on display at Manchester's Museum of Science and Industry.

Despite its appearance at a Farnborough show, photos of WG763 appear to be quite rare. This image was taken in July 1957 at RAE Bedford, on what appears to be an open day. Note the red cover over the air intake. *Terry Panopalis*

A static test airframe was also constructed and did not, as stated elsewhere, receive the serial WG765. These straightforward supersonic research aeroplanes were a great success, and the programme resulted in the development of an interceptor.

| The first P.1B Lightning prototype, XA847. *North West Heritage Group*

Rolls-Royce had produced the RA.24 version of the Avon while English Electric had designed a new annular air intake with two-shock, conical centrebody and revised fuselage to replace the P.1's pitot intake. This made the airframe viable for Mach 2. The new aircraft was designated P.1B and from then on WG760 and WG763 were referred to as P.1As. In June 1952 it was decided to order three P.1B prototypes to extend the Mach number range. The first of these, XA847, flew on 4 April 1957 and development of the type was taken through to the production Lightning, which entered service in 1960.

Preview handling trials with WG760 fitted with a cambered leading edge wing began at A&AEE on 25 November 1957. Later on, pilots from the Central Fighter Establishment (CFE; an RAF facility based at West Raynham and tasked with development of fighter tactics) commented that, within the P.1A's reduced performance envelope, the modified wing conferred a very significant improvement in handling characteristics and manoeuvrability. It was summarised as:

   a. Improved Stability. Unlike XA847 (which had the original, uncambered wing), WG760 settled into a turn at high speed and did not require constant attention and correction to bank and attitude – in short, the turn was stable.

   b. Improved Manoeuvrability and Control. Also unlike the P.1B, buffet was relatively unobtainable, and when it did occur it was at much higher applied 'g'. Control was smoother, more precise, more harmonious and had 'feel'.

In addition, control in the circuit, approach and landing was much better.

English Electric's results from flight tests with the cambered wing revealed the following benefits:

   a. Subsonic drag had been reduced by up to 20%, but increased supersonically

   b. Altitude performance and approach handling were both improved

   c. Ferrying range was increased by about 20%

   d. Lateral control was improved, though the rates of roll were slightly reduced (but still met specification requirements)

   e. Buffet performance was greatly improved

Airframe

Light aluminium alloys were used almost exclusively for the P.1's primary structure and the P.1As were built with heavier gauge metal than was usual, presumably to counter unknown supersonic effects. Some titanium was used in certain spots near the engines and jet pipes.

The tube-like P.1s were cantilever monoplanes with their mid-position wings built around five spars and swept at angle of 60° (leading edge sweep angle 57° 30'). The ailerons extended right across the wingtips, perpendicular to the fuselage – indeed, for the P.1 wing the angle of sweepback was such that the same position of the ailerons on less highly swept mainplanes would have corresponded to wingtips. There were large Fowler-type split flaps along most of the trailing edge, and notches were eventually introduced on the leading edge in lieu of wing fences. The P.1s had inner wing leading edge flaps, although these were used only on WG760's early flights and locked on WG763. Wing t/c ratio at the fuselage side was 5.27% and at the tip 6.19%.

The cantilever, all-metal, low-set slab tailplane was a one-piece all-moving surface that followed the shape of the wings, and there was a delta-shaped fin and rudder. The all-moving tail was essential for manoeuvrability at high speeds, but for structural reasons such a tailplane had to be kept as small as possible to perform its primary function as a trimming and manoeuvring device; it also contributed positive transonic damping in addition to that of the highly swept wing. For such advanced aeroplanes as these, the flying control system was completely conventional, ailerons, tailplanes and rudder all being driven by hydraulic power units.

The Armstrong Siddeley Sapphire engines were staggered one above the other within the fuselage, with the lower unit placed well forward of the upper. Internal fuel was housed in integral tanks in the wings, while the pilot and his Martin-Baker ejection seat were in a near flush cockpit set well forward in the fuselage. The P.1s had a polished natural metal finish throughout their careers. The only major differences introduced by WG763 were the ventral fuel tank and a pair of 30mm guns.

| The results of the P.1 (P.1A) flight test research came together in the fabulous Mach 2 Lightning. This is Lighting F.Mk 3 XP694.

21 FFA P-16 (1955)

FFA P-16

Type: single-seat strike fighter prototype

Span: 36ft 6.5in (11.14m)

Length: 47ft (14.33m)

Gross wing area: 322.58sq ft (30sq m)

Wing t/c ratio: 8% constant

Weights (Mk III): basic gross weight 20,475lb (9,287kg); overload gross weight 25,800lb (11,720kg)

Powerplant: first two prototypes 1 x Armstrong-Siddeley Sapphire Sa.6 8,000lb (35.6kN); third prototype and Mk III 1 x Armstrong-Siddeley Sapphire Sa.7 11,000lb (48.9kN)

Max level speed (Mk III): 603 knots (1,118km/h) or Mach 0.9 at sea level; 540 knots (1,000km/h) or Mach 0.92 at 32,810ft (10,000m)

Service ceiling: 46,000ft (14,020m)

Climb rate (Mk III): 12,795ft/min (3,900m/min) at sea level

Range: 970 miles (1,560km) at 30,000ft (9,144m)

Armament: 2 x 30mm Hispano-Suiza HS 825 cannon and MATRA launcher for 44 x 68mm folding fin rockets in fuselage. Four wing racks for 2 x 1,000kg (2,205lb), 4 x 454kg (1,000lb) or 8 x 204kg (450lb) bombs; 4 x 100-Imp gal (455-litre) napalm tanks; external fuel tanks; 4 x 68mm rocket packs; or 12 launch points for 48 Hispano R 80 80mm air-to-ground rockets

Switzerland's aircraft industry was once quite fertile in producing in-house designs for military aircraft. During the 1950s it was responsible for the development of two major jet-powered combat aircraft programmes the first of which, the FAF (F + W) N-20 Aiguillon and its scale model, the N-20-2 Arbalète, were covered in Volume I. The second was the Flug und Fahrzeugwerke Altenrhein AG (FFA, the Aircraft and Vehicle Works at Altenrhein) P-16 strike fighter, intended to combine very short take-off and landing runs with a heavy armament load and excellent manoeuvrability.

As a result of Switzerland's experience with nations in conflict all around it during World War II, and also in view of the nature of the country's topography, the Swiss Ministry of Defence decided to use its own aircraft industry to provide a new advanced jet-powered fighter. It would be a step towards gaining independence from acquiring all of Switzerland's combat aircraft from abroad and, to back it up, in a statement dated 3 July 1945, Major General Fritz Rihner of the Swiss Air Force stressed the importance of acquiring jet-powered aircraft.

It was some time before a specification was put together, but in 1948 a document was prepared for a new type combining transonic speed with a heavy external weapons load and yet possessing take-off and landing performance allowing it to operate from minor airstrips in narrow valleys. The document was issued to the two principal national aircraft companies and produced two programmes, the first of which came from the Eidgenössischen Flugzeugwerke (EFW, Swiss Federal Aircraft Works) at Emmen, with a radical tailless design designated N-20. The FFA, however, looked at a more conventional design that became the P-16.

Some sources (including the author in Volume I) state that the N-20 Aiguillon prototype performed taxi trials and short hops on 8 April 1952. It has now been established that its ground tests did not begin until the following year and this attractive aircraft never got beyond making brief hops.

The results of preliminary design studies indicated that the N-20 was more promising than the P-16 and on 15 July 1949 it received the official support of the Kommission fuer militaerische Flugzeugbeschaffung (KMF, the Commission for Military Aircraft Procurement). FFA's studies for a cheaper, single-engine fighter were accepted a few days later and would continue as a back-up. In the event, EFW's N-20, powered by four Armstrong-Siddeley Mamba turbojet engines exhausting through efflux slots in the aft mainplanes, proved underpowered. The chief of the Military Department (EMD) had also expressed doubts about the N-20's fuselage and engine configuration and then, following a Kriegstechnische Abteilung (KTA, War Technical Department) cost comparison of the two programmes, on 9 January 1953 the Federal Council decided to abandon the N-20 project.

It appears that N-20 ground testing actually began on 9 January, but due to reductions in the workforce allocated to the project, taxi trials and short hops were not completed until September. On 21 September 1953 the EMD chief declared that the N-20 was forbidden from making its first flight and the programme was officially closed. Despite offers by the design team to take responsibility for flying the aeroplane, with the workforce preparing the aircraft in their free time, the Federal Council would not lift the ban. The N-20 had missed its chance.

On 26 November 1949 FFA had submitted its "Project Investigations on Single Engine Jets P-14, P-15, and P-16" to the KTA. These designs shared a strong family likeness, although a layout based on the P-16 was favoured. After termination of the N-20, the P-16 was given priority under the direction of FFA chief engineer Dr Ing Hans L. Stüder.

An important advance made with the P-16 was its use of nose flaps (as distinct from slats, slots and droop-snoots) to provide extra lift. FFA stated that this was the first true use of the leading edge flap on a full-scale aeroplane anywhere in the world and it enabled the manufacturer to reduce the wing area to a minimum, while the P-16 still had good short take-off and landing characteristics and a low stalling speed. Dr Krüger, a German aerodynamicist working at Göttingen University, had made the first proposal for this type of leading edge flap during the Second World War. FFA's theoretical and wind-tunnel studies into the flap had started back in 1947, and since then it had been used on civil transport aircraft.

There were plans in early 1952 to modify the Aiguillon to use a pair of British axial turbojets, either the Avon or Sapphire, as the N-20.20 Harpon. This photo of the Harpon wind tunnel model was taken in the Museum of Transport in Lucerne in 1993. *Mike Kirk*

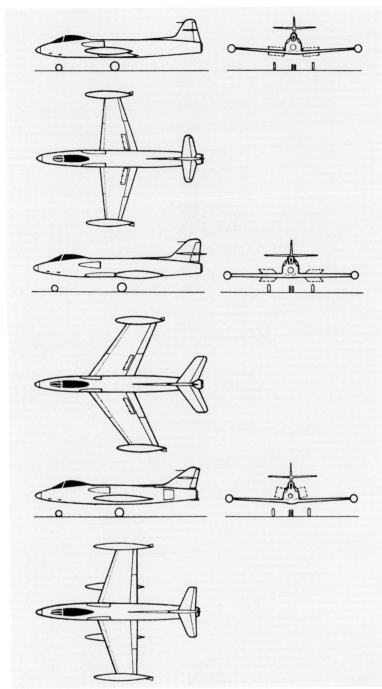

Top to bottom: FFA's P-14, P-15 and P-16 designs, as proposed in November 1949.

The first P-16 prototype, serial J-3001, made its maiden flight from Altenrhein on 28 April 1955, piloted by FFA chief test pilot Lt Hans Häfliger. It carried no armament, but showed most promising performance. J-3001's career was short lived, however, because on Flight 22, on 31 August, the engine suffered fuel starvation from a fracture in the main tank pressure line and flamed-out, the pilot having to eject, which he did safely. The aircraft crashed into Lake Constance (the Bodensee) and was lost. Because work on building the second P-16 had only just begun, a long break was caused in the flight test programme.

The second aircraft, J-3002 finally made it into the air on 16 June 1956, the opportunity having been taken along the way to introduce modifications compared to the first prototype. These included extending the air intakes forward along the fuselage ahead of the wing (they were also raised clear of the fuselage profile). There was a small plate or cap on top of the fin, and a bulged fairing covering a braking parachute was introduced over the tailpipe. Since this aircraft was also equipped with two 30mm guns, a Ferranti radar-ranging gunsight and underwing racks, it was used a good deal on bombing, and rocket and gun-firing trials.

Below Left: The short-lived J-3001. The entire flap system is deployed, including the section underneath the fuselage, with the ailerons providing additional area. The original empennage is also shown and there are no side-fuselage airbrakes. *Mike Kirk*

Below: This planform of J-3001 suggests the wing leading edge flaps were painted in a contrasting colour. Note the finlets on the outside ends of the tip tanks. *Mike Kirk*

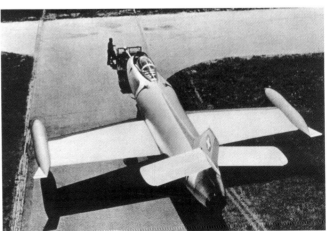

The first P-16, J-3001 taxis past the camera at Altenrhein. In the first photo the aircraft has a lower nose gun port, but this appears to have been obscured by the censor in the second picture. Note the original air intake position. *Mike Kirk*

J-3002 also had a Lear yaw-damper which, coupled with the type's stability, made the P-16 an excellent weapons platform with a hit probability of more than 60% with the guns. During Flight 18, on 15 August 1956, J-3002 exceeded the speed of sound for the first time in a slight dive and later the prototypes were often flown supersonically, even with a full compliment of rockets under the wings.

The Air Force evaluated the aircraft between 28 February and 12 March 1957, releasing its report in May. It noted: "The performance corresponds to expectations, and the flight characteristics are very good." However, there were problems with the brakes, while the servo control was considered insufficient, the report concluding: "The P-16 is not ready for production". FFA's engineers began making

Right: The second FFA P-16 prototype, J-3002. *Mike Kirk*

Below: J-3001 just after take-off. *Mike Kirk*

J-3002 introduced revisions to the air intakes and rear fuselage, as well as large perforated airbrakes on the fuselage sides and a cap at the top of the fin. *Mike Kirk*

improvements and altogether J-3002 contributed 310 flights to the programme, including landings on grass strips. The second P-16 flew for the last time on 7 March 1958 and was later scrapped.

Events surrounding the third P-16 did much to bring the programme down. On 15 March 1956 the Swiss Parliament proposed procurement of a further series of

The P-16's neat, clean design is highlighted in this view of J-3002, which also shows the twin wheels on each undercarriage leg. The aircraft is stated to have carried two guns, but many views of J-3002 have the ports obscured. *Mike Kirk*

four pre-production prototypes, one of them J-3003, which first flew on 15 April 1957. It had previously been earmarked for use as a static test airframe, but the loss of J-3001 led to its completion to "pre-series Mk II" flight standards, with a more powerful Sapphire engine. Most of the projected armament was now available to the aircraft, which also featured a fuselage weapons bay, although it carried only a single HS 825 cannon.

Right: Prototype J-3002 makes a fast flypast. *Mike Kirk*

Below and below right: J-3002 taking off with its nosewheel retracting, and then touching down. Its nose and dorsal spine/fin and tip tanks were painted red. *Mike Kirk*

Side view of J-3002. *Mike Kirk*

Rare photograph showing J-3002 and J-3003 together. *Mike Kirk*

Manufacturer's drawing of the P-16 Mk III. *Mike Kirk*

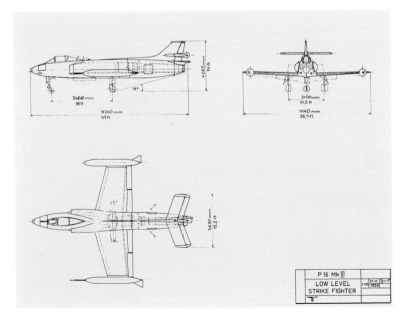

During Flight 102, on 25 March 1958, J-3003 experienced a sudden loss of control after a failure in the hydraulic system. The aircraft had entered final approach to land and the pilot (Lt J Brunner from the Swiss Test Establishment) ejected, being rescued from Lake Constance. As with J-3001, the vacated third prototype came to a watery end. The accident's cause proved quite complex, involving one material failure, two human errors and a physical phenomenon not previously fully understood.

The failure was in a coupling on the main hydraulic system supply tank. This allowed air to be pumped into the system, which was then absorbed by the hydraulic fluid to a far greater degree than earlier data had indicated was possible. A very high proportion of the hydraulic oil was turned into foam and the first human error came when groundcrew failed to spot that the hydraulic tank was full of foam rather than liquid. In fact there had been predominantly foam in the system for several flights after the coupling had cracked.

Finally, on the 25th, hydraulic pressure dropped to too low a level during final approach. With a hydraulic failure the pilot could usually control the aircraft manually if it was trimmed for the required flight configuration, but Brunner had made the second human error. After making high-speed runs with J-3003 trimmed nose heavy, he had not re-trimmed for the approach. With the hydraulic pressure below normal, Brunner suddenly had the stick yank forwards out of his hands to full deflection, and the aircraft went into a 40° dive. Left with no time to re-trim the aeroplane and insufficient strength to fly it manually, Brunner left and J-3003 went into the lake off the end of the runway.

It was impossible to raise the airframe and so the extensive enquiry involved a great deal of theory, which took time. The P-16's flying controls had a hydraulic stand-by system driven by a separate electric pump and also manual reversion, a supposed triple safeguard against this sort of failure. Its structural design had been based on British design requirements and so independent opinions were also solicited from foreign specialists, including three from Britain. Losing J-3003 through such a fault was most unlucky but, despite a relief valve being introduced into a revised hydraulic system to eliminate the possibility of it happening again, on 2 June 1958 the Swiss government cancelled an order it had placed for 100 P-16s and withdrew all support for the project.

In fact the situation had become very

political. The government claimed that the P-16 production contract had been terminated because FFA had failed to meet the British design requirements. As a result, the British Ministry of Supply was asked to send specialists from RAE Farnborough to investigate the affair. They analysed every aspect of the accident and their resulting report cleared the manufacturer of any technical blame for the failure.

A less obvious aspect, however, was changes in the staff at the Landesverteidigungskommission (LVK, National Defence Commission). One LVK man with significant influence was Lt General Georg Zueblin and he, along with several other officials, had advocated a new policy of 'Mobile Defence'. In mid-1958 the LVK defined how the Air Force would now employ 'Counter Air Operations' with missions flown beyond the Swiss border, some of which might also involve the use of atomic weapons.

These tasks would require different types of aircraft to the P-16, which had never been designed for such operations, or to carry nuclear weaponry, but rather for air superiority and close air support. The type was clearly unsuited to the new approach and the second crash brought an opportune moment to be rid of it. However, in his cancellation speech on 5 June 1958 the Federal Council's Paul Chaudet only reported that the government "had lost confidence in the technology of the aircraft" – he did not mention the change of policy. By then, however, the need for the Swiss Air Force to acquire a new ground attack type had become such that on 29 January 1958 the Federal Council had placed an order for 100 Hawker Hunters.

On top of this, in the spring of 1959 FFA was absorbed by a new company, Aktiengesellschaft für Flugzeugunternehmungen Altenrhein (AFA, literally 'Company for Aircraft Enterprises at Altenrhein'), though in due course it reverted to the old name. In spite of the official cancellation, the manufacturer elected to continue with the P-16 at its own expense and on 8 July 1959 flew the first full pre-series aircraft, J-3004, which it designated P-16 Mk III. This employed larger 208-Imp gal (945-litre) wing tanks and, since the work was now a private venture, received the civil-registration X-HB-VAC.

Hans Häfliger was no longer performing P-16 test flying and a reserve pilot, Ing Hans Bardill, began the test programme. His first job was to assess the revised hydraulic system, which proved satisfactory, to the point that when using the stand-by control system Bardill was able to take the aircraft through an aerobatic routine without trouble and up to Mach 0.92; in other words to

The fourth P-16, J-3004/X-HB-VAC, the first Mk III, did away with the nose pitot and, after appearing at first in 'bare metal', received full camouflage on its uppersurfaces as part of the manufacturer's export sales drive. The pitot was moved to the port tip tank, and note that a yellow bird emblem was painted beneath the forward part of the cockpit. *Mike Kirk*

J-3004/X-HB-VAC retracts its undercarriage after take off. *Mike Kirk*

almost full combat handling. Using manual control he was able to fly at Mach 0.8, affect 80° turns and stay in this configuration for flights of up to half an hour. After having demonstrated J-3004 in public during October 1959, in December FFA announced that the P-16 Mk III had completed a new flight test programme which, the firm claimed, completely vindicated it following the problems and controversy of the previous year.

Some elements of the P-16 Mk III's performance were quite remarkable, in part because of the heavily cambered wing and its lift devices. For example, it would not spin at all by accident, and when put into a spin deliberately, even if inverted, it would recover

The fourth P-16. *Mike Kirk*

The fifth P-16, X-HB-VAD is seen in its striking silver and red colour scheme, with external tanks on the inner wing pylons and bombs on the outer stations. *Mike Kirk*

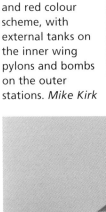

just a quarter of a turn after the pilot had released the controls. The Mk III could be flown under control in a fully-stalled attitude at vertical descent rates of up to 120ft/sec (36m/sec) and it never showed stalled wing drop, either in the high-speed or landing configuration, flying straight and level or in a tight turn. Stall warning buffet began when clean at about 129 knots (239km/h), and at 97 knots (179km/h) when the undercarriage and flaps were deployed.

Flying at Mach 0.8, the P-16 would roll at 200°/sec and the minimum landing speed was roughly l00 knots (185km/h). Its undercarriage allowed the aircraft to take off from difficult surfaces, including a soaked grass field that was so soft a jeep sank into the turf; the jet took of in less than 1,090 yards (1,000m).

At the time of its cancellation, two pre-series P-16 aircraft were under construction and the second of these, the fifth and last to fly, made its maiden flight on 24 March 1960. X-HB-VAD (J-3005) introduced a number of changes, including four instead of the earlier two underwing bomb or tank attachments, and the removal of the inner boundary-layer extensions from the intakes. Most important of all, this Mk III had a production wing with a single, taper-rolled thick skin, rather than the previous doubled wing skin with corrugations (the taper skin was easier to produce and saved weight). The fourth and fifth P-16s completed a full flight test programme and took the number of P-16 flights to over 470, though X-HB-VAD contributed only 19 of these for a total of 7.25 flight hours (including high-speed and full load tests).

The fifth aircraft was also the only P-16 displayed abroad. On 26 June 1960, Hans Bardill performed two flights at the

Above: X-HB-VAD demonstrates its larger, fixed tip tanks. *Mike Kirk*

Left: Detail of X-HB-VAD's flaps and jet pipe. *Mike Kirk*

International Air Day at Friedrichshafen, flying the aircraft at the extremes of 124mph and 684mph (200km/h and 1,100km/h) and performing a very short take-off and landing. X-HB-VAD was withdrawn from service directly afterwards (J-3004/X-HB-VAC had been grounded in April).

There were many proposals for improved P-16s. For example, the 30 May 1960 issue of the journal *Aviation Week* reported that one development would be powered by a 13,200lb (58.7kN) thrust Rolls-Royce RB.146 engine to provide a 20% to 35% improvement in take-off, climb and acceleration performance. There was also an attempt in 1965 to sell a version powered by a J79 engine to the US as the AJ-7, but none of these projects were built. But this was not quite the end of the story.

The fifth P-16, X-HB-VAD. *Copyright Pete West*

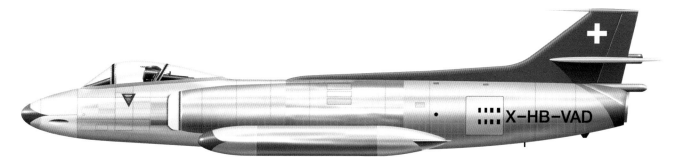

This photo of the last P-16 completed shows the airbrakes and how they retracted into large cut outs in the rear fuselage. *Mike Kirk*

In 1960 William P Lear Jr, an experienced US Air Force ground attack jet pilot and the son of the famous industrialist, flew J-3004 and rated it superior to any other type he had experienced in this class. Lear considered it "a joy to fly" and in a 67° dive from 40,000ft (12,192m) took the P-16 up to Mach 1.05. In due course his father also became enthusiastic, but he was able to take things a step further. Having formed the Swiss American Aviation Corporation in 1960, he produced the Learjet six-seat executive jet, which essentially had the P-16's wing with its tapered skins and fixed tip-tanks joined to a new passenger fuselage. The chief designer for the new project was Hans Stüder who had led the P-16 team, and the first example of this hugely successful aircraft was flown on 7 October 1963.

After their retirement from flying, both Mk IIIs were held at Altenrhein until 1979. In May and July of that year, respectively, X-HB-VAD and J-3004/X-HB-VAC were taken by train to Dübendorf. The latter was then cannibalised to provide parts for X-HB-VAD's restoration, though in fact this was really a case of producing one good airframe out of two. The remains of J-3004 were subsequently scrapped, while X-HB-VAD was put on display at the Flieger FLAB (Swiss Air Force) Museum at Dübendorf in 1980, where it remains, along with the N-20.

The handsome P-16 was an aircraft that offered so much promise and was perhaps unrivalled by any other aircraft of its type in the world. The project probably failed primarily because it suffered bad luck at the most critical moments of its development. The end of official support for the P-16 also brought the end to indigenous military aircraft design in Switzerland.

Airframe

The major aerodynamic feature of the conventional looking P-16 was its moderately swept, thin wing and very effective high-lift devices. It had full-span leading edge Krüger nose flaps which, when stowed, were flush with the wing, but had an extended deflection of 120°. The wing also had trailing-edge area-increasing Fowler flaps deflecting to 45° and extending to around half span, plus permanent tip-mounted fuel tanks that provided an endplate effect (the flap span extended right across the fuselage belly). Additional trailing-edge flap area came from drooping the ailerons through 18° when the flaps were at maximum

Comparative forward fuselage views of J-3002 and one of the Mk IIIs. *Mike Kirk*

Comparative rear fuselage views of J-3002 and J-3004, the latter with a fairing over the jet pipe. Early in its life, J-3004 has '04' on its nosewheel door. *Mike Kirk*

extension, and all of these features resulted in an extraordinary level of camber to give very high lift. The wing was swept 16° at quarter chord and the only cutout of any consequence made in the lower surface housed the main-gear strut of the tricycle undercarriage. This simplified the wing's structure, a multiple-box layout with vertical shear webs that, on the prototypes, was covered by a corrugated sandwich structure but on production machines by a one-piece tapered skin. As a result, the P-16's wing was very stiff, with a load factor of 12.75, 30% higher than for the majority of contemporary fighter aircraft.

The aircraft had a conventional fuselage with a spacious central armament bay for a MATRA Type 1000 rocket launcher, cannon in the nose and large airbrakes on the sides of the rear fuselage. There was no 'fixed' internal fuel, the tip tanks housing the majority of the supply – on the larger Mk III P-16 this came to 543 Imp gals (2,468 litres), rising to 890 Imp gals (4,045 litres) when auxiliary tanks were carried. But the fuselage bay also housed a 125-Imp gal (568-litre) fuel collector tank,

Relatively few photos seem to exist of the ill-fated J-3003, despite its flying career lasting almost a year. Here it has underwing bombs and rockets. Apart from red flashes on the nose, dorsal fin and tanks, as per J-3002, this aircraft had a grey metallic finish. *Mike Kirk*

which took its contents from the wingtips. There was provision for a fire-control radar in the nose, but this was never fitted. During trials the Mk IIIs were flown in an overload condition with 5,700lb (2,585kg) of external stores on board.

J-3004/X-HB-VAC shows off the P-16's leading edge flaps. *Phil Butler*

Armament boxes for X-HB-VAD's nose cannon and the retractable rockets housed in its fuselage bay are shown here. *Phil Butler*

22 Sud-Est SE 212 Durandal (1956)

Sud-Est SE 212 Durandal

Type: single-seat interceptor fighter prototype

Span: 24ft 5in (7.44m)

Length: 38ft (11.58m) with Atar 101F; 39ft 7in (12.07m) with Atar 101G

Gross wing area: 318.28sq ft (29.60sq m)

Loaded weight: 14,771lb (6,700kg)

Powerplant: initially 1 x SNECMA Atar 101F turbojet 8,490lb (37.7kN) thrust; 1 x SNECMA Atar 101G turbojet 9,920lb (44.1kN) fitted later; plus 1 x optional single-chamber SEPR 65 rocket motor 1,650lb (7.35kN)

Max speed: 1,036mph (1,667km/h) or Mach 1.57 at 38,715ft (11,800m)

Ceiling: 54,135ft (16,500m)

Climb rate: 39,370ft/min (12,000m/min) at sea level

Armament: 1 x Nord AA20 or MATRA R511 (R052) missile. Possible options for 2 x 30mm cannon or 24 x 68mm SNEB rocket projectiles, but never carried

During the 1950s France's aircraft industry produced a variety of jet fighter prototypes ranging from the extraordinary ramjet-powered Nord 1500 Griffon (*Volume I*) to the Dassault Mirage III, which was eventually exported all over the world. A type from this period that is sometimes overlooked is the Sud-Est SE 212 Durandal, named after a mythical medieval sword.

On 28 January 1953, the French Air Force published requirements for a lightweight interceptor. The aircraft was to weigh less than four tonnes, be capable of climbing to 15,000m (49,215ft) in four minutes and then fly at Mach 1.3 in level flight in order to catch up with enemy bombers flying at Mach 1. Its armament would include one air-to-air missile.

The design team at Société Nationale de Constructions Aéronautiques du Sud-Est (SNCASE), led by Pierre Satre, had by then put together a long and detailed study of the delta wing and prepared a series of projects for delta interceptors in the X-212 series (in addition to swept wing studies under designation X-207). Some of the designs used a combination of jet and rocket motors, others rocket power only, and one mixed-propulsion design became the SE 212C Durandal II proposal. It was rejected, but a jet-only design was ordered against the specification (though this would have an optional auxiliary booster rocket mounted externally, rather than within the fuselage).

Of the designs submitted against the specification, three were ordered as prototypes – the Dassault Mirage I, Sud-Ouest Trident (featured in *Volume I*) and SE 212. Two SE 212 Durandal prototypes were ordered and built at Sud-Est's facility in Toulouse. The SE 212 was initially fitted with a reheated SNECMA Atar 101F turbojet plus the auxiliary rocket, the Atar fed by a large nose intake. Satre attempted to persuade the Air Force with an alternative configuration featuring side intakes, but this was turned down, while the officials pressed Satre to retain the nose intake without any form of centrebody shock cone, a step that some observers felt was short sighted. The possibility of replacing the rocket motor with pods containing either two 30mm cannon or 24 68mm SNEB rocket projectiles was also considered.

The first SE 212 Durandal in in its initial configuration with short nose and original jet pipe arrangement. Note the large fin, undercarriage doors and small dorsal air inlet in the upper fuselage, level with the main gear doors. *Wolfgang Muehlbauer*

By mid-March 1956 the first airframe was almost complete and taxi trials were expected by the end of the month. However, Sud-Est's preoccupation with producing its Caravelle jet airliner had pulled a great deal of the manufacturer's effort away from the Durandal and both prototypes experienced considerable delay, to the point that at the end of 1954 it looked like their contract might be terminated. There was also controversy regarding some of the Durandal's design features.

Taxi trials undertaken by Sud-Est flight test team leader Pierre Nadot at Blagnac airfield revealed problems with undercarriage vibration, and the flying controls were also out of balance. The wheels were equipped with a new and highly effective braking system, but made the undercarriage legs vibrate. The situation gave rise to pessimism regarding the quality of the aircraft as a whole, with some technicians expecting serious problems in flight – it was even stated that the aeroplane should be scrapped rather than flown.

This angered Nadot, who had the first SE 212 taken from Blagnac to Istres to complete its tests. Once there, however, on its third taxi run the Durandal lifted very slightly off the runway and that was enough for Sud-Est test pilot Pierre 'Tito' Maulandi to state that the controls were not balanced and the aircraft "unpilotable". The required adjustments proved fairly easy and two days later Maulandi repeated the test, this time declaring that he was satisfied that the Durandal was ready to fly.

The first Durandal, F-ZWUC made its maiden flight on 20 April 1956 from Istres, piloted by Pierre Maulandi; apparently the trip went very well. However, on a subsequent flight test pilot

The first Durandal in 1956, early in its flying career.

Roger Carpentier had to land with the nosewheel retracted, though the resulting damage was slight and the SE 212 back in the air three days later. A considerable volume of development flying was completed after the first sortie but, due to problems with the SEPR 65 motor, the first "rocket-propelled" flight was not made until 19 December 1956. The second aircraft, F-ZWUD first flew on 30 March 1957 and made its first sortie with the rocket during April.

Development of the SEPR 65 by Société d'Etudes de la Propulsion par Réaction had begun in December 1953 and the first ground test was performed on 4 November 1954, the boost motor being designed to run for two minutes. Unlike other SEPR-designed liquid-propellant rocket motors, the 65 used a single small chamber rated at approximately 1,650lb (7.34kN) thrust. It was longer than previous designs, but made into a self-contained pack to fit underneath the Durandal's Atar jet engine. Because the rocket exhaust was angled downwards, the ground tests were conducted with the Durandal's rear fuselage standing over a deep pit – and they were very noisy!

Rare photo of SE 212 No. 01 'C', on the runway in its original form.
Phil Butler

At the end of June 1956, CEV made an initial assessment of the Durandal's characteristics. At a take-off weight of 13,999lb (6,350kg) the first prototype was taken to Mach 0.91 at 2,500ft (762m) and Mach 1.20 at 30,000ft (9,144m). The maximum altitude achieved was 45,000ft (13,716m), the minimum flying speed was 140 knots (259km/h) and the landing speed was 125 knots (232km/h). In the climb on full engine power and at an optimum 500 knots (927km/h) and a constant Mach 0.90, the

Detail of 01 on the approach, or during a low pass with the undercarriage down. Note the tailskid.
Wolfgang Muehlbauer

SE 212 Durandal first prototype.
Copyright Pete West

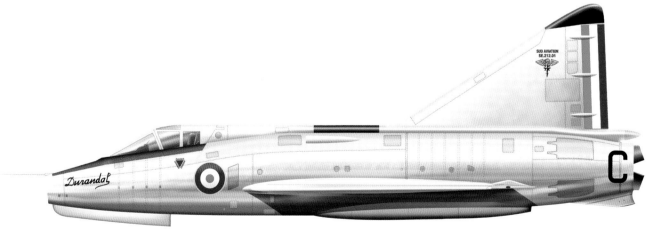

The first Durandal, with a nose intake guard in place. *Wolfgang Muehlbauer*

Below: The strake under the nose and its extent rearwards over the nosewheel door are shown here.

Durandal reached 10,000ft (3,048m) in 2 minutes 6 seconds, 30,000ft in 3 minutes 35 seconds and 43,000ft (13,105m) in 5 minutes 50 seconds. Also on full jet power, Mach 1.15 was recorded between 30,000ft and 40,000ft (12,192m), and when flying at Mach 1.41 the aircraft could be rolled through 360° in four seconds.

After 26 flights the aircraft had met most of its technical requirements, except that the stall had still to be explored and the airbrakes were temporarily limited to operation at no faster than Mach 0.94. At times the controls proved a little sensitive at subsonic speeds, but the prototype showed good transonic behaviour; its lateral and longitudinal stability were good (the latter after the fitting of an auto stabiliser), and the airbrakes were excellent.

Fitting the more powerful Atar 101G in July brought disappointment, however, since

manufacturer and CEV flight tests showed that the aircraft's maximum speeds were down on those obtained previously, a maximum Mach 1.17 at 35,000ft (10,668m) being some way off the original estimate of Mach 1.50. The main problem was the design of the nose air intake, which limited the aircraft's performance.

Adding the SEPR 65 did not provide the Durandal with the performance expected of an interceptor, the best achieved (in March 1957) being Mach 1.57. In addition, the ceiling on dry turbojet power only was around 40,000ft (12,192m), and with reheat thrust only 50,000ft (15,240m), and it took 5 minutes and 68 miles (110km) for the aircraft to accelerate from Mach 0.90 to Mach 1.33 in level flight at 37,000ft (11,278m). These figures were far short of the performance required to catch an enemy bomber flying at Mach 1.

Aircraft 01 still as built. The wider angle has been badly retouched around the nosewheel area. *Wolfgang Muehlbauer & Michel Cristescu*

An evaluation by the Centre d'Essais du Matériel Aérien (CEAM, Air Force Test Centre) at Mont-de-Marsan made in 1957 also revealed that the Durandal's behaviour at low speeds and low level was poor. The aircraft's centre of gravity had been deliberately set well back, Sud-Est claiming this was intended to simplify landing the aircraft. CEAM found, however, that when the Durandal was flying at low speeds and altitudes it came close to being longitudinally unstable and was quite sensitive to control. Suggestions that the autopilot should remain operating during the entire flight brought worries that this situation might lead to accidents in the case of auto-stabiliser failure.

By June 1956 Durandal 01 had been fitted with an additional ring around its jet pipe and afterburner. The tailskid had also been removed. *Phil Butler*

Manufacturer's views of the first Durandal during its flight test programme.

The first machine, with a good view of the outwards angle of the main undercarriage legs. The open cockpit canopy shows its heavy framing. *Alain Pelletier*

By June 1957 Durandal 01 had a slightly extended nose intake and white paint on the dorsal spine, just aft of the cockpit. This view shows the aircraft taxiing out in its final form. The rocket motor has been removed. *Phil Butler*

These characteristics weighed heavily against Sud-Est's light interceptor contender, but other events were also against it. The interceptor requirements as laid down in 1953 could only work if the aircraft received accurate of guidance from ground-based radars and equipment, but the increased possibility of electronic and other countermeasures by the enemy confirmed that the new fighter required greater autonomy of operation, which meant that it would have to have a radar of its own. On top of this, the performance of fighters and bombers had improved very quickly and by 1956 it was clear that the speed requirements

of 1953 were no longer sufficient. More powerful engines and improved aerodynamics meant that the lightweight interceptor as it existed was out of date.

Therefore, in July 1956 the Air Force Staff proposed a new Stage II Interceptor intended to destroy enemy aircraft with very little help from outside the cockpit: it would have its own radar and carry an air-to-air guided missile with a range of at least 10km (6 miles). These requirements were in part shaped by a new proposal from Dassault for a design designated Mirage III, a very much scaled up Mirage I fitted with a more powerful engine and radar.

This photo of 01 making a pass at the Paris show a rare image of the aircraft with its undercarriage retracted. *Phil Butler*

The Durandal's later jet pipe arrangement is shown in this Paris photograph. Note the small tailskid fitted to the rear end of the rocket installation. *Wolfgang Muehlbauer*

The lightweight fighter was dead, but Sud-Est offered a revised design against the Mirage III, with many changes including the installation of an Aladin radar. The project was designated Durandal IV but was not ordered, and by now the Air Force no longer needed the two Durandal prototypes either. The SE 212's armament of a solitary air-to-air missile meant it could only ever have had one opportunity to hit its target, and after that it would be unable to defend itself. This fact alone limited the its potential quite severely.

The two Durandals completed 45 rocket flights between them before the programme was terminated in May 1957. At the Paris show in late May 1957 the SE 212 (which for the event did not have its rocket motor) seemed to observers to have a quite long take-off run but, according to *Flight*, it climbed "…as nearly vertical as makes no difference". The second prototype was there on static display, with an AA20 missile beneath its fuselage.

Many published sources have recorded that during flight testing a speed of 897mph (1,444km/h) Mach 1.36 was attained at 40,355ft (12,300m) on jet power alone and 1,036mph (1,667km/h) Mach 1.57 at 38,715ft (11,800m) with the rocket running as well;

these figures were apparently achieved by the Durandal without armament.

After cancellation, the first Durandal passed to SNECMA in late 1957 for use as an engine test bed, but few details are available for the final stages of its flying career. Prototype No. 02, F-ZWUD, was abandoned. The far more capable Dassault Mirage III was the way ahead for the French Air Force and the arrival of this promising fighter brought an end to a number of other experimental aircraft covered in Volume I of *X-Planes of Europe*. Sections of the first Durandal are held in store by the Musée de l'Air et de l'Espace at Le Bourget. The SE 212 was the last fighter-type produced by Sud-Est – from then on the firm concentrated on airliners and helicopters.

Airframe

The SE 212 was a compact aeroplane and its delta wing had a wing thickness/chord ratio of 4.5% and was swept 60° at the leading edge. The wing was built as a multi-cellular box structure with five main spars perpendicular to the fuselage and the box itself was divided into three integral fuel cells. Elevons extended along the trailing edge. The central fuselage was classic monocoque and had the Atar engine in the rear, fed by a nose air intake. An air-to-air missile was carried externally on the fuselage centreline, as was the complete detachable housing for the SEPR 65 rocket, placed towards the rear.

The main weapons were either a Nord Type 5103 AA20, the development of which had begun in 1953, or the MATRA R511, which started out in 1949 as the experimental R052. The Atar drove the fuel pumps for the rocket through an auxiliary gearbox, and the motor ran on a combination of nitric acid and triethylamine xylidine or TX. Airbrakes were placed on each side of the rear fuselage and the tricycle landing gear retracted into the

Above: SE 212 01 lands at Paris.

Right: Most photos of the second prototype appear to have been taken at the 1957 Paris Show, when the aircraft was displayed with a MATRA R511 missile but did not fly. This angle shows how the R511 was attached beneath the rocket motor. No photos have been found showing a Durandal carrying an AA20. *David Hedge*

fuselage. A long under-fuselage strake extended from the lip of the intake back to the level of the wing leading edge, crossing the nosewheel bay door, and there was a large fin.

Both aircraft were in bare metal, although for the 1957 Paris show the first prototype (coded 'C') appears to have had its dorsal spine immediately behind the cockpit painted white, with a short darker section behind that.

Below: Here detail of the SEPR 65 rocket motor and 02 'D's' thin delta wing is revealed. Note the natural-metal finish, the company logo on the centre of the fin beneath the text, and the new fairing for the dorsal air inlet. *Nicolas Gauthier*

23 Ambrosini Sagittario 2 and Aerfer Ariete (1956 and 1958)

Ambrosini Sagittario I

Type: single-seat research aircraft

Span: 24ft 7in (7.50m)

Length: 30ft 6in (9.30m)

Gross wing area: 157sq ft (14.60sq m)

Max weight: 3,858lb (1,750kg)

Powerplant: 1 x Turbomeca Marboré turbojet 838lb (3.73kN) thrust

Max level speed: 348mph (560km/h) at sea level; 342mph (550km/h) at 16,405ft (5,000m)

Climb rate: time to 19,685ft (6,000m) 16 minutes 30 seconds

Aerfer Ambrosini S. Sagittario II

Type: single-seat jet fighter prototype

Span: 24ft 7in (7.50m)

Length: 31ft 2in (9.50m)

Gross wing area: 155.9sq ft (14.50sq m)

Loaded weight: 7,275lb (3,300kg)

Powerplant: 1 x Rolls-Royce Derwent 9 turbojet 3,600lb (16kN) thrust

Max level speed: 646mph (1,040km/h) at sea level; 634mph (1,020km/h) at 27,230ft (8,300m)

Climb rate: time to 39,370ft (12,000m) 10 minutes

Service ceiling (possibly estimated): 46,000ft (14,020m)

Range: 475 miles (765km); 1,240 miles (1,995km) with underwing tanks

Armament: 2 x fixed 30mm cannon in forward fuselage (not fitted and ports faired over); underwing pylons for 2 x 225kg (496lb) bombs, 2 x napalm tanks or 18 unguided rockets

Aerfer Ariete

Type: single-seat, mixed-powerplant jet fighter prototype

Span: 24ft 7in (7.50m)

Length: 31ft 6in (9.60m)

Gross wing area: 155.9sq ft (14.50sq m)

Loaded weight: 7,793lb (3,535kg)

Powerplant: 1 x Rolls-Royce Derwent turbojet 3,750lb (16.7kN) thrust, plus 1 x Rolls-Royce Soar RSr.2 turbojet 1,810lb (8kN) thrust

Max level speed: 671mph (1,080km/h)

Climb rate: time to 39,370ft (12,000m) 4 minutes 20 seconds

Armament: 2 x fixed Hispano Suiza HDD-825 30mm cannon in nose

In the years immediately following the end of World War II, the Italian aircraft industry received little support from the government and several firms went out of business. In the mid-1950s, however, Aerfer was created as part of an industrial group set up with the assistance of public capital to undertake work for the Air Force. Besides turning out parts for Italy's Republic F-84 jet fighters, the factory was responsible for a family of three light fighter designs, the Sagittario II, originally designed by the Ambrosini company, the follow-on Ariete and the Leone mixed-power interceptor, which was never completed. An aerodynamic research aircraft from Ambrosini preceded the programme.

Ambrosini Sagittario I

Post-war, Ambrosini produced a wooden piston-powered military trainer designated S.7. In 1952 it took a basic S.7 fuselage and fitted it with a 45° swept wing and swept tail surfaces. As the Freccia (Arrow) and serialled MM550, it was first flown in mid-July under piston power. The Freccia achieved a maximum 211mph (340km/h) on the level at sea level and 230mph (370km/h) in a dive, and its flight trials lasted until 1 August.

Next the Alfa Romeo piston engine was replaced by a small Turbomeca Marboré jet engine and in this form the aircraft was initially named Turbofreccia, but from October 1952 it became the Sagittario (Sagittarius – the Archer). It was the first jet aircraft designed and built in Italy. After completing ground tests

in December, the newly modified aircraft made another maiden flight on 4 January 1953, piloted by Ing Guidantonio Ferrari, Ambrosini's chief experimental test pilot.

The Marboré could be accessed from the front by opening the upper and lower covering sections (or doors) of the fuselage nose. The Freccia's tailwheel undercarriage was unsuitable for a jet aircraft however, a problem solved by the installation of a separate retractable long-leg 'tail' undercarriage, placed mid-way along the rear fuselage. The standard S.7 main undercarriage units were retained and for its initial testing with the piston engine the aircraft's new wing had fixed leading edge slots, fences, dive brakes and aileron spoilers. Once the aircraft's handling characteristics had been sampled, the Ambrosini engineers removed the

The Ambrosini Sagittario I, MM550. *Achille Vigna via Angelo Romano*

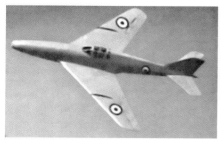

MM550 early in 1953. *Angelo Romano*

Planform view of the Ambrosini Freccia piston-engined research aircraft.

Planform view of the Sagittario I, the Freccia airframe now fitted with a jet engine.

dive brakes and faired over the slots. When the aircraft was modified as the jet-powered Sagittario the wing was cleaned up rather more, while at the same time the rearward part of the two-seat canopy was closed in.

Initially there were thoughts towards building up to three Sagittarios, since the design was thought to be capable of around Mach 1.05, though of course the wooden airframe had structural limitations and was not expected to go beyond 350mph (563km/h) in level flight. However, the third machine would be built in metal and allow the design's higher speed potential to be realised.

Nevertheless, in its first 30 flights the Sagittario provided a wealth of information on the aerodynamics and control of a 45° sweep wing. The spoilers were effective, manoeuvrability and especially rate of roll were very good, and there was no tendency to 'Dutch roll'. On take-off the Sagittario's heavy tail left the ground after around 1,000 yards (915m), at which moment the tailwheel would be retracted and the consequent removal of drag and jet spoiling effect (the wheel sat directly in the path of the underfuselage jet pipe) cleared the way for a rapid acceleration with the machine airborne after another 500 yards (457m). The landing run was long because, with the tail wheel coming down last on the approach, the hold-off angle of attack had to be reduced. However, trials showed that this large drag-producing tailwheel was ideal for operation as an airbrake, and very good indeed from a trim point of view.

On 26 March 1953 the Sagittario passed into the hands of the Aeronautica Militare Italiana (AMI, Italian Air Force) for further trials. The innovative short cuts made by Ambrosini to produce the Sagittario so quickly provided great rewards in the acquisition of jet flight experience, despite the wooden airframe making for a relatively heavy aeroplane. In the end, only the one Sagittario was built and plans for series production in several forms, including the 'Sagittario Viper', powered by the British Armstrong Siddeley Viper jet engine, came to nothing – the design process had moved beyond this basic research machine. The arrival of the Sagittario II meant that this first jet project would now be referred to as the Sagittario I.

Aerfer Sagittario II

The designer behind Ambrosini's effort to produce a jet fighter was Ing Sergio Stefanutti and one of several studies he made in the years after World War II looked at a sleek interceptor named Vindex, drawn up in 1950. It was to be powered by a French SNECMA Atar axial turbojet engine which, coupled with a highly swept wing, would provide supersonic performance. It was the need to gather back-up data for a project like the Vindex that prompted the decision to build scale model research aircraft including the Freccia/Sagittario I, but the AMI rejected the type. In the meantime, the concept of a light fighter for NATO countries was beginning to gain interest, and would eventually result in the design competition outlined in the next chapter. One of the competitors was to have been the Sagittario II.

Almost all known photos of the Sagittario II appear to show the first example, MM560. Here the aircraft was photographed before any markings had been applied. *Achille Vigna via Angelo Romano*

Studies for what became the Sagittario II began in early 1953 with funding from the US via the Mutual Defense Assistance Program (MDAP). (During the 1950s, as part of its foreign policy, the US made grants of money and supplies to 'free' nations to help build up their defences.) Some of the money allocated to Italy went towards the new fighter, but the Aeronautica Militare subsequently decided that the responsibility for any project that was going to be more complex that the Sagittario I should pass to Aerfer. A new company based at Pomigliano d'Arco near Naples, it was formed in 1955 by the merger of Industrie Meccaniche Aeronautiche Meridionali (IMAM) and Officine Ferroviarie Meridionali. The move resulted in the transfer of rights and project data from Ambrosini, the aircraft's official title now becoming Aerfer Ambrosini S. Sagittario II.

A project brochure dated May 1955 highlighted an estimated combat speed of 540 knots (1,000km/h) and the document also made reference to a Sagittario IV, with a combined Derwent and Soar powerplant (this became the Ariete). An order was placed for two Sagittario II prototypes and plans laid down for 400 production machines. The basic production version was to be used for the tactical support of ground forces, but further developments with more powerful or different engines were to have been multi-role, covering air supremacy and ground attack, which would have required a heavier weapon load. A Bristol Siddeley Orpheus-powered Sagittario III was also considered and would have had a length of 31ft 6in (9.6m).

Construction of the prototype Sagittario II, serial MM560, moved forward quite slowly. The first ground runs were made at Pomigliano d'Arco from 28 March to 5 April 1955, and in October the airframe was taken to Pratica di Mare, close to Rome, the new home of the Aeronautica Militare's Experimental Flight Unit. From there it made its maiden flight on 19 May 1956, in the hands of Commandante (Cdt) Constantino Petrosellini.

The first Aerfer Ambrosini S. Sagittario II, MM560. *Achille Vigna via Angelo Romano*

Below: The first Ariete prototype. *Copyright Pete West*

Detail of MM560's underfuselage jet pipe. The majority of sources give the aircraft's designation as Sagittario II, but the prototype had 'Sagittario 2' written on its lower fin; the reason for this variation is unknown. Note the airbrakes on the rear fuselage underside. *Phil Butler*

This image shows MM560, most likely in May 1956. *Achille Vigna via Angelo Romano*

This view confirms that the Sagittario II was left in bare metal, with only roundels and markings applied, and an anti-glare panel on the nose. The guns ports shown here are thought to be false. The Ariete had a very similar finish. *Achille Vigna via Angelo Romano*

Walkaround views of the first Sagittario II, taken during its flight test programme by a visitor from A&AEE Boscombe Down. *Phil Butler*

The test flying was made in some secrecy and early flights revealed problems with a weak undercarriage, but on 26 June MM560 was unveiled to the public at the MAF 56 air show at Fiumicino. On 20 July the pilot made an emergency landing following engine seizure, causing a break in the flight test programme. After the necessary light repairs had been completed, Lt Col Giovanni Franchini, commander of the Italian flight-test centre at Pratica di Mare, took over the test flying.

On 3 December Franchini began looking at the Sagittario II's performance and behaviour in a dive when approaching supersonic speed, taking the aircraft to its maximum diving speed firstly from 41,995ft (12,800m) and then from 32,152ft (9,800m). In the process he went supersonic but, since he was flying well out over the sea, few if any heard the sonic boom. On the 4th he repeated the test over the base and, having started a vertical dive at 47,572ft (14,500m), went supersonic between 42,650ft and 13,123ft (13,000m and 4,000m), reaching a maximum of Mach 1.15 at 26,247ft (8,000m).

These were the first occasions that an aircraft of Italian design had broken the sound barrier, and US pilot Major Arthur Murray repeated the feat in the Sagittario II on 19 December. The only problem encountered during supersonic flight was some inversion of the controls at Mach 0.94-0.98 and the manufacturer claimed that the Sagittario II was probably the first aircraft in the world to have exceeded Mach 1 easily in a dive with only 3,600lb (16kN) of thrust available. The achievement created a great deal of national interest and on 27 March Franchini displayed the prototype to Italian officials from the civil and military sectors.

By 11 June 1957 Franchini had completed a further 50 flights in the first prototype. During the month he also demonstrated MM560 at the Paris Air Show, *Flight* commenting how the aircraft: "…unsticks nimbly, darts around, and for no obvious reason comes in for an undershoot, throw-on landing. Then in an instant it is off and up again, rolling *a grande cadence.*" The journal added that the Aerfer Sagittario II "has the appeal of an Italian sports car."

On 25 April 1957 Franchini performed the maiden flight of the second Sagittario II prototype, MM561, from Pomigliano d'Arco. After nine flights this machine was also despatched to Pratica di Mare, for a further seven trial flights that included carrying North American F-86E Sabre external fuel tanks under the wings. On 6 July Franchini took MM560 to Linate Airport in Milan for the Baracca Air Show (the Manifestazione Aerea Baracca or MAB 57), but after a hydraulic failure prevented the flaps from operating fully and stopped the brakes working properly, the aircraft ended on its belly after landing.

The Aerfer Sagittario II was a candidate in the 1957 international competition for a NATO light tactical support aircraft. The British technical press stated that the Sagittario II was an outsider among the rival designs, but in fact it never had a chance at all because Aerfer's proposal was submitted after the deadline had passed, which meant it was automatically rejected, despite Aerfer's pleas. After MM560's damage had been repaired Capt Enzo Cauda from the Pratica di Mare flight test centre took up its flight trials.

The Sagittario II was characterised by good manoeuvrability, even at low speeds, and good performance overall. It was capable of short

MM560, about to roll for a test flight.
Phil Butler

take-offs and landings and (a quality confirmed by the crash landing) its airframe was very strong. With the flying programme over, both prototypes remained at Pratica di Mare until MM560 was selected for a series of drop tests using an Agusta-Bell 204 helicopter, the Sagittario II being released from height to fall to the ground. These tests gradually wrecked the airframe. However, MM561 survives at the Museo Storico dell'Aeronautica Militare (Italian Air Force Historical Museum) at Vigna di Valle near Lake Bracciano, along with Ariete MM569.

The first Sagittario II, in AMI markings at the June 1957 Paris show. Note the panel removed from directly behind the cockpit and the engineer working inside the fuselage.

Since this aircraft is carrying external fuel tanks it is thought that it might be the second Sagittario II prototype, MM561.

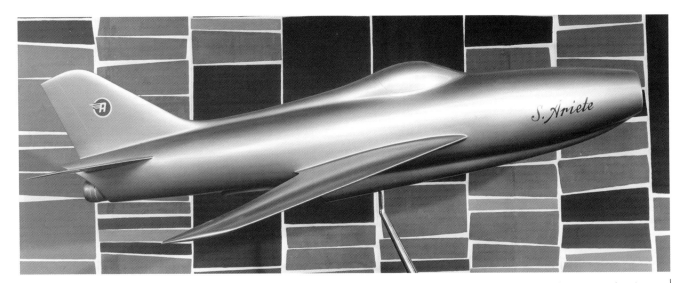

Model of the Aerfer Ariete displayed at the October 1957 'Technical Salon' Exhibition in Turin. Note the fatter rear fuselage compared to the Sagittario II, making space for the Soar engine.

Ariete

Despite the Sagittario II's qualities it was clear to the designer that the aircraft lacked power. Stefanutti therefore joined the Sagittario II's wing to a revised body housing not only a more powerful Derwent, but also a supplementary Rolls-Royce Soar jet engine breathing air supplied from a retractable intake in the top of the fuselage. This new version was named Ariete (Aries – the Ram) and a model of it was displayed at the 'Technical Salon' Exhibition in Turin in October 1957.

To increase its thrust the new version of the Derwent turbojet introduced a 'hot' turbine and a special combustion system, while the Soar's thrust would be used to bolster the aircraft's take-off and climb performance, and during combat. When the Soar was not required its intake would close flush with the fuselage, rising open by 11.8in (30cm) again for use. Compared to the Sagittario II, the Ariete's fuselage was 3.9in (10cm) longer and its cockpit canopy was lowered. Wind tunnel tests indicated a potential maximum speed of Mach 1.2.

Again assisted by US funding, Aerfer began assembling the first of three Ariete prototypes in 1955, although only two were completed. The first was MM658, which was taken on its maiden flight from Pomigliano d'Arco by Enzo Cauda on 27 March 1958. By November, only 31 flights for more than 17 hours in the air had been completed, because there were problems with the powerplant, which on several occasions had flamed out in flight.

Due to variations of pressure experienced in the air, the Soar intake would suddenly independently open or close. There were other problems as well, which brought a February 1959 decision to permanently ground the Ariete, well before the aircraft's full flight envelope had been explored. MM569, the second prototype, was completed, but never flew. Ing Stefanutti had planned an Ariete II powered by the Soar plus a Bristol Siddeley Orpheus engine, but the problems surrounding the Soar installation killed this idea and led him to look at rocket propulsion to provide the required additional power. After a period in store at Pratica di Mare, MM568 was used for fire practice, but MM569 is preserved.

The Ariete prototype, MM568, pictured as new in 1958.

Leone

The mixed-power Leone (Lion – another constellation) is the final part of this story, but was abandoned before a prototype had flown. For the initial Leone studies and proposals the powerplant was a combination of Bristol Siddeley Orpheus turbojet and de Havilland Spectre Junior controllable-thrust rocket, the latter using kerosene fuel with hydrogen peroxide. In a stroke the problems caused by the retractable dorsal air intake were removed, although much of the airframe was unchanged from that of the Ariete II.

Despite the fact that the Leone was really only a mixed powerplant test bed, tunnel tests indicated that its performance would be on a par with modern fighters from abroad. This time, however, in 1956 a NATO Mutual Weapons Development team from the USA turned down funding, primarily because of the limited time for which the rocket motor was expected to run.

As a result, Stefanutti revised the Leone thoroughly into an altogether larger design with a longer, rather sleeker fuselage and 50° sweep wing. To cope with the higher speeds the nose intake would now have a shock cone (inside which there would be a radar scanner), but the mixed powerplant concept was retained. To begin with the main engine, placed further back than on the earlier designs, to beneath the pilot, was to be a 6,800lb (30.2kN) Orpheus Or.12, but later a 7,000lb (31.1kN) de Havilland Gyron Junior would be installed, both of them having reheat and with the exhaust angled downwards slightly to exit under the rear fuselage. A 10,000lb (44.5kN) de Havilland Spectre rocket would go in the end of the rear fuselage and predicted top speed appears to have been in the region of Mach 2.

Contemporary press reports indicate that the Leone would climb to 65,000ft (19,812m) in just two minutes, but official documents give 68,900ft (21,000m) in just under 5 minutes and an absolute ceiling of 82,020ft (25,000m). As a supersonic day interceptor it would have been armed with two de Havilland Firestreak air-to-air missiles, although it carried no guns.

A full size wooden mock-up was built and work began on the first of five prototypes, but funding was still in short supply and the first Leone progressed to 80% completion and no more. In due course Italy went on to build the highly supersonic Lockheed F-104 Starfighter under licence.

Airframe

The Sagittario II was a small, all-metal light alloy (aluminium) aircraft with a one-piece, all-moving tailplane and a low-position, swept tapered wing equipped with modest mid-wing fences. The wing was swept 41° at quarter chord and built in one piece with very thick skins. It was attached to the lower fuselage above the jet pipe and its trailing edge had plain flaps stretching from fuselage to aileron, which could deploy to an angle of 70°. All of the aircraft's flying controls were fully powered and had manual reversion.

The fuselage was built around four longerons and there were two main fuel tanks of 110-Imp gal and 88-Imp gal (500-litre and 400-litre) capacity, respectively. This would be the only fuel carried on interception duties, but for ground attack more fuel would be housed in the lower nose and in the central wings, to give a maximum load of 255 Imp gals (1,160 litres).

The engine was positioned in a nose cone ahead of the main fuselage structure, with the jet pipe discharging under the fuselage, level with the wing trailing edge, the under-fuselage being covered with a sheet of stainless steel to prevent any damage by the exhaust gases. The Sagittario II had a tricycle undercarriage and its pilot was seated beneath a clamshell cockpit canopy. Production machines would have been armed with two internal 30mm Hispano-Suiza 825 cannon.

The rear fuselage of the Ariete was enlarged to make space for the supplementary Soar turbojet and its dorsal intake, otherwise its structure was little changed from that of the Sagittario II.

The full-size wooden Aerfer Leone mock-up with its port wing only in place, but carrying a Firestreak missile inboard and a drop tank. Note the shock cone inside the nose intake. *Alberto Trevisan*

24 Breguet Br 1100 and 1001 Taon (1957)

Breguet Br 1100

Type: single-seat lightweight fighter prototype

Span: 25ft 8in (7.83m)

Length: 41ft 1in (12.52m)

Gross wing area: 209.9sq ft (19.52sq m)

Wing t/c ratio: 6%

Gross weight: 14,429lb (6,545kg)

Powerplant: 2 x Turbomeca Gabizo turbojets each 2,645lb (11.6kN) dry and 3,750lb (16.7kN) with reheat

Max speed: Mach 0.94 at sea level

Climb rate: time to 32,810ft (10,000m) less than 5 minutes

Range at altitude: 1,336 miles (2,150km)

Armament: 16 x armament combinations available, but prototype appears to have carried none. 2 x 30mm DEFA cannon or 4 x 0.5in (12.7mm) Browning machine guns and MATRA rocket pod for up to 35 rounds carried internally. External armament on four wing pylons could include 500lb (227kg) bombs, napalm tanks, rocket launchers or fuel tanks. Production aircraft would have carried 400kg (882lb) or 1,000lb (454kg) bombs

Breguet Br 1001 Taon

Type: single-seat light tactical fighter prototype

Span: 22ft 3.7in (6.80m)

Length: Prototype 01 during CEV trials 37ft 8.8in (11.50m)

Gross wing area: 155.9sq ft (14.50sq m)

Wing t/c ratio: 6%

Max permissible take-off weight: 11,900lb (5,398kg) on concrete; 10,450lb (4,740kg) on grass

Powerplant: 1 x Bristol Orpheus B.Or.3 turbojet 4,850lb (21.6kN)

Max speed: CEV assessment, clean 580 knots (1,075km/h) or Mach 0.91 at 2,000ft (610m); 450 knots (834km/h) or Mach 1.10 at 28,000ft (8,534m) in a dive; with 2 x bombs 580 knots (1,075km/h) or Mach 0.89 at 3,000ft (915m); 470 knots (871km/h) or Mach 0.97 at 20,000ft (6,096m); after development Mach 0.95 at sea level; Mach 0.98 at 29,528ft (9,000m)

Max range: 1,150 miles (1,850km)

Armament: 4 x 0.5in (12.7mm) Browning machine guns (to be replaced by 2 x 30mm guns and two 68mm rocket launchers, each containing 15 projectiles). Four underwing hardpoints for external stores

During 1957 Breguet flew two very similar light fighter prototypes for quite different roles. For much of the time the work undertaken on the firm's Br 1100 and Br 1001 projects ran in parallel, with the Br 1100 intended for service with l'Armée de l'Air and Aéronavale, while the Br 1001 Taon was Breguet's entry into the NATO Basic Military Requirement 1 competition.

Models shown at a public display (probably a Paris show) of the then still unbuilt Breguet Br 1001 (left) and Br 1100.

Breguet Br 1100

In 1954 two prototypes of the Br 1100 were ordered for l'Armée de l'Air, later followed by another for the Aéronavale, the latter as the 1100M ('M' for Marine). Much of the development for the 1100 and the 1001 was common, since although they designed to rather different specifications, the two types were fairly similar and indeed had identical front fuselages.

Despite looking conventional, the Br 1100 had several advanced features. The fuselage side air intakes, for example, had plateau fairings both below and forward, with boundary layer bleeds venting upwards only, a result of extensive wind tunnel testing. Some observers felt that there might be problems with this arrangement, for example with gun gas ingestion, since the guns were mounted in the plateau. But these fairings were designed mainly to keep gun smoke out of the engine, while Breguet added that the feature did not affect the intake performance at high angles of attack. In fact the firm claimed that five times more wind tunnel work had been conducted on the 1100 than for most other fighters, some of it at the Cornell Laboratory in the USA during January 1956 (work which also benefitted the Br 1001). Georges Ricard led Breguet's design office.

After completing engine test runs at its Villacoublay birthplace, Breguet Br 1100-01 was dismantled and transported to Istres for flight trials. Yves Brunard (Breguet's chief test pilot) performed its first flight on 31 March 1957, apparently exceeded Mach 1.0 during the trip, which lasted 15 minutes. Particularly bad weather conditions prevented further flying until 13 April, but Brunard and Bernard Witt subsequently moved the flying programme forward at a considerable pace.

In the weeks that followed the machine flew regularly at Mach 0.9 and showed an ability to exceed Mach 1 in a dive at very low altitude, while its system of flaps and spoilers gave a roll rate of 200°/sec at Mach 1. The aviation press quoted the pilot as saying that the aircraft was "right from the start" and it was so simple to fly that he was "waiting for Breguet to produce a touring version".

In fact, at low speeds the 1100 exhibited the expected qualities, but at higher speeds there was clearly an aerodynamic problem because the aircraft was not as fast on the level as had been anticipated (the team had hoped for a maximum speed at height slightly above supersonic). The main problem was considerable drag around the rear fuselage, coupled with a lack of thrust – in essence the rear of the aircraft needed redesigning, although in the end only the extreme aft fuselage was tweaked, when something much more substantial might have cured the problem fully (significantly, the single-engined Br 1001 did not experience drag problems).

Information on the other Br 1100 prototypes is sketchy and at times contradictory, but author Jean Cuny reports that the second Air Force machine was abandoned when it was 80% complete. It was to have been designated Br 1101 since it introduced a stronger structure and could accept different engines – either two

The Br 1100.
Michel Bénichou

Hispano-Suiza R-800s or two SNECMA R-105s. The Air Force General Staff decided to withdraw from the 1100 project at the end of 1957, in part due to budget concerns.

The second completed prototype was therefore the Br 1100M naval version for carrier operation. A naval prototype for the Aéronavale had been requested on 23 March 1955, and the order (No. 2240/55) was confirmed on 23 September. The aeroplane would differ from the Air Force machine by virtue of its naval equipment, including an arrestor hook, but in fact the desire for 'commonality' between the land and sea versions resulted in compromises. The airframe strengthening necessary for naval operations was introduced as standard on the land version, for example, while the Navy was forced to drop its demands for the aircraft to have a span of less than 23ft (7m) and a sliding canopy.

Here the Br 1100 jet pipes are in their original form. Curved fairings were later added around the end fuselage and pipes in an effort to reduce drag. *Michel Bénichou*

Here the 1100's landing gear and leading edge wing root fillets are shown to advantage. No guns are fitted. *Michel Bénichou*

The first Br 1100, still in original form, is prepared for a test flight. The aircraft's nose undercarriage leg was particularly long, presumably in keeping of its potential role on aircraft carriers and need for catapult launches. However, this particular aircraft was the first Air Force prototype. *Michel Bénichou*

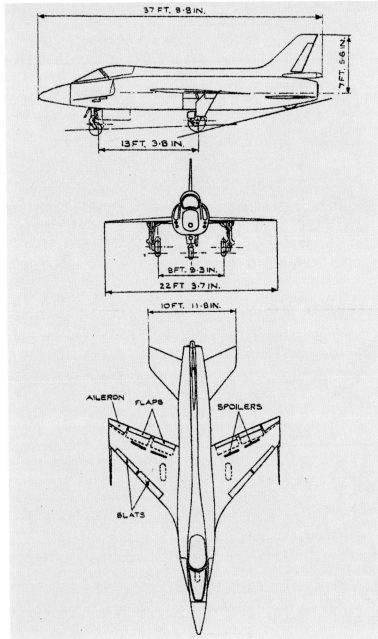

Above: The Br 1100 was displayed at the 1957 Paris Air Show, where it is seen just after touching down and trailing a drag chute (out of picture). Note the drooped leading edge. *Phil Butler*

Cuny reports that Bernard Witt performed the aircraft's maiden flight on 15 November 1957. The sortie was also its last, because the Br 1100M had by now been abandoned. There had been some criticism of its gradual increase in weight which, coupled with a lack of engine power, would have made catapult launches and carrier landings difficult. It appears that the flying Br 1100 and 1100M prototypes were scrapped, but no details of their fates have been discovered.

Breguet 1001 Taon

The Br 1001 Taon was Breguet's entry into the competition against NATO Basic Military Requirement 1 of 1954.

For quite some time after the Second World War there were conflicting opinions as to the need (in this new age of nuclear weapons) for a tactical strike fighter. The Republic F-84F Thunderstreak was supplied to a number of NATO countries to fill the role, but eventually the feeling grew that a new, specialised aircraft should be produced to perform tactical roles with Western European air arms.

When the United States decided that it could no longer maintain F-84F supplies, it was clear that the time had arrived for Western Europe to become self-sufficient in this category of aeroplane. Accordingly, NATO sponsored a design study for an aircraft

Boscombe Down three-view drawing of the Breguet Br 1001. *National Archives*

capable of performing strike operations from semi-prepared fields, while in the meantime the conflict in Korea had also highlighted a dire need to reduce aircraft weight.

As a result the requirements, known collectively as NATO Basic Military Requirement 1 (NBMR.1), gave a high priority to light weight, suggesting a maximum of 8,000lb (3,629kg). NATO also apparently outlined 35 different types of unprepared surface from which the aircraft might have to operate, ranging from ploughed land to English lawn, with tyre pressures and sizes arranged according to the surface from which the machine would fly. The document originally outlined two missions, close support and reconnaissance, but by the time of the official review the exact mission requirements were yet to be confirmed.

Besides the Sagittario, Italian submissions to NBMR.1 included the G.91 from Fiat, which was already on order, the Aermacchi MB.327 and SIAI-Marchetti SM.133, neither of which left the drawing board. In 1950 Aermacchi opened its MB.324 interceptor project which, powered by a de Havilland Ghost 103 engine and armed with four guns, had an estimated top speed of 640mph (1,030km/h).

In 1951, a two-seat MB.324 research aircraft was drawn with a Turbomeca Marboré, the objective being to test a highly swept wing. In 1953/54 the MB.324 was revised as the MB.327 lightweight tactical fighter specifically for the NATO competition. Having begun with two engines (possibly the British Armstrong Siddeley Viper 8), in due course it was proposed for a Bristol Siddeley Orpheus. The internal armament remained as four machine guns, but it is understood that designer Ing Ermanno Bazzocchi did not submit his MB.327 project officially because he believed there was no chance of it winning.

In appearance, SIAI-Marchetti's small SM.133 proposal looked quite advanced. A delta winged aircraft, it had a slim fuselage and canard surface at the nose. Its two Viper ASV.5 engines were housed in elegant 'nacelles' situated on the upper rear fuselage either side of the fin. The expected maximum speed was 680mph (1,094km/h), but it was not ordered. These Italian studies have been highlighted primarily to illustrate the amount of work going on behind the scenes for NBMR.1, but also because they have rarely (if ever) been published before.

Besides the Br 1001, other known designs submitted directly against NBMR.1 by French

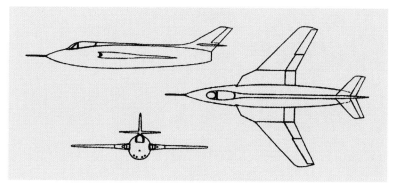

One of the NATO NBMR.1 contenders was intended to be the Aermacchi MB.327, which had four guns in the lower forward fuselage.

The Sud-Est SE 5000 Baroudeur was another prototype assessed during the NATO trials at CEV Brétigny. *Terry Panopalis*

manufacturers, either initially or later on, were the Dassault Etendard II and VI, Morane-Saulnier MS 800, Nord 1540 and 5010 Harpon, SIPA S 800 and S 801, SNCASE SE 5000 Baroudeur, and SNCASO SO 6150 Requin. From Britain came the Avro 727 and a variant of the Folland Gnat, but it is unknown if these were submitted officially, while Messerschmitt in West Germany also seems to have produced a design.

The wind tunnel work at Cornell had resulted in major changes to the Br 1001 design (including the application of area ruling), so that there was quite some delay in building the first prototype. The 1001 was named Taon (Gadfly), the name also an anagram of NATO, and two prototypes were ordered in August 1955. Construction of the first (F-ZWUX) began at Villacoublay and the completed aeroplane was conveyed in one piece by road to Melun-Villaroche.

When Bernard Witt made its maiden flight from there on 25 July 1957, the NATO assessment for all the contestants that had reached flight status was just a few weeks away. Despite the lack of time before the deadline, Breguet's engineers worked hard to cure faults and flaws revealed in the early test

Right: The first Br 1001 Taon, at end of its first flight on 25 July 1957. It has the original ventral nose finlet that was later moved to the rear fuselage, and the leading edge and trailing edge flaps are deployed. For its first flight, 01 had a Taon (Gadfly) symbol painted beneath its cockpit on the starboard side.
Michel Bénichou

Right: Taon 01 without fuselage code letters. Note the NATO artwork on the outside of the air intake.

In this early Taon shot the aircraft is flying at slow speed with everything down. The twin gun ports in the lower intake extension and the bleed door behind the intake are well shown.
Michel Bénichou

230

flights. Alterations made to the airframe during August 1957 included removing the side fuselage airbrakes and fitting a new brake beneath the fuselage, changes to the air intakes, and moving the nose 'underfin' to a position under the rear body. The last of these was a partial counter to lateral instability encountered early in the flight test programme.

The five aircraft types that took part in the official NBMR.1 assessment, held at CEV Brétigny, were three built using NATO funding – the Breguet Br 1001 Taon, Dassault Etendard VI and Fiat G.91, all powered by a Bristol Orpheus – and two entered as private ventures, the SE 5000 Baroudeur (described in *Volume I*) and Dassault Etendard IV. Both the latter used a SNECMA Atar turbojet and were present because it was thought they might also prove satisfactory for the envisaged role. An important point was that by the start of the flying programme, Fiat already had orders for 27 of its G.91.

These aeroplanes were test flown by an international evaluation team of three pilots from the USA, plus one apiece from France and Italy, and two from the UK (supplied by A&AEE Boscombe Down). They reported on each aircraft's stability and control, its manoeuvrability at low altitudes, performance in level flight and the climb, and its suitability in respect of the intended tactical mission. In addition, the field characteristics were determined for each type, including ease of maintenance, turn-around time for refuelling and rearming, and the quality of the cockpit layout.

The trials lasted from 16 September until 5 October and the British pilots' report on the Taon was based on 1.75 hours in the air. It concentrated on the close support role, which would involve attacks on troops, vehicles and so on, using guns, cannon, bombs and rockets. By the time of the trials the first Taon had received its four Browning machine guns and two wing pylons for weapons. The aircraft made 31 flights in all during the assessment.

To begin with the A&AEE pilots reported that the Taon suffered from its lack of development and, in addition to the many aerodynamic deficiencies for which Breguet had already planned modifications, there were other defects that prevented completion of the assessment. The proposed future aerodynamic changes were considerable and included lowering the wing by 6in (15.2cm), making the second stage of spoilers operative and providing mechanical connection between the ailerons and spoilers, reducing the range of tailplane movement, and increasing fin and rudder areas.

The trials confirmed the need for these alterations. There was a marked over-sensitivity of the tailplane at high indicated airspeeds and this remained to an unacceptable degree, even at supersonic speeds. At low speeds the controls gave only a sluggish response. The rudder was very late in becoming effective during the take-off ground roll so that in crosswinds the take-off run could be prolonged by the need for differential braking for steering. The need for continuous rudder retrimming during flight was unacceptable and the apparent weakness of the dropped leading edge mechanism was another serious criticism. There was a lack of ground clearance for the airbrakes, which prevented their extension on the ground or their use during landing (another undesirable feature), but the trim changes due to airbrake operation were commendably small, although the deceleration provided by the brake at lower speeds was inadequate.

In tactical manoeuvres the Taon's rolling performance and aileron feel characteristics were quite satisfactory, but the tailplane forces for sustained manoeuvres, though tolerable, were too high to be pleasant. Here the absence of trim changes with airbrake operation was again a good feature. The Taon's performance in regard to buffet-free manoeuvring was appreciably inferior to that of its rivals, only around 2.5g being available without buffet at 300 knots (556km/h) IAS at low altitudes and 4g at 500 knots (927km/h). Some of this was doubtless attributable to the Taon's wing loading being higher than that of the other aircraft tested, but at the same time it was noted that there were no fences, notches, vortex generators or leading edge camber, which had been used to a great extent on other aircraft to improve their flow and lift distribution. Another undesirable feature was the masking of any pre-stall warning buffet in the approach configuration by airframe buffet that appeared when the landing gear was extended.

Finally, the Taon's take-off distances were excessive, even without underwing stores and when operating from a dry concrete runway. About 1,200 yards (1,095m) of ground roll was required in zero wind, and about 1,700 yards (1,555m) to reach an altitude of 50ft (15m). The aircraft was clearly underpowered for its wing loading and the take-off speed of 140 knots (259km/h) was considered high. (Prior to the NATO assessment Breguet had not had time to examine the aircraft's characteristics when operating from grass runways or when carrying external stores.)

In conclusion, the British assessors noted that none of the aircraft tested met the spirit of the specification in that they all materially exceeded the proposed maximum weight of 8,000lb (3,629kg). The immediate consequence of this was a deficiency in take-off performance for all except the Fiat G.91, which just satisfied the requirement. The report added that if the ability to land on the roughest of surfaces was supreme, then the Baroudeur appeared to be the only contender. If excellent handling and aiming qualities were all important then the Etendard VI was by far the best, but if time had been available for its development, then the Taon could easily have become a serious contender. In the end, it was the G.91 that was ordered in quantity (although France, in due course, acquired the Etendard IV for its Navy).

It was unfortunate for Breguet that the Taon had done relatively little development flying prior to the competition – in many respects the assessors were handling a raw prototype. Clearly it was an aircraft possessing significant potential and the results of the assessment might have been quite different had 01 been in the air for a few months longer before it began. One very important aspect of

Early photo of the second Br 1001 prototype. It lacked the nose pitot, but introduced additional windscreen framing. The type's slimmer fuselage compared to the Br 1100 is evident. *Michel Bénichou*

NBMR.1 was the requirement for rapid turn-around times for refuelling, rearming and engine changes, and the Taon performed particularly well in this respect.

After the CEV trials, Taon 01 received some of its modifications. Bulged fairings known as 'carènes' were added to the wing roots, the contours of the intake lips modified to improve airflow, and bleed doors were introduced aft of the intakes. As built, Taon 01 had received only partial area ruling and the primary object of the wing root bulges was to cut drag at transonic speeds, although they provided space for another 55 Imp gals (250 litres) of fuel.

In the meantime Br 1001-02 (F-ZWVE) made its maiden flight on 18 January 1958. Compared to the first machine, Taon 02 featured a slightly larger rudder and revised tailcone, while spoilers were introduced ahead of the flaps, the upper lip on the exhaust had been extended to improve local aerodynamic flow, there was an improved nose profile, and the aircraft was fitted with British equipment rather than the French items used in 01.

These changes pushed the Taon's length up to 38ft 4in (11.68m). The second aircraft was intended primarily for armament trials, while the improvements made only a slight difference to 02's performance compared to 01. In fact, at low altitude the second aircraft had lost a little speed, but at altitudes up to 25,000ft (7,620m) it was slightly faster than the first prototype.

With the NATO trials complete, the Taons were subject to an intensive flight development programme and by September 1958 the two aeroplanes had accumulated in the region of 250 hours of flying. Now their potential began to stand out and was underlined graphically on 25 April 1958, when Bernard Witt set a new 1,000km closed-circuit world speed record in 01. He flew for almost an hour at "near-sonic speed", recording an average of 649.7mph (1,045km/h) at 25,000ft and covering the distance in a time of 57 minutes 23 seconds. On 23 July the same aircraft and pilot, flying at 20,000ft (6,096m), broke the record again, with a time of 56 minutes 3 seconds for an average speed of 668mph (1,075km/h).

These records were achieved using only the modest thrust provided by the Orpheus Or.3, and by an aeroplane designed to give its best at low altitudes, although 01 had received minor modifications before the first attempt was made. Its guns were removed and replaced by fuel, and the gun ports faired over, while the carène bulged fairings brought the

Images showing how the Orpheus engine was removed from the Taon, in this case prototype 02. *Michel Cristescu*

Taon more in line with the area rule; these changes together raised the aircraft's maximum speed in increments to the point where Mach 1.0 would be possible in level flight at altitude. On both occasions the circuit used for the record attempts was Istres to Cazaux and back to Istres.

On landing there was very little clearance between 01's rear fuselage and the ground and it was easy to drag the jet nozzle along the landing surface; this was one of the factors behind the 02's redesigned tailcone. The carènes did not feature on 02, which came rather closer to the planned production standard. Following NATO's rejection of the Br 1001, the two Taons found employment as support prototypes for the 1100 and 1100M. At the beginning of July 1958 one of them took part in a NATO flying display at Liege, but with the failure of the Br 1100 to win production orders, the 1001s eventually went into reserve. Taon 02 is now preserved at the Musée de l'Air et de l'Espace at Le Bourget. It is thought that 01 was scrapped.

Various proposed developments and upgrades were suggested for the Taon, including the supersonic Br 1003 and the Br 1005, but none were built. In the end perhaps the NATO competition proved rather a waste of time, since the G.91 had been

The second Breguet Br 1001 prototype in its vivid blue colour scheme. *Terry Panopalis*

Taon 02 was registered F-ZWVE and marked with an 'E' on its rear fuselage. Note the extension over the jet pipe upper lip to improve to local airflow, and the shorter nose leg compared to the Br 1100. *David Hedge*

The first prototype Taon F-ZWUX ('X') is shown here in its 'second' configuration, showing the changes made in part for the speed records. Aerodynamic bulges or carènes were added at the wing roots and the gun ports faired over. This photo was taken after the records had been set, as signified by the thin coloured bands painted around the nose. *Michel Bénichou*

Rare photo showing both Taons side-by-side. Note the differences in their jet pipes. *Michel Cristescu*

ordered in quantity prior to the event (over 750 were eventually built for Italy, Germany and Portugal). France also went ahead and bought its own designs of light fighter, but NBMR.1 was a most interesting exercise.

Airframe

The Breguet Br 1100 was a slim, elegant design. It had a low-position, swept trapezoidal metal wing and a low tailplane set below the level of the wing. The sweep angle at the wing leading edge was increased slightly at the roots with small fillets, and the wing torsion box was formed in a honeycomb-filled structure. Both leading edge and large span, very narrow chord tailing edge flaps were installed, while wide chord, narrow span ailerons worked with spoilers that rose vertically out of the wing ahead of the flaps – the leading edges of the wing drooped sharply to provide high lift at low speeds. The elevator was a single slab, an airbrake was fitted on the fuselage underside just forward of the tail and a brake parachute was housed in a fairing beneath the rudder.

The NATO 'winner' was the Fiat G.91. Here Italian Air Force examples are refuelled.

The fuselage employed metal construction with the engine bay protected by stainless steel. Br 1100 was designed to operate from unprepared airfields and therefore had low-pressure tyres, the whole undercarriage retracting into the fuselage because of insufficient space in the thin wing. The aircraft was pressurised, but in accordance with NATO requirements the 1001 was not (although provision had been made for it).

The Br 1001 Taon also had leading and trailing edge flaps, ailerons, spoilers, rudder and slab-type elevators. Its wing was swept 43° at quarter chord and its structure employed the same manufacturing techniques as the Br 1100, in particular the use of bonded honeycomb sandwich. The airframe made very extensive use of this new manufacturing technique, which rigidity and lightness, the wings for example having variable thickness sheet metal coverings bonded to the aluminium honeycomb core to form a box. Some of the armament and four fuel tanks (total capacity 402 Imp gals/1,830 litres) were housed in the 1001's central body and the four guns were mounted below the air intakes.

25 Hispano HA-300 (1964)

HISPANO HA-300

Type: single-seat light interceptor prototype

Span: 19ft 2in (5.84m)

Length: 40ft 8in (12.40m)

Gross wing area: 179.57sq ft (16.70sq m)

Wing t/c ratio: 3%

Full loaded weight: first prototype 7,055lb (3,200kg); E-300 (probably estimated) 12,000lb (5,443kg)

Powerplant: first prototypes 1 x Bristol Orpheus 703-S-10 turbojet 4,190lb (18.6kN); third prototype 1 x Brandner E-300 6,300lb (28kN) dry and 10,575lb (47kN) with afterburning

Max speed: Orpheus prototypes subsonic in level flight; E-300 (estimate) Mach 2.0 at altitude

Service ceiling: E-300 (estimate) 59,055ft (18,000m)

Climb rate: E-300 (estimate) 39,960ft/min (12,180m/min)

Range: E-300 (estimate) 870 miles (1,400km)

Armament: Never clarified, but potentially 2 x 30mm or 4 x 23mm cannon, plus 2 x air-to-air missiles

The Hispano HA-300 jet fighter was in the main developed outside Europe and strictly speaking it falls outside the parameters of this book. However, within its story it has several direct European connections – its origins were in Spain, where a full-scale model glider of the aircraft was flown, and the type's designer was German.

The HA-300 light interceptor project was the work of Professor Willy Messerschmitt, the German aircraft designer who had been so successful during World War II. After initially being financed in Spain, the programme was transferred to Egypt before any metal had been cut on the first prototype, a country that in truth was entirely unsuited to building such an advanced aeroplane.

In the late 1950s Spain formulated its Ejercito del Aire requirements for a new daytime point-defence interceptor fighter with Mach 1.5 capability. A Germano-Spanish design team led by Messerschmitt produced the resulting HA-300, for Hispano Aviación 300. Messerschmitt had established the Hispano Aviación company at Seville, Spain and his studies for an ultra-lightweight fighter had been ongoing since 1951. The powerplant for the rather small HA-300 was intended to be a new, reheated version of the Bristol Orpheus, the B.Or.12, while the advanced nature of the aircraft's very highly swept and very thin delta wing prompted the construction of a model test glider designated HA-300P (Hispano apparently gave this aircraft the production reference HA-23P).

Hispano drawing from January 1959 showing the HA-300 in its original form, without horizontal tail.

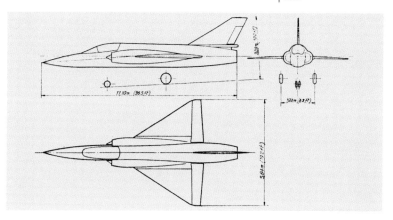

The Hispano HA-300P (HA-23P) research glider. *Wolfgang Muehlbauer*

The HA-300P glider just lifting off the ground. It is understood that this craft contributed little to the fighter programme. *Wolfgang Muehlbauer*

Designed to acquire data at low speeds, this mixed construction craft was a fair representation of the fighter, but lacked the tailplane of the HA-300 prototypes. It was painted in orange, yellow and white, and the mid-section of its wing was formed from an all-metal box structure. The forward fuselage, inboard wing and main spar were all in metal, but the rear fuselage, wing leading edges (swept at 57.5°), outer wings and spars were all in wood. The skins were of ply.

The outer wing sections had a single spar and two beams perpendicular to the body (one in metal, the other in wood), there were two small fences on each outer wing, and inboard and outboard elevons along the trailing edge (for trimming, the inboard elevons used 'Plasticel' Flettner tabs). Inside the fuselage were two tanks for water, which could be drained as required to adjust the centre of gravity position and rebalance the aircraft. The undercarriage was fixed.

Little information has emerged in regard to the HA-300P's flying career, but its first flight came in 1959 and contemporary published sources report that the rudder became effective at a speed of 50mph (80km/h) and the aircraft left the ground at 121mph (195km/h); the towing cable was cast off at between 124mph and 155mph (200km/h and 250km/h).

A later source adds that its initial towing trials were made using a jeep, and then preparations were made to tow it into the air behind a 'B.21' aircraft (a CASA 2.111 bomber, the Spanish version of the German Heinkel He 111). However, on its first full flight the glider displayed a violent directional and lateral instability from the moment it left the ground, to the point that the Spanish pilot had to pull the towline release lever immediately. On that evidence it appears that the HA-300P's only attempt at flight, lasted mere seconds.

In the meantime, wind tunnel testing had revealed that the HA-300 would most likely experience flutter and there was also the potential for longitudinal instability. Hence the airframe was redesigned with a tailplane, which caused delay, a situation not helped by Bristol Siddeley's unwillingness to continue with the afterburning B.Or.12 purely as a private venture (the engine was eventually abandoned). The cost of the HA-300 project was growing all of the time and by 1960 the Spanish government had concluded that the HA-300 was just too expensive to be continued. When an official approach was made by Egypt to take the project on in its entirety, Spain was very happy to accept.

The HA-300 programme and some of its workforce now made their way to the other side of the Mediterranean. In the early 1960s, with his country reliant on acquiring combat aircraft from the Soviet Union, Egypt's President Nasser had ambitions of establishing and expanding his own aircraft industry, and the HA-300 seemed an ideal way to help reach this objective. At the same time a licence was also acquired to manufacture Hispano's HA-200 Saeta jet trainer, and even the HA-23P glider was apparently sold to Egypt (its final fate is unknown). HA-300 design and development work passed to Helwan Aviation (meaning that no change in the fighter's designation was required).

The first two HA-300 prototypes were to be powered by available examples of an earlier version of the Orpheus, the 703, but there was now no suitable engine for production aeroplanes. The Egyptian government therefore opted to develop a brand new jet engine of its own, a move that automatically added cost and complexity to the programme. There were several external influences on this decision, not least the fact that acquiring a large quantity of engines from Britain would not be a good political move for Nasser after British forces had invaded Egypt just four years earlier during the Suez Crisis.

An Austrian, Ferdinand Brandner, designed the new engine and a recruiting drive for his engine company and for Helwan to build the HA-300, saw 470 technical staff hired from European countries (the level of German involvement was kept secret). Helwan's design, manufacturing and test facilities were expanded and the nation's aerospace programme came under the control of the Egyptian General Aero Organisation (EGAO). Messerschmitt controlled the airframe Factory 36 to the southeast of Cairo, while Brandner looked after turbojet Factory 135 next door.

The new, lightweight engine was designated E-300, fitted with an afterburner and expected to provide as much as 11,465lb (51kN) of thrust, thereby making the HA-300 capable of Mach 2.0 speeds and reaching 40,000ft (12,192m) in about two and a half minutes. Work on the engine began in the spring of 1962 but, as might be expected, it

suffered delays and did not run on the bench until July 1964. The E-300 was first test flown in an Antonov An-12 'Cub' test bed, replacing the Soviet four-engine freighter's port inner turboprop, and the first flight with the E-300 running was made in June 1966; it still took nine months to complete 30 hours of flight time with the unit. In March 1968 an example with reheat was installed, but after just five hours in the air the trials ended and the An-12 was returned to its normal role with the Egyptian Air Force.

However, an Indian HAL HF-24 Marut jet fighter was also supplied to Helwan (along with a support team from India), to test the Brandner engine at transonic speeds. This particular aircraft had already been used to test two reheated Orpheus engines in an enlarged rear fuselage making it ideal for the E-300. The new power unit replaced the Marut's starboard Orpheus and was carried on more than 100 test flights, the Marut operating under the designation IBX.

Initial design work on the HA-300 (also designated XC-6) was apparently the responsibility of Georg Madelung, one of the Messerschmitt people employed by Hispano Aviación in Seville. First metal for the first prototype was cut in early 1961, the airframe being known to the German contingent as V-1 following German wartime practice. It proved impossible to keep the HA-300's configuration

The first HA-300 prototype just after take-off on its first flight in March 1964. The undercarriage was not retracted during the trip. *Wolfgang Muehlbauer*

HA-300 V-1 lands at the end of its first flight.

The second prototype at Helwan in 1966. The aircraft featured a longer, more pointed nose than V-1. Note the relatively high rudder and that the tips of the tailplane have mass balances. *Wolfgang Muehlbauer*

secret because of the need to conduct wind tunnel testing and other work in Western Europe (a complete, fully-equipped cockpit underwent ground pressure testing at Normalair in Somerset, UK for example).

Since Egypt had no test pilots of its own, Gp Capt Kapil Bhargava was brought in from India, but after inspecting the finished HA-300 prototype he put together a long list of flaws and hazardous design features, then called the fighter a "death trap". In July 1963 Bhargava taxied the aircraft in front of President Nasser as part of Egypt's Republic Day celebrations, but the arguments regarding its safety, and the long time taken to address the issues once it had been acknowledged that the prototype was unsatisfactory, meant that the first flight did not take place until 7 March 1964. Full-scale taxiing trials had been performed in February and its first flight lasted 12.5 minutes. During its initial flight trials V-1 was towed to the end of the runway at Helwan to save the fuel normally used in taxiing out.

By now the HA-300 had regularly been compared to the Folland Gnat and in the air Bhargava found the new aeroplane was very similar to the British aircraft, both in terms of its performance and handling (India had bought the single-seat Gnat). It flew well, but the HA-300's innovative design caused problems. Since the aircraft had an extremely thin wing, flutter was always a potential problem at the back of the pilot's mind. As the flight envelope was expanded, modifications were made to counter flutter in the form of hydraulic dampers intended to delay its onset in the ailerons and elevators. A single hydraulic system was eventually installed, looking after the rudder as well – all very advanced work for Egypt, which was new to high technology aeroplanes.

On top of this, given its small wingspan and rudder position relatively high above the aircraft's centreline, inertia coupling might have afflicted the HA-300 at high rates of roll at high altitude; the prototypes were never tested for inertia coupling, however. The low-power Orpheus also brought restrictions, including a ceiling of just 39,370ft (12,000m), while to go supersonic the aircraft had to enter a shallow dive. Nevertheless, Bhargava recorded Mach 1.13 in prototype V-2 and overall he found the HA-300 a very pleasant aircraft to fly.

The second Orpheus-powered prototype flew on 22 July 1965, while V-1 took part in the Republic Day celebrations on 23 July and the HA-300 also featured in the 1966 event. The Six-Day War with Israel in 1967 caused little in the way of handicap to the project, but opened the government's eyes to the fact that there would be little point in seeing the project through to its end. In addition, Indian officials had hoped that Egypt was going to acquire

From the side the HA-300 was similar to the single-seat Folland Gnat.

HA-300 prototype V-2 at Helwan in 1966, giving a suggestion of the aircraft's compact dimensions. *Wolfgang Muehlbauer*

production examples of the Marut powered by the E-300, but when it became clear that this was not the case, India's interest in the engine died. The Egyptian government officially abandoned the HA-300 in May 1969. Many in West Germany were relieved by the decision because there had been concerns that this German-designed fighter might go into combat against Israel. These same concerns may also be the reason that it was never armed.

Bhargava, however, pushed to have the third prototype, the first with the E-300, test flown a few times so that at least some data could be gathered from the effort that had gone into the project. The fat lipped, semi-circular intakes used by the first two aircraft were replaced on the E-300 machine by a new form fitted with shock cones, and the third and fourth machines also had a longer fuselage for the afterburner and altered vertical tail surfaces.

It was November, before Bhargava was able to make high-speed runs to near take-off speed. These were sufficient to indicate that the third machine's characteristics seemed pretty similar to the those of its predecessors, but problems with fuel contaminating the oil supply, and the fact that all of the foreign engineers had by now returned home, meant that the aircraft's E-300 was never made airworthy. The third HA-300 never flew.

Since 1997, V-1 (serial 51-100) has been on display in the Deutsches Museum at Oberschleißheim near Munich. The other prototypes were presumably scrapped, the first two HA-300s having accumulated 135 test flights without accident. The only real moment of worry had come when Egyptian test pilot Major Sobhy El Tawil (who had been trained in the role by Bhargava) experienced flutter after firing a "thruster" on the left wing (at the time of writing it is uncertain what "thruster" refers to). In response, Tawil prevented the aerodynamic loads on the aircraft from becoming any larger, easing the aircraft out of its dive and returning safely with only a cracked hinge on the port flap/aileron.

This very expensive project put a strain on Egypt's troubled economy and in the end the HA-300 proved something of a fiasco. Contemporary accounts in the aeronautical press called the project a status symbol and labelled the HA-300 programme a folly for Egypt, but in retrospect it was also a brave decision and Egypt's engineers acquired a great deal of knowledge and experience (and facilities) in the design of modern combat aircraft. The HA-300 would probably have been out of date by the time it entered service and was unlikely to have provided much of an improvement in capability over the Soviet Mikoyan-Gurevich MiG-21 'Fishbed' then serving with the Egyptian Air Force. The HA-300 was Prof Messerschmitt's last design and his first supersonic aeroplane.

Airframe

The single-seat HA-300 tailed delta-wing interceptor was built in aluminium and had a very thin wing swept 57.5° at the leading edge. The wing was revolutionary for its thickness/chord ratio of just 3%, making it the thinnest aluminium (Duralumin) aerofoil to have flown at the time of its creation. The tailplane was placed immediately behind and slightly below the wing, and the rudder had an external mass balance. The engine was fed by semi-circular intakes blended into the fuselage and the tricycle undercarriage that gave the aeroplane something of a crouched appearance on the ground; the nose gear had small twin wheels. The Orpheus-powered prototypes were in grey or a natural metal finish with red trim.

Manufacturer's display model of the E-300-powered HA-300, with shock cones in the redesigned air intakes.

26 BAC TSR.2 (1964)

BAC TSR.2 (1964)

Type: two-seat supersonic tactical bomber prototype

Span: 37ft 1.6in (11.32m)

Length with nose probe: 89ft 0.5in (27.14m)

Gross wing area: 702.9sq ft (65.37sq m)

Weights: normal loaded 95,900lb (43,500kg); overload 105,000lb (47,628kg)

Powerplant: 2 x Bristol Siddeley Olympus 22R (Mk 320) turbojets each 19,600lb (87.1kN) thrust dry and 30,610lb (136kN) with reheat

Max speed: 725 knots (1,343km/h) at sea level; Mach 2.05 at 36,000ft (10,973m)

Ceiling: 55,000ft (16,764m)

Climb rate: 55,000ft/min (16,764m/min) at sea level

Radius of action: 1,500 miles (2,414km) with underwing tanks

Armament: See text

During the Second World War Britain placed the de Havilland Mosquito into service, an machine that can perhaps be considered as the world's first true multi-role combat aircraft; it was used in the fighter, fighter-bomber, and bomber roles, against naval targets, for reconnaissance and even as a high-speed passenger transport. With the arrival of the jet age the creation of a 'jet-Mosquito' was a key programme for the late 1940s and again the British got it right, in the shape of the English Electric Canberra. However, this aircraft was subsonic and by the mid-1950s there was a growing need for a Canberra replacement. The outcome was the British Aircraft Corporation TSR.2, among the most controversial aircraft ever and, from a British point of view, perhaps THE most controversial.

Opinion grew over several years during the 1950s that the RAF needed a new tactical strike/reconnaissance aircraft to succeed the Canberra, but concentration on the development of the strategic V-Bomber force to provide a nuclear deterrent had prevented any real effort being applied. During 1956 however, the absence of this type of aircraft from forward plans became increasingly marked, and especially so during the Suez episode that year, and support for the project strengthened.

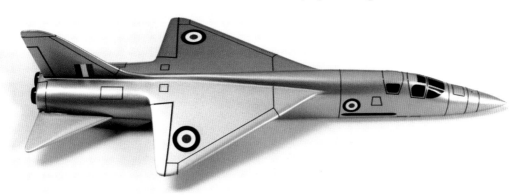

Model of the English Electric P.17 proposal to GOR.339.
Joe Cherrie

The deficiencies of the Canberra with advancing technology were seen as its lack of self-contained blind bombing/reconnaissance system, relatively slow speed at medium altitude and limited fatigue life at low level. In 1957 the need for a new aircraft was confirmed and covered by General Operational Requirement 339 (GOR.339), issued in March. This was written around the widest possible application, covering not only commitments to Supreme Allied Commander Europe (SACEUR), but also those under various treaties with other nations and operations in Colonial wars. The requirement included a radius of action of 1,000nm (1,855km), of which 200nm (370km) was to be at low level, the warload would embrace tactical nuclear weapons or high explosives in bomb and rocket form, and the aircraft was to be highly subsonic at low altitudes and highly supersonic at medium altitudes.

Industry submitted ten different designs to GOR.339 and the final selection saw the best elements of Vickers-Armstrong's Weybridge single-engine Type 571 proposal and the English Electric (EE) Warton P.17 design combined to create TSR.2. Splitting the work 50/50, and the airframe near the trailing edge of the wing box, it was agreed that Vickers would manufacture the fuselage and everything forward of that point, while EE would produce the wing, rear fuselage, powerplant installation and tailplane.

Bristol Siddeley Engines (BSE), a company formed in 1959 by the merger of Bristol and Armstrong Siddeley, would develop a new version of the Olympus engine specifically for the aircraft. According to an Air Staff review, the design team at Warton, under Freddie Page, was the only group with extensive experience of Mach numbers up to 2 (with its Lightning) and had therefore centred upon the aerodynamic, stability and control aspects of the design. Vickers, on the other hand, had instituted a far-reaching study into electronic systems and airborne equipment, and in consequence had produced a more refined design.

Other factors were also in play and require at least brief mention. Firstly, the 1957 *Defence White Paper* was intended to end development of future manned fighters in the UK (except for the Lightning), so that much of the cost of the research work generic to high-performance aeroplanes would now be heaped upon TSR.2 alone. Second, to ensure they would continue to win government orders, most of Britain's aircraft companies had amalgamated into two competitive groups – Hawker Siddeley Aviation (HSA) and the British Aircraft Corporation (BAC).

In February 1960, the companies already forming Hawker Siddeley (Avro, Armstrong Whitworth, Gloster and Hawker) joined with Blackburn, while Bristol, English Electric, Hunting and Vickers came together as BAC.

In example of the heavy engineering behind TSR.2, High Duty Alloys at Redditch produced the aircraft's 'tailplane frame', a huge, hand-forged and machined slab of RR.58 aluminium for the rear fuselage. It was 119in (302cm) wide, 46in (117cm) tall and 9in (23cm) thick. Sixty-five had been manufactured by the time the project was cancelled. Here forged and rough-cut pieces are ultrasonically tested for internal flaws.

(For the record, Hawker Siddeley also acquired de Havilland in 1960, but kept it as a separate company until 1963, while Handley Page resisted any attempt by the government to merge into a larger entity and consequently went into liquidation in 1970.)

On 1 January 1959 Aubrey Jones, the Minister of Supply, announced publicly that Vickers-Armstrong and English Electric were to develop a new strike aircraft designated TSR.2 ('TSR' for Tactical Strike and Reconnaissance, not Torpedo, Spotter, Reconnaissance as some sources have recorded). Sir George Edwards of Vickers was to lead the project and in May GOR.339 was replaced by an updated and more precise requirement, OR.343, specifically to cover the new aeroplane. The most significant changes were a minimum flying altitude of 200ft or less, replacing the previous 1,000ft, Mach 2 operation at altitude, the introduction of electronic countermeasures (ECM) equipment, and that the aircraft should now be capable of operation from lower grade airfield surfaces.

Originally the aircraft was to have been known as OR.339, but during 1958 a study was made comparing the upcoming, but as yet unnamed Blackburn Buccaneer for the Royal Navy, the OR.339 and the embryonic Hawker P.1127 vertical take-off research aircraft, which was being considered for ground attack. For the purposes of the study the three types were labelled TSR.1, TSR.2 and TSR.3, and when Jones announced the new aircraft to the public he mistakenly called it TSR.2. In a memo dated 1 January 1959, government official JE Herbecq wrote "OR.339 – or TSR.2 as I gather

we must learn to call it". Government circles in fact became quite fussy about the publication of just a number for the aeroplane – there was no name as yet and in the event, TSR.2 did not last long enough to get one.

Flying at high speed and low level brought problems in providing a comfortable ride for the aircrew. In just one example of the lines of research required to bring all of the elements of TSR.2's design together, in 1960 the 'Swifter Flight' of six Canberras operated around the Mediterranean theatre, kitted out with instrumentation to record turbulence and accelerations when flying extensively at low level over the sea and all manner of terrain, from mountains to desert.

Such factors eat away at an airframe's fatigue life and analysis of the data resulted in the adoption of a flexible, multi-spar wing to help ensure TSR.2 had a high fatigue life. TSR.2's wing had many attachment points to the fuselage, but with none of them rigid – each could move in a different plane, allowing the wing to spread twist or flexing loads across its span without passing stresses to the fuselage. As a result, the low level ride for the crew was smooth but the resulting small wing was incompatible with the need for short field performance. Hence the aircraft also had to have very high thrust engines and virtually full span, blown flaps, the requirement for the latter leading to the adoption of differential, all-moving tailerons for pitch and roll control. In addition, the powerful wing flaps required the tailerons to have flaps with a geared surface for use when the wing flaps were in the down position.

After full machining, a 'tailplane frame' is readied for the heat treatment that optimised the material's properties.

TSR.2 had a comprehensive electronics suite, the design of which broke new ground in many areas. Another piece of advanced design was TSR.2's all-moving, single-surface fin, used for auto-damping but kept to a minimum size to reduce weight and drag. In consequence, the aircraft would be unstable directionally above Mach 1.7, so an artificial system was fitted, a new feature for a planned production aeroplane. Another was the development of a terrain-following system allowing the aircraft to hug the contours of the landscape, over hills and into valleys, which was another huge step forward at the time.

Backing up the development programme was a host of test bed aircraft – an Avro Vulcan modified to accommodate a test engine in a belly-mounted fifth nacelle flew the new Olympus, while Canberras and Buccaneers were employed on avionics trials.

During these early years assessments were also conducted to see if TSR.2 was actually needed. One in particular in September 1960 compared the BAC aircraft to a design that would become a rival throughout the saga, the Blackburn Buccaneer naval striker.

TSR.2 was expected to be in service in the strike role in 1966 and a full contract for nine development aircraft (XR219-227) was placed on 6 October 1960 under KD/2L/02/CB.42(a), with a first flight expected during March 1963. On 28 June 1963 a further 11 aircraft (XS661-671) were ordered against KD/2L/13/CB.42(a), to be built to a pre-production standard at Preston, Samlesbury and Warton, and then on 20 March 1964 an order was placed for 30 production aeroplanes (XS944-954 and XS977-995). A cockpit mock-up was examined officially at Weybridge on 14 January 1960.

When Minister of Defence Harold Watkinson raised the issue of a strategic nuclear role for the TSR.2, the gradual expansion of the aircraft's performance requirements began, along with the amount of equipment and weaponry it would carry, inflating the programme's cost and leading to arguments in the press and in government over whether the aircraft really was required. In truth TSR.2 did not have the required range to satisfy a full strategic role and yet it was considered as such to fill an upcoming gap between the V-bombers and the submarine-launched Polaris strategic missile, bought by Prime Minister Harold Macmillan in 1963.

In the meantime, Specification RB.192D had been issued around OR.343 in August 1960 and included a tactical nuclear 'lay-down' weapon for low-level use. By 1961 the arguments and policy outlined by the 1957 White Paper had faded and other aircraft programmes were up and running, while in the US the General Dynamics company was building a swing-wing strike aircraft designated F-111 and this, in due course, became the TSR.2's nominated replacement.

An important driver of TSR.2 costs was the use of exotic structural materials, including titanium alloys, high-grade steels and aluminium-lithium alloy sheet. The aircraft was to operate at speeds close to the limits of normal aluminium alloys and X2020 aluminium-lithium (AL-Li) was lighter than the copper-based Duralumin and other aluminium alloys normally used in aircraft construction. It also offered high strength and on TSR.2 was used for the skinning around the cockpit, lower fuselage bomb bay, rear fuselage, and fin and tail, but not near the intakes or engine tunnels. Using Al-Li saved weight (estimates made in 1960 suggested 844lb/383kg for the whole airframe), but the material was sensitive to fatigue and crack propagation. How well Al-Li would have lasted on production airframes is open to conjecture.

Powerful forces were soon lobbying against the TSR.2 project. Two severe in-house critics were the Chief Scientific Advisor to the Minister of Defence, Sir Solly Zuckerman, and Admiral of the Fleet Lord Mountbatten, the Chief of the Defence Staff, both of whom leaned heavily towards the Buccaneer. There was also much hostility to the project from the opposition Labour Party, led by Harold Wilson. But the Conservative government had serious doubts of its own.

On 15 November 1963 Prime Minister Alec Douglas-Home minuted to his Minister of Defence Peter Thorneycroft: "I am rather troubled about this project. It seems to be turning out to be considerably more expensive than we thought; and its military value is also being called into question." The controversy went on, a few snippets here illustrating just how insecure TSR.2 was throughout most of its existence.

The whole programme was hindered by the often less than cordial relationship between Vickers and EE, and the level of co-ordination required between many companies across the country, contracted or subcontracted into the programme, via a large committee system. In practice this impeded the decision making process. The industry problem was in part an outcome of the substantial programme of mergers, while a post-cancellation government review later added: "Part of the project's

unhappy life was due, not to deliberate mismanagement, but to the fact that government and industry were still only learning how to handle the procurement of such complex weapons systems."

By February 1963 a total of 138 TSR.2s was planned for the RAF, with production to be completed in 1973. The first nine aircraft would be retained by the Ministry of Aviation (MoA) for development tasks, the next five would go to A&AEE Boscombe Down for MoA acceptance test flying, and airframes fifteen to twenty were earmarked for the RAF's TSR.2 development squadron at Coningsby, to provide flying and maintenance experience in advance of operational release. It was to conduct intensive flying trials, aircraft numbers ten and fourteen swelling its ranks after being brought up to production standard. On 23 September 1964 it was agreed that the type's overseas trials would take place at Edinburgh Field and the Weapons Research Establishment in Australia.

The salient features of TSR.2 were released to the national press on 28 October 1963, but a substantial blow to the project was Australia's decision that same month to buy the US F-111 instead of TSR.2. Australia had for some time been a leading contender for export orders, indeed it was the only other country to express a strong interest in the aircraft, and an order had been crucial to the prospects of the aeroplane reaching the RAF. During September 1963 West Germany had also shown interest as a replacement for its Lockheed F-104G Starfighters, but the Ministry of Aviation felt that this was never serious.

The front and rear halves of the first aircraft, XR219, were joined at Weybridge in March 1963, with the agreed target date for flight now January 1964. But this slipped again and the prototype was not taken by road to A&AEE

Boscombe Down until 4 March 1964. Engine troubles then delayed flight testing further (during April there were failures on three engines, in part due to resonant vibration of the main shaft), before, in August, the first prototype was finally cleared for taxi trials. These commenced on 2 September and reached speeds of 100 knots (185km/h) with the nose raised. On 9 September the second TSR.2, XR220, was moved to Boscombe by road to be prepared for its contribution to the flying programme, but suffered fuselage damage when its trailer overturned and the aircraft fell onto its side. It came as a relief when XR219 finally made its initial flight (of 14 minutes) from Boscombe, on 27 September 1964, piloted by chief test pilot Wg Cdr Roland 'Bee' Beamont and with Don Bowen accompanying him as navigator.

Engine changes, other modifications and minor problems prevented the second flight being made until 31 December which, at 13 minutes, was virtually a repeat of the first. An attempt was made to raise the undercarriage for the first time on Flight 5 on 14 January but the port bogie, despite rotating, failed to retract. Beamont was able to land safely. The undercarriage was kept down for Flight 6 (15 January, Wg Cdr James 'Jimmy' Dell's first trip), but Flight 7 on the 22nd saw another attempt to retract it; this time the starboard bogie rotated but failed to retract. At last, the undercarriage was raised fully and safely on Flight 10, allowing the flight envelope to be expanded, a speed of 500 knots (927km/h) being recorded on this sortie. In the meantime, on 28 January the TSR.2 static test rig had failed at 85% of its ultimate load in the underside of the starboard wing. The failure point was near the "apex corner fitting" and the crack travelled rearwards through several panels.

Preparations for the maiden flight, with crew aboard, 27 September 1964. BAC via Terry Panopalis

XR219 lands at Boscombe Down, most likely at the conclusion of its maiden flight. TSR.2 needed a large drag chute.

The TSR.2's undercarriage was a primary source of trouble during the limited test programme. Other major issues came with the engines, especially before the maiden flight. *North West Heritage Group*

Flight 11 was made on 8 February and saw 511 knots (947km/h) achieved at low level, and an investigation of the aircraft's high-altitude handling, while No. 13, on 16 February, recorded Mach 0.98 at 29,000ft (8,839m). On 22 February 1965, during Flight 14, XR219 reached its highest ever speed while flying over the Irish Sea and with just one afterburner lit. Starting out on a transfer from Boscombe to Warton, Beamont maintained an IMN of 0.992 with intermediate dry rating on both engines before port engine reheat was selected and taken to maximum. XR219 was still accelerating and climbing when reheat was cancelled at 30,200ft (9,205m) with the IMN reading 1.124. As he passed through the sound barrier Beamont experienced no vibration or trim change.

Chased all the way by a Lightning (which required both its afterburners to keep up), Beamont performed a 10-minute flying demonstration in front of TV cameras, press and assembled employees, before landing at BAC's factory airfield. For the first time a version of the Olympus engine had been taken supersonic on the level. All of XR219's remaining flying would be conducted from Warton.

High-level and low-level fuel consumption checks were made in the next two flights, but undercarriage vibration was experienced during landings, affecting the cockpit by approximately 2-2.5g. It was expressed as a violent motion of the forward fuselage and was rather unpleasant for the crew, so for Flight 17, on 8 March, BAC reduced the oleo pressure from the undercarriage components. This time there was no vibration on touchdown and during trip XR219's handling characteristics were investigated at 200ft (61m) and speeds in excess of 500 knots (927km/h). The 19th flight on 11 March achieved 580 knots (1,075km/h) at 2,000ft (610m), and the next day a final sortie was made before XR219's engines scheduled for inspection using X-ray analysis.

On the 15th, George Edwards summed up the flying so far in a message to the new Minister of Aviation, Roy Jenkins. He noted that the initial flight envelope had been explored and exceeded, and the aircraft's stability and control were shown to be as predicted or, in some areas, better. In these tests the primary high-speed, low-level design point had been cleared with ease. In particular, the TSR.2's control standard was such that, from low speed through to supersonic speed,

The prototype, during its first flight. The distinctive 'streamers' running off the wingtips were formed by powerful vortices. Note the open auxiliary doors on the intake sides.

On its early flights XR219's undercarriage remained down. This view shows the trailing edge flaps and downward angle of the wingtip. *North West Heritage Group*

XR219 taken with its gear down. *BAC via Terry Panopalis*

XR219 photographed during Jimmy Dell's first flight in the aircraft on 15 January 1965. *North West Heritage Group*
XR219 at low speed. *BAC via Terry Panopalis*

Prototype XR219 at Boscombe Down. *North West Heritage Group*

Above: XR219 in clean configuration, during Flight 13 on 16 February 1965. *North West Heritage Group*

Left: Here the aircraft's high wing position is well illustrated. Almost all the air-to-air photos of the TSR.2 were taken from behind the aircraft. *David Eagles*

XR219 deploys its petal airbrakes. The TSR.2's Olympus engines produced a great deal of black smoke. *North West Heritage Group*

Above: The prototype TSR.2s were painted Anti-Flash White, but for RAF duties production machines would have been camouflaged. *Terry Panopalis*

Left: This underside view of XR219 shows the wing shape and the large tailerons, which had their own flaps. *North West Heritage Group*

no development work would be necessary on aerodynamics and control, and the aeroplane was fit from the engineering and aerodynamic aspects to carry out its basic low-level design mission in its present form without modification. Only one engineering problem of magnitude had been encountered, the undercarriage vibration, but a modification programme was in hand.

The second TSR.2, XR220 was photographed during repairs at Boscombe Down after falling off a lorry on delivery. The aircraft just missed its chance to fly, but survived to go on museum display. *North West Heritage Group*

One of the more advanced TSR.2 airframes, XR226 is chopped into sections at Samlesbury before despatch to a commercial scrapyard. *North West Heritage Group*

During this break, XR220's engine runs were completed and a first flight date of 27 March was scheduled, while XR219 returned to the air on the 26th, with fixed struts fitted to its undercarriage to cut out the landing vibration. In fact, XR219 performed Flights 21 and 22 that day, engineers turning it around in just 40 minutes. Don Knight became the third pilot to fly it on 27 March (other navigators crewing the aircraft were Peter Moneypenny and Brian McCann) and the 25th and final flight took place on 2 April. Total flying time had reached 13.25 hours, but the project had been cancelled.

The general election of October 1964 elected a new Labour government and the cost analyses and questions over the need for the TSR.2 began all over again. In December a fact finding mission was sent to Washington and to General Dynamics at Fort Worth to gather information on the F-111 (the prototype of which had made its maiden flight on 21 December 1964). By 7 January 1965 there were strong rumours in the national press that the TSR.2 would be cancelled, though it was not until the Chancellor of the Exchequer's budget speech on 6 April that this became fact, the Cabinet having decided to axe the programme five days earlier. Work now began on a new collaborative strike project with France, known as the Anglo-French Variable Geometry Aircraft (AFVG).

During May 1965 plans were made to use the two airworthy TSR.2s in a programme of experimental flying trials (after delays, XR220 had been due to fly on the very day that cancellation was announced). In part this was to assist with the general research required for the Anglo-French Concorde supersonic transport, gathering data on aerodynamic stability at high Mach numbers, kinetic heating, drag at supersonic speeds, and subsonic and supersonic engine handling (a further supersonic development of the Olympus was used on Concorde). But the proposal was turned down.

After the end of flying, XR219 appeared as a static exhibit at a semi-public Families' Day event at Warton on 10 June 1966, before going to the target ranges at the Proof and Experimental Establishment at Shoeburyness. Here it was subjected to fire from modern weapons in an assessment of how a contemporary airframe would respond to such treatment. Official documents indicate that the brittle Al-Li airframe cracked readily and it was suggested that a single 20mm round could have downed the aircraft with ease. It was joined at Shoeburyness by the near complete XR221 and XR223, which had received its wings. All thee airframes were scrapped at the end of their 'working' lives after having been destroyed as complete structures in what were termed "vulnerability and lethality trials".

XR219 as a static exhibit at a Families' Day event at Warton on 10 June 1966. *Terry Panopalis*

During 1966 XR220 was used at Boscombe as a non-flying Olympus test bed for Concorde, for which duties it used a Cullum muffler to reduce noise. The aircraft was nominally attached to B Squadron before being Struck Off Charge on 11 April 1967. XR222 was allocated to the College of Aeronautics at Cranfield and arrived there in October 1965. XR220 now resides with Royal Air Force Museum Cosford and XR222 is a major exhibit at IWM Duxford. Lastly, after reaching various degrees of completion, XR224 to XR227 and XS661 to XS671 found their way into private scrapyards, the more advanced early serials having been cut into sections at BAC in September 1965 in readiness for despatch.

The aircraft selected as an alternative to TSR.2 faired no better. As a direct replacement the government ordered the Anglicised F-111K, but this was cancelled in January 1968. The AFVG was also abandoned. Faced with a severe economic crisis in 1967, the government abandoned Britain's commitment 'East of Suez', rendering one of the primary roles envisaged for TSR.2 as no longer necessary. In due course the RAF ordered the Buccaneer, the aircraft it had tried for so long to avoid, and the type proved so good that it remained in service into the 1990s. The Buccaneer order was accompanied by the setting up of the multi-national Multi-Role Combat Aircraft (MRCA) programme that produced the Panavia Tornado, which benefited in particular from the avionics development undertaken for TSR.2.

Government papers indicate that extreme cost was the primary reason for cancelling TSR.2, but contrary to many reports, the decision was not taken hastily or easily. Other facts have emerged in regard to the development programme that show TSR.2 was far from being as a service aeroplane at the time of its cancellation. Among the issues, it is understood that wind tunnel testing had indicated that flutter would occur on the all-moving fin at around Mach 1.7, a speed not yet achieved in flight. This type of problem was common during a new aircraft's development, but indicates that a great deal more money was needed to take TSR.2 through to maturity. Furthermore, it is believed that the first-generation solid-state electronics used in the aircraft were very complex for their time, unproven and most likely to have generated problems. Although brilliant for their day, much of the avionics used analogue technology that would have made the equipment very large, heavy and a nightmare to maintain.

A telegram dated 10 April 1963 (oddly from the Foreign Office, author unknown) noted that TSR.2 was not, and was never intended to be the basis for a British deterrent. The type was seen to begin with as a relatively simple aircraft, but from the late 1950s onwards the concept became progressively more complex. As a result, TSR.2 outgrew its original tactical duties and eventually nuclear weapons became its primary armament to allow it to fulfil an additional strategic role.

Then, by 1964, as Damien Burke revealed in his book, even the RAF had lost faith in the aeroplane, completing a report called *The Shortcomings of the TSR.2*, which outlined how the world situation had changed and the aircraft no longer met the Service's requirements, particularly in the conventional role. For its time TSR.2 was the most advanced military aircraft ever attempted by the British aircraft industry and had it been continued as a pure Canberra replacement at a more modest cost then perhaps it might have been successful.

| XR219 after its move to Shoeburyness in 1966, before it was used as a target. A Bristol 188 sits behind. *Terry Panopalis*

Airframe

The TSR.2's clipped delta wings were swept at 58° 19' at the leading edge and spliced together as a single piece before being attached to the fuselage. They were covered in a thick skin and built up around a forward main spar and auxiliary rear spar, with four intermediate spars set in between. Trailing edge flaps were attached to the aft spar, and some of the fuel also went into the wing. TSR.2's near full-span blown flaps used high-pressure air bled from the engine compressors to increase lift at low airspeeds.

The fuselage was formed in four sections, the forward fuselage with radome, crew and main avionics bay; a forward centre section embracing the semi-circular variable-geometry air intakes and some of the fuel load; a centre section with the wing sitting on top and containing the engine and weapons bays beneath with more fuel; and the rear fuselage with petal airbrake panels, the tailerons and all-moving slab fin. Total internal fuel capacity was 5,588 Imp gals (25,408 litres), with another 600 Imp gals (2,728 litre) in the weapons bay for ferry flights, 1,000 Imp gals (4,547 litres) in a ventral drop tank and a 450-Imp gal (2,046-litre) drop tank on each inboard wing pylon.

Production TSR.2s were to have employed an extensive avionics suite including a US central computing system manufactured under licence by Elliott, an automatic flight control system, Ferranti terrain-following radar, also used for radar ranging and conventional weapon aiming, and sideways-looking EMI radar. The latter was described as a navigation fixing radar and would have used known points on a map to correct navigational errors. As such it formed part of a sophisticated navigation system. Much of this equipment was entirely new to British industry.

The 20ft 6in (6.25m) long bomb bay could hold tactical nuclear stores (two ASR.1177 [WE.177] Type 'A' or 'B') or six 1,000lb (454kg) bombs (high explosive or retarded HE), while a WE.177 or Martel air-to-surface missile could also go on each of the inner underwing pylons. All four wing pylons could take a 37-round 2in (5.1cm) rocket pack or 1,000lb (454kg) bombs, and in the latter case four bombs could be mounted on the inner pylons with single weapons on the outers. With HE bombs also occupying the internal bay, the TSR.2 could carry sixteen thousand-pounders. Bomblet dispensers were another option, although prototype XR219 was unable to carry live weapons. The bay could also take a reconnaissance pannier containing cameras, line scan and sideways-looking radar.

The rough runway requirements demanded large low-pressure tyres on a two-wheel bogie undercarriage, which resulted in a complex retraction process to accommodate the gear into the tightly packed fuselage.

27 Dassault Mirage IIIV (1965)

Mirage IIIV 01

Type: single-seat V/STOL fighter prototype

Span: 26ft 11in (8.20m)

Length: 57ft 5in (17.50m); IIV 02 63ft (19.20m)

Weights: normal VTOL weight 26,455lb (12,000kg); max take-off 29,542lb (13,400kg)

Powerplant: 1 x SNECMA TF104 turbofan 9,340lb (41.5kN) dry and 13,800lb (61.3kN) with reheat, plus 8 x Rolls-Royce RB.162-1 lift jets each 4,410lb (19.6kN); later 1 x SNECMA TF106 delivering around 10,800lb (48kN) dry and 19,070lb (84.8kN) with reheat

Max speed: Mach 2.04 at altitude

Dassault's story is one of great determination, effort and success from a manufacturer that has for a long time been a world force in military aircraft design. Marcel Bloch established the Societe des Avions Marcel Bloch (MB) in 1929. After the Second World War, Bloch changed his German sounding name to Marcel Dassault and in January 1947 the company was renamed Avions Marcel Dassault. In 1971 Dassault acquired Breguet to form Avions Marcel Dassault-Breguet Aviation, which in 1990 was renamed Dassault Aviation.

From the late 1940s, Dassault was responsible for an astonishingly successful series of jet fighters – the Ouragan, Mystère and Super Mystère, the naval Etendard and Super Etendard, then the Mirage series of I, III, 5 and 50 deltas, plus the Mirage IV bomber, the Balzac and Mirage IIIV, followed by the swept-wing 'F' and swing-wing 'G' families, then the Mirage 2000 and 4000 and, today, the Rafale.

The fact that no Dassault designs have featured previously in these pages is perhaps a reflection of the success the company had in winning production orders, but after a search began in the 1960s for a new-generation French combat aircraft, Dassault produced a handful of 'prototype only' programmes. The Mirage IIIV was primarily prepared against a NATO design competition for a new vertical take-off and landing (VTOL) aeroplane, but received considerable government support.

NATO Basic Military Requirement 3 (NBMR.3) sought an all-weather, supersonic, vertical take-off, strike, reconnaissance and tactical support aircraft with a minimum sea level speed of Mach 0.92 and radius of action of at least 250 miles (402km). The aircraft's operating altitude would be between 500ft (152m) and 40,000ft (12,192m), with as high as possible maximum speed at medium altitude. Weapon load would comprise 2,000lb (907kg) of stores, including nuclear weapons.

NBMR.3 was circulated to European industry in June 1961, with design proposals to be submitted by the end of the year. Service entry was expected four years after the winning design had made its maiden flight. The full list of contenders was long and today not absolutely certain, but from the UK came the BAC/Vickers 584, Hawker P.1150/3 (later redesignated P.1154) and Short PD.56; from France the Breguet Br 1115, Dassault Mirage IIIV and Nord 4210; Germany offered the supersonic Focke-Wulf Fw 1161 and subsonic Fw 1262; Italy the Fiat G.95/6; Lockheed proposed its CL-704 project (a V/STOL derivative of the F-104 Starfighter that was used by some European countries); Holland and the US joined

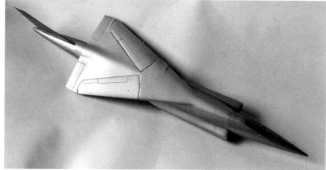

Model of the extraordinary Dutch-US D.24 Alliance, showing its swing wings spread and then fully swept. The model's span with wings swept was 6.4in (16.25cm) and 12.5in (31.75cm) fully spread. It was 23in (58.4cm) long.

forces in an extraordinary combined effort known as the Fokker-Republic D.24 Alliance; and Avro Canada proposed its P.51. (Aviation magazines published from June 1962 indicate that the Breguet Br 1110 and 1116, and the Hawker P.1155 were also offered, although recent research shows that the latter was not submitted in the competition.)

The British designs feature in the author's books on *British Secret Projects*, while the French types will appear in the publisher's forthcoming volume *French Secret Projects* by JC Carbonel. The P.1154 was schemed for a new Bristol Siddeley Pegasus engine development designated BS.100, a power unit also selected for the intriguing D.24 Alliance. The complex engineering requirements for obtaining supersonic speed and VTOL capability were compounded on the D.24 by its variable-geometry wing.

Fokker designed the Alliance, working in collaboration with Republic Aviation, the effort in both countries falling under the management of Alexander Wadkowsky. The D.24 had a polymorphic wing – essentially a highly-swept delta (70° at the leading edge) fitted with a pair of auxiliary wings that could be spread during

flight to increase wing area by a significant amount and thereby improve low-speed handling and performance. With plenum chamber burning, the BS.100-3 was expected to power the D.24 to Mach 1.25 at sea level and Mach 2.4 above 40,000ft (12,192m).

Although based on the F-104G, Lockheed's CL-704 retained little more than the Starfighter's forward fuselage, tail, undercarriage and overall configuration. Powerplant was to be 14 Rolls-Royce RB.181 lift jets, seven each in wingtip pods, plus an RB.168R for propulsion, the latter requiring enlarged, redesigned intakes.

The prime German contender was the Fw 1161, a design based on the Hawker P.1127 experimental prototypes. Power would have come from a developed Bristol Siddeley BS.53 Pegasus engine, plus Rolls-Royce RB.162 lift engines fore and aft (P.1127 design details had been passed to the West German company).

Fiat's G.95 designation covered a series of vertical/short take-off and landing (V/STOL) projects produced under the leadership of chief project engineer Giuseppe Gabrielli. The objective was to replace the firm's earlier G.91, the G.95/6 NBMR.3 submission being the

Internal detail of the Fiat G.95/6, showing the two groups of three lift jets, the main engines in the rear fuselage and a bomb housed in the centre weapons bay.

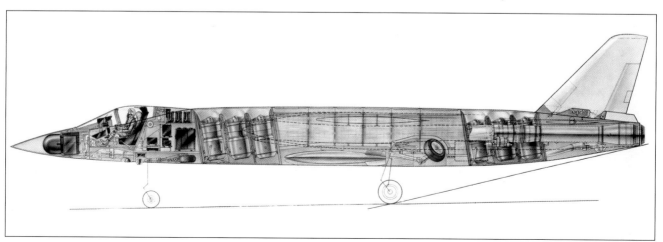

largest of the series and powered by a battery of six ultra-lightweight 4,400lb (19.6kN) thrust Rolls-Royce RB.162 lift engines in groups of three ahead and behind the wing, plus two RB.153 afterburning propulsion engines in the rear fuselage (and fed by extremely long air intakes). Each group of lift jets had two hinged doors covering their inlets and exhausts, and they were tilted to assist the transition from hovering to forward flight. Fiat described this arrangement as a double engine system – one for lift and the other for propulsion and, since the latter could not be fitted with jet deflection, the former would supply all of the lift, similar to the Mirage IIIV and CL-704.

The centre fuselage contained a large volume of fuel and a weapons bay. At medium altitudes the G.95/6 would be capable of Mach 2.0. Its span was 27ft 6in (8.38m) and length around 61ft 6in (18.75m). A model was displayed at the 1961 Paris show. The G.95/6 was shelved, but smaller G.95/4 remained under consideration until the mid-1960s and featured heavily in the aviation press of the time. It was a rival to the German VAK 191 covered in Volume I and a hovering rig was built to represent it.

The first meeting of the NBMR.3 Design Studies Evaluation Group took place over 26-27 February 1962, and the field was narrowed down to two lists, A and B. From now on work concentrated only on the designs in List A. Because of national sensibilities those on List B had not been officially eliminated, although the Evaluation Group would perform no further work on them. The lists were (in no order of preference):

A. Hawker P.1154, Dassault Mirage IIIV, Fokker-Republic D.24, BAC 584 and Breguet 1115

B. Lockheed CL-704, Focke-Wulf Fw 1161 and Fw 1262, Short PD.56 and Avro (Canada) P.51

An official request from West Germany to allow the late inclusion of a re-designed EWR VJ 101C tiltjet (Volume I) was rejected. However, by October 1962 the NATO standing group charged with selecting the winning design had virtually given up, since by then it was clear that national considerations would block any single design from being adopted (NATO had no budget, so the 'winner' had to be funded by all the NATO nations that wanted it).

By the time of Dassault's NBMR.3 submission in December 1961, the French government had been supporting the Mirage IIIV for eighteen months, the Air Staff having shown interest in V/STOL concepts since the late 1950s. However, this situation meant there was bound to be a problem if another design was selected as the NBMR.3 winner. By the middle of 1962 NBMR.3 was pretty much defunct, however, and work on the IIIV continued independently. In fact, freed from NBMR.3's restrictions, the aircraft grew in size in order to meet the latest l'Armée de l'Air specification. Changes included the larger-diameter RB.162-31 lift jet, which was 25% more powerful than the version planned for installation in the first prototype.

The Mirage IIIV retained the general characteristics of the Mirage III, but with a modified wing and substantially enlarged fuselage. As a mixed-powerplant project (separate lift and propulsion engines), the French Air Staff first accepted it in late 1959 and a full-scale mock-up was built at Dassault's experimental Saint Cloud facility. Considerable effort went into saving weight, including the use of light alloy honeycomb or polyester sandwich-type materials in the airframe, and integral fuel tanks in the wings and fuselage.

Two prototypes were ordered in August 1961, in addition to a "half-thrust, half-weight" scale model that became the Balzac, described in Volume I. François Cordié led the IIIV design team, supported by Jacques Alberto. Dassault was prime contractor and Sud Aviation a partner.

Design and development of this large V/STOL fighter proved more complex than originally expected and full-scale wind tunnel testing on a half-fuselage and wing, built by Sud Aviation at Rochefort, did not commence until February 1963. Fitted with two pairs of early RB.162-1 jets, this half airframe was tested extensively in the wind tunnel at Rolls-Royce Hucknall, before being moved to the Office Nationale d'Etude et de Recherches Aéronautiques' (ONERA's, National Office of Aerospace Studies and Research's) largest wind tunnel, at Modane, in August. Rolls-Royce and ONERA made a considerable contribution to the Balzac and Mirage IIIV programmes as tunnel testing continued well into 1966.

A specific development problem was the difficulty in starting the RB.162s and then equalising their lift thrusts, delaying IIIV flight trials for some time. In forward flight the lift engines had to be sealed to reduce drag, but for transition to the vertical it was essential to have scoops or cascades in place to ensure good airflow distribution across the intake face of each vertically- mounted unit.

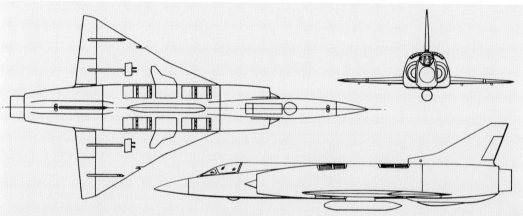

Above: The Dassault Balzac pictured in the hover. *Dassault*

Left: Dassault Mirage IIIV general arrangement, as of December 1963.

Below: The Mirage IIIT 01 test bed in July 1972.
Terry Panopalis

Initially the IIIV's main propulsion engine was a TF104 turbofan, a Pratt & Whitney JTF10 suitably modified by SNECMA. The French engine company also built the definitive TF106, fitted later in the IIIV programme, and both engine types were flight tested separately in a conventional take-off Mirage IIIT trials and test bed aircraft. This made its somewhat delayed first flight, with a TF104B installed, on 4 June 1964 at Melun, piloted by Jean Coureau. The first flight with a TF106 installed took place from Istres on 25 January 1965.

The contribution made by the Balzac to the IIIV was vital. Tethered hovering with a fixed undercarriage began on 12 October 1962, with free hovering just six days later. Extensive modifications, including installation of a retractable undercarriage, were necessary before the Balzac could fly for the first time as a conventional aeroplane, on 2 March 1963. Its eight RB.108 lift jets (predecessors of the RB.162) were started in flight for the first time on 14 March, and on 18 July the prototype was hovered with one lift jet shut down, all valuable experience for the IIIV. Ten days later it took off from concrete rather than its special metal platform for the first time.

A specific Balzac development to find its way onto the Mirage was the use of thrust deflector doors mounted ahead of the nozzles in the belly. For ground running these were inclined aft at an angle of 45°, blowing hot gasses and debris away from the Balzac. When the engines were opened up to full power the doors dropped automatically to a 90° setting to ensure maximum lift thrust was available. On rough surfaces covered in loose materials and debris a rolling take-off could be performed, the pilot releasing the brakes and allowing the Balzac to accelerate for a short distance, after which the RB.108s would cut in for a vertical take-off. This technique would permit the IIIV to make short rolling take-offs. To highlight the diversity of Balzac flying, by October 1963 it had recorded forty-eight hovers, eleven take-off transitions, four landing transitions, twenty-two double transitions, and just four conventional flights.

In early December 1963, with two more IIIV prototypes recently ordered, the fuselage of Mirage IIIV 01 was structurally complete and being equipped. Its wings were not yet fitted but these too were complete, although the engines had still to be installed. At this point, powerplant plans for the prototypes were:

The Mirage IIIV's greatest rival in the NBMR.3 race was always the Hawker P.1154, shown in Royal Navy form by this model.

01: one TF104 delivering about 10,000lb (44.4kN) thrust dry and 15-16,000lb (66.7-71.1kN) in full reheat, plus eight 4,100lb (18.2kN) RB.162-1; first flight expected May 1964;

02: one TF106 delivering about 11,000lb (48.9kN) dry and 17,000lb (75.6kN) in reheat, same lift jets; first flight expected August 1964;

03: one TF106(+)delivering about 14,000lb (62.2kN) dry and 20,000lb (88.9kN) reheated, eight 5,500lb (24.4kN) RB.162-31; first flight due spring 1966;

04: powerplant as 03; first flight to be confirmed.

At that stage firm orders had been placed only for the prototypes, any decision on pre-production machines being based on flight test data. Neither of the first two machines would carry military equipment, although the planned installation included a terrain-following radar, podded sideways-looking radar for reconnaissance and inertial platform for auto-navigation. Digital and analogue airborne computers were being developed for navigation, attack and bombing, and auto-landing, and the emphasis throughout was to be on 'self containment'.

However, when Minister of Defence Pierre Messmer released the news that each IIIV would cost around six times as much as a contemporary light strike and attack aircraft, it became clear that supersonic V/STOL was going to be expensive. One outcome of this was a study made with the British Aircraft Corporation of a version fitted with a Rolls-Royce Spey main engine, and to help spread the cost there were also attempts to interest Boeing. However, when it came to supersonic V/STOL in the UK, the Hawker P.1154 was preferred to the Spey Mirage IIIV. The jet's production as the new French Air Force fighter now appeared unlikely.

Ground running with 01 was successfully completed in early 1964, but flight testing was held back by further problems and the fact that the prototype was overweight and required more lift thrust. Interestingly, the design team considered that the Mirage IIIV and Balzac before it were sufficiently similar to the conventional Mirage III in terms of their aerodynamics to remove any need to begin flight tests with normal take-offs. Dassault chief test pilot Rene Bigand performed 01's first tethered hovering trials at Melun-Villaroche on 10 February 1965, taking the aircraft just a few inches off the ground. Free hovering trials began on the 12th, to an altitude of about 65ft (20m), and then between 25 March and 30 April initial attempts were made to achieve a forward speed of around 100 knots (185km/h).

It was vital to collect data on balancing 01's weight against its lift thrust and how this would change as the aeroplane began to move forwards. But progress was ponderous and at one stage the lift engine fairing doors had to be removed to reduce airframe weight. There were several reasons behind the slow progression. One was pitch-up when the lift jets were started while the IIIV was airborne, caused by airflow going into the upper fuselage intakes; large deflections of elevon were required to counter this and care was needed by the pilot to retain control. This had

Mirage IIIV 01 at Melun-Villaroche very early in its trials programme. The aircraft stands over a grid to prevent re-ingestion of exhaust gases, while a chain under the centre fuselage secures it to the ground. *Dassault*

Mirage IIIV 01 performs its first hover at Melun-Villaroche. Efflux deflector doors (also known as scuttles, or shovels) hang beneath the fuselage forward of the lift jet exhausts to help provide forward thrust for ground-running and short take-offs; these were removed late in the aircraft's career. *Dassault*

also happened on the Balzac, as did another problem caused by the lift engines, in what was termed the 'shower effect', when their exhaust efflux induced a down flow over the aircraft, causing a loss of lift.

Once the transition to wingborne flight had been accomplished, the next phase was to decelerate in readiness to perform a vertical landing. Testing confirmed that the optimum approach for a vertical landing was to fly into wind while decelerating at an altitude no lower than 33ft (10m) to zero forward speed, the pilot alighting in a flat attitude as soon as possible. The IIIV had to decelerate below a 200 to 250-knot (371km/h to 463km/h) limiting speed before the lift jet air intakes could be opened (the figure was 180 knots/334km/h for the Balzac). To assist with the VTOL trials a mobile grid platform with twin-cascade exhaust deflectors was built for operations away from the IIIV's home base and used by the Balzac at the 1963 Paris show.

Another problem now came to light. The IIIV's transition from vertical take-off to forward flight took a long time and covered a great deal of ground, and the airfield at Melun-Villaroche was just too small to ensure that the aircraft would remain inside its boundary before this most delicate manoeuvre was completed. At the beginning of June 1965 prototype 01 was therefore transferred by road to Istres in a dismantled state. For this reason it missed that year's Paris show, the Balzac taking its place.

The TF106 engine was also now installed, but there had been troubles with this as well, to the point that SNECMA took Pratt & Whitney's TF30P engine and developed it into what it called the TF306. A decision was subsequently made to fit the TF306 in prototype 02.

Mirage IIIV 01 made its first flight from Istres on 24 July 1965, piloted by Jean-Marie Saget. Towards the end of the year it became the first V/STOL aeroplane to achieve supersonic flight on the level, the TF106 taking it up to around Mach 1.35. During the winter of 1965/66, prototype 01 was grounded for an inspection, but returned to flying in February 1966. On 24 March Saget at last completed the aircraft's first full double transition – a vertical take-off, accelerating transition to wingborne flight, decelerating transition to the hover and a vertical landing – at Istres (on the 23rd 01 had been flown at the other end of the spectrum in high-altitude, supersonic flight). In contrast, the Balzac had accomplished the double transition in under 20 flights.

By now, however, such was the cost of the IIIV that the Air Force had begun to look for a different aeroplane. Former test pilot Colonel Roland Glavany, Air Force Chief of Plans and Material, declared that the limitations of the RB.162 lift jets would prevent production aircraft from having sufficient operational range (it was not possible to carry enough fuel for long range). Consequently, the possibility of producing 120 Mirage IIIVs had been discussed, but was dropped on 28 March 1966 because the type was so expensive and required considerable further development. Orders went instead to the new Anglo-French SEPECAT Jaguar strike aircraft project, while Air Force development moved on to the Mirage F and G series, programmes that ran side-by-side. Mirage IIIV prototypes 03 and 04 were cancelled, but Dassault reached an agreement with CEV Director General Engineer Pierre Tamagnini to continue with 02 purely for research.

By then the lighter IIIV prototype 02 was almost ready (new manufacturing techniques and the use of new materials, including plastic, had shaved off some of the excess weight). The aircraft's weight was officially given as 28,748lb (13,040kg), while the air intakes over the lift engines had also been improved. Sud Aviation built the second aircraft at Suresnes and delivered it to Dassault Saint-Cloud (just over the road) on 1 April 1965.

The aircraft was configured to represent the two-seat version and despite its weight loss, 02's fuselage was actually longer than 01's. In addition the more reliable and more powerful TF306 had replaced the TF106. Saget took the aircraft on its first free hover, at Melun-Villaroche, on 22 June 1966, the first conventional flight was made on 1 July, and on 5 September, 02 was flown to Istres (the ferry sortie was Flight 9).

Flights 10 and 11, on 9 and 12 September, respectively, took the aeroplane through the sound barrier, Flight 11 reaching a landmark when 02 became the first V/STOL type in the world to record Mach 2. Saget was again the pilot, and recorded Mach 2.04. It is worth noting, however, that the prototype never exceeded Mach 1 in a flight that had begun with a vertical take-off and after the record was set, conventional flights were abandoned, the RB.162 lift units were refitted and the second machine was devoted entirely to the study of vertical flight, beginning with Flight 12 on 8 October. Dassault was interested solely in acquiring information on vertical flight, since it already had plenty of knowledge of high-speed flight from the Mirage III.

A rare inflight photo of a Mirage IIIV (prototype 01) with its undercarriage retracted. The aircraft was near to Bordeaux when the picture was taken. *Terry Panopalis*

The Dassault Mirage IIIV 01 relatively late in its career after Air Force markings had been applied. A dragon was painted on the fuselage side beneath the cockpit. *Terry Panopalis*

In hovering fight the Mirage IIIV was difficult to handle, prototype 02 more so than 01, and both rather worse than the Balzac. Stability, low-speed control and auto-stabilisation were extremely difficult during transitions and in this respect 02 was very touchy and delicate, tending to roll from side to side. This was expressed at its worst on 28 November 1966, when CEV pilot Colonel Michel Jarriges, flying the aircraft for the first time, had to eject over Istres after experiencing control problems.

Following a vertical take-off and translation into slow forward flight, the aircraft began a roll oscillation at an alarming and increasing rate. By the time 02 was moving forward at about 75 knots (139km/h), the roll angle on both sides had reached some 45°. When this reached 70° it was time for Jarriges to leave. He escaped successfully, but after just 38 seconds in the air, 02 crashed and was burnt out.

Throughout Dassault's Mirage IIIV programme the two prototypes suffered such problems of control at slow-speed that they were never allowed to operate vertically away from their gridded platforms – in fact it was impossible to fly the IIIV away from its home facilities. In addition, exhaust gases were sucked back into the engines, causing them to stall, and debris ingestion was another problem. The aircraft's short take-off possibilities were never fully explored either. At this stage in the development of advanced V/STOL during the late 1960s, it was the Hawker Siddeley P.1127's vectored-thrust engine principal that won the day – there was no room for lift engines, which were dead weight in wingborne flight (though the Soviet Yakovlev Design Bureau tried its best with the Yak-38 'Forger', first flown in 1970 using vectored thrust and lift jets). Simplicity was key and the advanced, supersonic Hawker Siddeley P.1154 with plenum chamber burning never flew either – the subsonic Harrier reached service, but was nothing like as complex as the much larger IIIV or P.1154. As Dassault's Jean Cabrière declared: "Eight vertical jets, one horizontal, and another motor for the electricity generator – just getting them all going was a headache!"

Prototype 02 carried a little more in the way of a colour scheme, with a red stripe along its sides and flames painted on the outside of the air intake (it carried the insignia of 2ᵉ Escadre de Chasse (2nd Fighter Wing). The aircraft had a new lift engine intake system, with sideways-opening upper doors and petal scoops over the intakes replacing the original sprung grille panels. Early in the flying programme its ventral exhaust doors and deflectors were removed to save weight, and in late 1965 they were replaced by new 'bomb bay' style doors. Again the aircraft is chained to the ground and note the ram air turbine deployed near the fin.

With 179 flights completed by the Balzac, forty by Mirage IIIV 01 and twenty-four by 02, Dassault had nevertheless compiled a substantial volume of experience and data in combined high-performance and V/STOL flying. The IIIV was the first and remains the only V/STOL aircraft to exceed Mach 2, although not after a VTO, due to excessive fuel consumption in vertical flight. In an article for *Fana de l'Aviation* magazine in 1997, test pilot Jean-Marie Saget remarked that the Mirage IIIV was: "…a very complicated aircraft, very heavy, relatively fragile, and when operating the slightest damage to the lift systems or stabilisation would have made it impossible to perform a vertical landing." Clearly quite a handful! The extraordinary Mirage IIIV prototype 01 is preserved in Le Bourget's Musée de l'Air.

Airframe

The Mirage IIIV was the heaviest V/STOL fighter to have flown at the time and considerably larger than the conventional Mirage III. Its design followed standard Dassault practice in using a delta wing and a sleek fuselage. The wing, based on that of the Mirage IIIC production fighter, was slightly cranked at the leading edge, swept 67° inboard and 60° out to the tips. When compared with the long fuselage, the wing appeared small.

The aircraft had eight Rolls-Royce RB.162 lift jets and making space for them and the propulsion engine, required a very long fuselage that was not area-ruled. The RB.162s were placed in tandem pairs around the centre fuselage and supplied with air from retractable intake grills. In normal forward flight the lift jet intakes and exhausts were covered by flush-fitting fairings. The lift jets were inclined forward at around 9° to provide an element of forward thrust. Hydraulically-extending deflector doors (scuttles) placed forward of and beneath each pair of lift jet exhausts gave further forward thrust.

There was a centre fuselage weapons bay, the nosewheel of the long-stroke undercarriage folded forwards and the mainwheels inwards (flight trials revealed that the undercarriage had been made unnecessarily strong) and both prototypes had a predominantly unpainted finish.

The first Mirage IIIV.
Copyright
Pete West

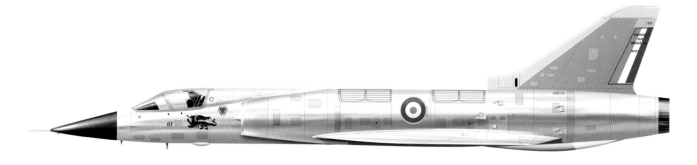

28 Dassault Mirage F2 (1966)

Dassault Mirage F2

Type: two-seat low-level penetration fighter and research prototype; also served as an engine test bed

Span: 34ft 5in (10.50m)

Length: 57ft 9in (17.60m) including pitot

Gross wing area: 387.10sq ft (36sq m)

Wing t/c ratio: 4.5 to 4.2%

Max loaded weight: 40,388lb (18,320kg)

Powerplant: 1 x SNECMA TF306 turbofan 19,840lb (88.2kN) with reheat; 1 x Pratt & Whitney TF30 A22 turbofan 18,825lb (83.7kN) with reheat initially installed

Max speed: 1,460mph (2,350km/h) or Mach 2.2; 1,450mph (2,333km/h) with TF30

Service ceiling: 65,615ft (20,000m) with TF30

Climb rate: climb to 50,000ft (15,240m) 4 minutes 48 seconds

Armament: None carried, but original documents indicate plans to carry an underfuselage pod housing 1 x Nord AS30, AS33 or AS37 air-to-surface missile, 2 x MATRA M530 air-to-air missiles or 2 x 400kg (882lb) bombs. The inner wing hardpoints were for 2 x JL100 rocket launchers, 2 x 400kg bombs, or 2 x AS30 or M530 missiles. Outer wing hardpoints for 2 x 400kg bombs or 2 x Sidewinder air-to-air missiles. No guns were to be carried

During the mid-1960s Dassault embarked on a series of prototype and research aircraft, covered in this book and two chapters of Volume I. After the VTOL Mirage IIIV, however, the primary objective was to find a successor to the conventional Mirage III, as a new and larger type specialising in the low-level penetration role. Dassault looked at fixed wings with the Mirage F2 and the swing-wing 'G' series, but the scaled-down fixed-wing F1 eventually won the production orders.

The Mirage F2 was a one-off swept-wing prototype, although when research for the project commenced through 1962 and 1963, delta and swept-wing studies were also undertaken under the Mirage IIIT and Mirage IIIF designations, respectively. Dassault used the name Mirage for the majority of its fighter programmes from the Mirage I right up to the 4000, and its use of suffix letters to differentiate between types frequently created confusing designations. The F2 began life as the Mirage IIIF2, abandoning the delta wing that Dassault had favoured for the Mirage III to introduce swept wings and a slab tailplane (the latter also a feature of the 'G').

Dassault received a contract for a single prototype of its new twin-seat type early in 1964, its F2 suffix standing for 'fixed-wing, two-seater'. The aircraft was primarily to serve as a test bed for the new SNECMA (Pratt & Whitney) TF306 turbofan, although initially power came from a Pratt & Whitney TF30, the engine from which the TF306 was derived). The Mirage F2 would also test weapon systems for new fighters. The TF306 was a slightly modified, licence-built TF30 fitted with a new SNECMA reheat system. The aircraft was designed under the direction of Jacques Lefeuvre and Mirage F2 No. 01 was assembled at Dassault's Saint-Cloud facility.

In early 1966 the completed prototype was taken in sections to Villaroche. However, as a security measure it had by then been officially decided that first flights for all new aeroplanes should take place at Istres, and so the F2 was

The Dassault Mirage F2 at Villaroche in April 1966. Note the lowered flaps and leading edge slats. *Dassault*

moved there in April. Test pilot Jean Coureau completed a 40-minute maiden flight in the aircraft on 12 June 1966, using an 18,825lb (83.7kN) TF30 A22 engine. At a take off weight of 30,335lb (13,760kg) the Mirage reached 23,000ft (7,010m) and a speed of 450 knots (834km/h), or Mach 0.8. Little trouble was experienced, although buffet was experienced when the flaps were lowered to 35°.

Succeeding flights pushed the weight up to 35,802lb (16,240kg) as the fuel load was taken to its maximum, while back on the ground minor improvements were made to the airframe and an all-metal nose 'radome' fitted. By 7 July a total of 15 flights had been recorded, with CEV's Capt Cousson piloting the last two. Next the flight envelope was expanded up to 600 knots (1,112km/h) at 5,000ft (1,524m), 750 knots (1,390km/h) at 33,000ft (10,060m) and Mach 1.64 at 40,000ft (12,192m) and, apart from the buffet coming from the flaps (which increased with speed), the F2's flying qualities were found to be very satisfactory.

Back at Villaroche the F2 received further modifications, including strengthening of the main undercarriage, alterations to the tailplane and other changes. On 20 September it returned to Istres and the flying programme began to concentrate on reducing drag, work that saw a decline of at least 10%.

Now at last the TF306 was ready and with this installed the aircraft flew again on 29 December, its 34th flight, the extra power enabling it to exceed Mach 2.0 – it reached Mach 2.06 at 38,000ft (11,580m). Next the F2 carried a pair of 1,300-litre (286-Imp gal) external tanks, but these appear to have adversely affected longitudinal stability and made rolling the aircraft "touchy". Large 2,000-litre (440-Imp gal) tanks were carried from Flight 42, at which point it was decided to limit the flaps to 30°, although there were still problems with buffet. On the next flight the aircraft took two crew aloft for the first time, engineer Jean Cuny accompanying Coureau.

On 16 May 1967 and with 66 flights under its belt, the sole Mirage F2 passed into the hands of CEV, although Coureau was soon displaying the aircraft at the Paris Air Show. *Flight* noted that the F2 took off with afterburner and what appeared to be almost

The Mirage F2 on its maiden flight, with 'Mirage III F2' on its nose.
The Mirage F2 taking off with just the pilot on board. *Henry Matthews*

The F2 begins a display at the 1967 Paris Air Show. *Henry Matthews*

Another shot from the 1967 Salon – images of the Mirage F2 seem to be relatively rare.

The F2's type's smaller stablemate, the Mirage F1 was built to the extent of more than 700 aeroplanes. This is the second F1 prototype.

full flap. Dassault displayed three Mirages at the show, the F2, the Mirage IVA supersonic bomber and the Mirage 5, based on the older technology of the Mirage III, "all with blasting afterburners and making high-speed runs and snap rolls." The F2 returned for the 1969 show, this time in the static park because by then its flying career was over, the Air Force having chosen the Mirage F1.

Directly after the 1967 show, the F2's air intakes were replaced by more robust versions, but prior to this, on 18 May the single-seat Mirage F1 prototype had crashed with the loss of its pilot. The accident was caused by rear fuselage

and tailplane flutter and as a result the F2 empennages were put through a programme of static resonance tests to prove their integrity.

Back in the air, the F2's next series of tests included work with the TF306's reheat in readiness for the swing-wing Mirage G, which was to use the same engine. By the end of the year the F2 was also being used to assess flap modifications designed to postpone the onset of buffet, while other alterations to the flying surfaces examined problems that had been encountered on the prototype F1. One outcome of this work was the introduction of two small ventral fins under the F2's rear fuselage.

The F2 carrying two seemingly enormous 2,000-litre external tanks late in January 1967. The outer wing leading edge saw-tooth is also visible. *Alexis Rocher*

Into 1968 the Mirage F2 continued to serve as a test bed for the Mirage G engine installation and other equipment earmarked for the G and F1. In early 1969 it performed a few TF306 development flights for SNECMA, within the limitations of 700 knots (1,297km/h) up to 20,000ft (6,096m) and Mach 2 above that altitude. Thereafter, boundary layer measurements were made on its rear fuselage, before tests were conducted with the TF306C and TF306E versions of the new engine.

In all, the prototype accumulated 243 hours of flying time in 214 flights, the last of which was apparently made on 19 May 1969 (it is not known if the Paris show, which began on 30 May that year, involved any transit flying). After being held in store at Istres, the F2 was moved to Toulouse for a new role as a ground instruction airframe for students.

The F2 effort proceeded alongside Dassault's studies for the swing-wing 'G' series and the F2 could be described as a fixed-wing version of the Mirage G discussed in Volume I, since the two types shared a near identical fuselage design. Such was the profusion of Dassault prototypes in the 1960s that work also proceeded on a single-seat version of the F2, designated F3. It was to be powered by a 22,820lb (101.4kN) TF306E for a top speed of Mach 2.2, but in due course l'Armée de l'Air changed its requirements and opted for the smaller and simpler Mirage F1, which Dassault had built and flown as a private venture in parallel with the F2. The prototype F1 made its maiden flight on 23 December 1966 and in due course also won export orders, while the F3 never flew.

A mock-up of the single-seat Mirage F3 at Saint-Cloud, as it looked in 1966 or 1967. *Wolfgang Muehlbauer*

Airframe

The single prototype F2 provided much data for Dassault's ongoing series of new fighter designs. Apart from important aerodynamic trials, its work with the TF306 provided France with new a fighter engine that offered high thrust coupled with low specific fuel consumption. Other than the flap buffet, the F2 never experienced major problems in flight. Today it resides at the Centre d'essais aéronautiques de Toulouse (CEAT, French National Aeronautics Test Centre) at Balma, east of Toulouse, a facility that undertakes ground trials for military and civilian aircraft, including stress and strength testing of complete airframes or separate components, such as undercarriages.

The Mirage F2's airframe was essentially metal. It featured a high wing, swept at of 52° at quarter chord, with an extended chord leading edge, or saw-tooth towards the tip. Two large trailing edge flaps were installed on the inner wing and there were leading edge flaps inboard of the saw-tooth.

The F2 had a low-set, all-moving tailplane and its sleek fuselage featured the characteristic Dassault shock cone air intakes and sharp, pointed nose. The tricycle undercarriage mounted twin main wheels and retracted into the fuselage, while the crew was seated in tandem. Internal fuel capacity was 1,449 Imp gals (6,590 litres), while two 1,300-litre or 2,000-litre external tanks could be carried on underwing hardpoints. The F2 was flown in a basic natural metal finish throughout its career.

The Dassault Mirage F2. *Copyright Pete West*

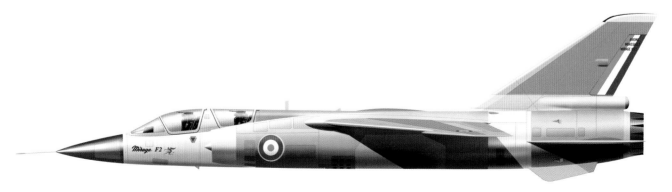

29 Dassault-Breguet Mirage G8 (1971)

Dassault-Breguet Mirage G8

Type: two-seat fighter prototype

Span: spread 28ft 6.5in (8.70m); fully swept 50ft 6in (15.40m)

Length: prototype 01 62ft 4in (19m); prototype 02 66ft 3in (20.20m)

Gross wing area: 365.6sq ft (34sq m)

Wing t/c ratio: 11.5 to 8%/5.4 to 3.3%

Weights: take-off as a single-seat interceptor with two missiles and underwing fuel 45,988lb (20,860kg); as a single-seat striker with AN22 and underwing fuel 47,090lb (21,360kg); max 67,240lb (30,500kg)

Powerplant: 2 x SNECMA Atar 9K50 each 10,845lb (48.2kN) dry and 15,565lb (69.2kN) with reheat

Max speed: Mach 1.2 at sea level; Mach 2.3 at altitude

Ceiling: 55,775ft (17,000m)

Range: 547 miles (880km) with four external tanks and AN22

Armament: See text

The swing-wing Mirage G8 was a follow-on development of the Mirage G described in Volume I. Two prototypes were built and continued the manufacturer's research into variable geometry to its conclusion. In 1971, the year that the G8 first flew, Dassault acquired and merged with Breguet to form Avions Marcel Dassault-Breguet Aviation, abbreviated to AMD-BA.

Mirage G and G4

L'Armée de l'Air had initially wanted a V/STOL strike fighter, but the idea ended with the complex, expensive Mirage IIIV. The need for a low-level penetration fighter remained, however and two aircraft configurations, the Mirage F2 with swept wings and high-lift devices, and the variable-geometry Mirage G were commissioned for comparative studies against the requirement. The G was an experimental aircraft intended to trial and prove the swing-wing formula aerodynamically and structurally, aims it successfully achieved.

After an earlier hop during taxi trials, the Mirage G made its first flight on 18 November 1967 and completed 316 sorties before being lost in a crash on 13 January 1971. It had a span of 22ft 11.5in (7m) with the wings swept fully back and 42ft 8in (13m) spread, a of length 55ft 1.5in (16.8m), wing area 268.82sq ft (25sq m), maximum weight 39,683lb (18,000kg) and maximum speed Mach 1.2 at sea level and Mach 2.2 at altitude.

When France withdrew from the Anglo-French Variable Geometry Aircraft (AFVG) project in 1967 (an aircraft planned in Britain as a replacement for the TSR.2), the l'Armée de l'Air looked towards a home-grown, twin-engine type powered by the SNECMA Atar 9K50 for its future strike/reconnaissance needs. In mid-September 1967 Jean-Claude Brabant's design team at Dassault was given the job of defining the initial specification for a variable-geometry aircraft to satisfy the requirement.

On 6 September 1968 a pair of two-seat prototypes of this Mirage G development were ordered under the designation Mirage G4, and on 11 October the Air Force's Materials Programme Bureau released a specification clarifying that the aircraft must carry either a

The first Mirage G prototype on 27 May 1967, during its official presentation to the aeronautical press.

nuclear weapon for release at low altitude and high subsonic speed (later revised low supersonic speed) or a heavy load of conventional ordnance. Using the 9K50 limited the G4 to Mach 2.2 but Dassault was asked to make the all-metal airframe capable of Mach 2.5, since there might be the possibility at some stage of fitting the new SNECMA M53 engine.

In the meantime, economic problems suffered by France during 1968 put the programme on hold, an order for 60 G4s proving to be beyond the Air Force's means. In addition, the Service had now made the interceptor role its primary mission for the new aircraft, reducing the required range and setting the programme off in a new direction.

The Mirage G pictured at the 1969 Paris Air Show. *Terry Panopalis*

This model of the Mirage G4 was exhibited at the 1969 Paris show. Marcel Dassault is standing behind it on the left. The family likeness between the G series and fixed-wing Mirage F1 and F2 was obvious. *Dassault*

Mirage G8

The two G4 prototypes were not cancelled, but instead modified to fit the new role with the revised designation Mirage G8. Prototype 01 was assembled in Dassault's experimental workshop at Saint-Cloud and differed from the earlier G in many respects, the fuselage and vertical tail surfaces having been substantially redesigned for example. Nevertheless, *Flight* described the G8 as a "minimum step" evolution of the G to explore the flight envelope more fully. The completed aircraft was trucked to CEV at Istres, from where it made a 60-minute maiden flight on 8 May 1971 in the hands of Jean-Marie Saget, Dassault's chief test pilot. Throughout the trip the wings were held at their fully spread position of 23°, up to the maximum attained speed of Mach 0.73, and the undercarriage was cycled.

The first Mirage G8, prototype 01. *Dassault*

Rapid progress was made with the flying programme, 01 reaching Mach 1.25 with the wing swept at 55° on its second sortie on 11 May. The next day, during Flight 3, the wings were swept fully back to 70° and Mach 1.6 recorded, but it was on Flight 4, on the 13th, that the aircraft really displayed its speed potential. Saget reached Mach 2.03 with the wing fully swept, while the aircraft's acceleration was staggering, the pilot reporting how it took just 10 seconds to go from Mach 1.2 to 1.3, and 6 seconds from Mach 1.9 to 2.0.

The G8's acceleration from Mach 0.9 to Mach 2 was 50 seconds faster than the earlier G, but there were problems with the gloves or 'curtains' that sealed the wing/fuselage junction, as they deformed under load. In addition, buffet appeared at low speeds when the angle of attack reached 11° and became pronounced at 16°. The aircraft's longitudinal stability was very good. The benefits of variable geometry (coupled with sophisticated high-lift devices) were illustrated by the fact that 01 was able to land at a speed of 118 knots (219km/h).

The flow of early flights was interrupted by the June 1971 Paris Air Show at Le Bourget. Marcel Dassault did not want to stop the trials because there was a risk in displaying a prototype that had recorded so few flight hours, but neither did he wish to miss the chance to show off his new aeroplane. Discussions on how best to display the G8 became quite heated, but Saget's performance for what was only the prototype's 11th flight, with wing sweep angles altered during the display, impressed the crowds.

Above: Mirage G8 01 takes off. Note the leading edge flaps. *Henry Matthews*

Left: 01 with its wings fully swept. The wing trailing edge flap arrangement shows up well. *Dassault*

Top: First Mirage G8 probably taken at the 1971 Paris Air Show. *Terry Panopalis*

At the beginning of November a new phase of trials began and by early December had accumulated around 50 hours of flying in 39 flights, with the objective of making a precise analysis of the G8's flying characteristics in all configurations at speeds up to and considerably in excess of Mach 2, and at altitudes up to 40,000ft (12,192m). At the end of the year 01 went back into the factory for necessary strengthening of the airframe for continued supersonic flying. It returned to the air in March 1972.

Next came the official CEV review and test pilot Robert Galan flew the aircraft regularly between April and September 1972, and again from November 1972 to March 1973. A full evaluation of the prototype's flying qualities included an assessment of its limitations in terms of manoeuvrability and control, the programme including low flying at supersonic speed over the Gulf of Lion, off the French Mediterranean coast, very high-speed sorties at high altitude, and a landing made with the wing set at the intermediate angle of 45°.

Mirage G8s 01 (two-seat) and 02 (single-seat) photographed when they were parked side-by-side at the 1973 Paris show. The extended, more pointed nose on 02 was to accommodate a radar. The difference in the intakes and size of the shock cones is evident. *Both Terry Panopalis*

CEV's pilots declared that the G8 was in many respects a quite brilliant aircraft with generally very good flying qualities, although directional control was a little heavy, and light buffeting was still experienced in the approach configuration up to a 17° angle of attack, regardless of the wing sweep angle.

However, from a manoeuvring point of view 01 was not so good. It was built for high speed and when the wings were swept back it could not turn sharply because of the high wing loading. There was also some instability in roll when the wing was positioned at angles between 25° and 55°. But the speed performance continued to impress, Saget reporting that 750 knots (1,390km/h) could be reached with ease at low altitude. Flying at Mach 2 at 40,000ft (12,190m) (which happened regularly) brought an interesting problem as the pilot attempted to prevent the aircraft from accelerating so much that kinetic heating from air friction would overheat and damage the aluminium airframe. The solution was to keep one engine in afterburner at Mach 2 and the other throttled back – with both afterburners lit the aircraft's speed continued to accumulate.

Prototype 01 was back at Paris for the June 1973 show, this time performing together with 02, Saget flying the original aircraft and Dassault test pilot Guy Mitaux-Maurouard the second. On 18 June G8 01 made the last of its

Paris 1973 provided an opportunity to fly the G8s together. This photo was taken during the last such flight on 18 June. The larger intake shock cone on 02 (nearest) is again visible as is the outline of its painted-over rear canopy. *Terry Panopalis*

210 flights. During its career the aircraft had recorded a minimum speed of 104 knots (193km/h), reached a maximum speed of Mach 2.2, or 750 knots (1,389km/h) IAS at 65,000ft (19,800m) and confirmed that the variable-geometry wing presented few problems. After a period in storage, in 1977 Mirage G8 01 was transferred to the Musée de l'Air et de l'Espace (Air and Space Museum) at Le Bourget, where it remains on display.

The extremities of wing sweep available to the G8 are shown by the two prototypes in flight in 1973, with 01 trailing. *Alexis Rocher*

G8 prototype 02 taxis at Paris in June 1973.

Mirage G8 01 approaches to land.

Since the Air Force really wanted a single-seat aircraft, the second Mirage G8 was turned out as such, although only in as much as the second seat had been deleted and the rear canopy covered in metallic paint. An enlarged 'false' nose for the G8's Cyrano IV radar stretched 02's length to 66ft 3in (20.20m), but the most important difference from the first prototype came with the air intakes, which had been redesigned to allow 02 to reach Mach 2.5. However, the Atar engine was limited to Mach 2.3 due to the risk of metal creep in the compressor disks, and there were still some speed limitations on the airframe because of the potential effects of kinetic heating. Plans to fit a titanium wing were dropped for reasons of economy.

Jean-Marie Saget took 02 on its maiden flight, again from Istres, on 13 July 1972 and he soon found that the aircraft's flight performance and behaviour came close to what had been experienced in 01. Flight 2, on 18 July, had the

wing fully swept to 70°, allowing Mach 1.5 to be recorded. Test pilot Robert Galan began CEV's assessment on 5 October and went on to take the aircraft to Mach 2.1. On 31 October the second machine was taken to its highest altitude so far of 52,990ft (16,150m), and then on 4 January 1973 Guy Mitaux-Maurouard made his first trip in the aeroplane.

During February and into early March airframe work had to be done adjacent to 02's wing pivot brackets before the aircraft could resume flying on 14 March. Apart from this, and the need to make detail adjustments to the air intakes, there was little to deal with in the way of technical issues.

On 15 March, during Flight 32, Saget took 02 from 30,020ft to 61,025ft (9,150m to 18,600m) in just 3 minutes 24 seconds, in the process accelerating from Mach 1.5 to Mach 2.12, while the very next day Mitaux-Maurouard stayed at Mach 2 for 14 minutes. Then, exactly a year after its maiden flight, during Flight 74 on 13 July 1973, prototype 02, with Saget again at the controls, set a speed record for an aircraft operating in Western Europe, a figure of Mach 2.336 being recorded at an altitude of 41,000ft (12,500m). Incredibly this was achieved with less than full afterburning because, with its airframe and engine limitations, 02 was only permitted to fly at this speed for 30 seconds before the structure experienced heat damage. At the time of writing this European record had not been beaten.

In 1974 prototype 02 moved on to trials carrying stores on underwing pylons (including two AS37 Martel anti-radar missiles), looking at the problems these gave when changing the wing sweep angle, and the way in which they affected the flying characteristics overall. Flight 112 on 28 March was used for an inflight refuelling trial with an Air Force Boeing C-135 tanker aircraft. For its final flights the second G8 had its wings set permanently at 55° as part of the research for a new Air Force aircraft programme to provide air defence, strike and reconnaissance, the ACF or Avion de Combat Futur.

In reality, despite their advantages, by the early 1970s the G8's variable-geometry wings had made the aeroplane too expensive for France to buy in quantity and for export, adding to their complexity and the inevitable weight compromise that VG brings. In addition, new-generation advanced types including the General Dynamics F-16, first flown in January

1974, would demonstrate that swing wings were no longer needed to give a fighter aeroplane excellent performance.

Despite its qualities, doubts began to grow regarding the validity of the G8 configuration, and on 22 December 1972 the French Defence Minister announced that test flying would end in 1973, apart from specific flights related directly to the ACF to determine the new type's optimum wing angle. After these trials Dassault-Breguet confirmed that 55° was the best compromise for a fixed wing multi-role fighter with a bias towards air superiority. The fixed wing was also cheaper to produce than a swing-wing (by as much as 10%) and its use simplified the carriage of external stores.

Back at Dassault-Breguet the G8 was recast as the fixed-wing Mirage G8A 'Super Mirage' strike/interdictor with a 55° swept wing to comply with the ACF requirements. In service it would have been designated Mirage F8 and carried two 30mm cannon, missiles and bombs; top speed would have been in excess of Mach 2.5. An initial prototype contract was signed in late autumn 1973 and on 13 January 1974 General Claude Grigaut, Chief of Staff of the French Air Force, publicly announced the project's go-ahead.

Model depicting the fixed-wing Dassault-Breguet G8A 'Super Mirage' Avion de Combat Futur, which followed the G8 but was abandoned in late 1975. *Dassault*

By 1975 two prototypes had been approved for manufacture at Saint-Cloud, but once again strains on the defence budget were jeopardising the timetable – the first prototype had been due to fly in October 1976, but this was expected to slip to early 1977, while construction of the second was reported to have either slowed drastically or even stopped temporarily. The ACF became the subject of increasing doubt through its rising costs and minimal export potential, and on 18 December 1975 France's National Defence Council decided to abandon the project.

At the point of termination the first prototype's fuselage was almost complete and appeared ready to receive its wing and equipment (it was presumably scrapped). By that time work on the succeeding Mirage 2000 was under way, with a return to the delta wing. The first prototype made its maiden flight on 10 March 1978. The type went on to become very successful at home and on the export market.

Mirage G8 02 made the last of its 137 flights on 22 November 1974, bringing the grand total for the two prototypes to 347. Performance-wise, the G8 was clearly an astonishingly fast aeroplane. But its Achilles Heel was its lack of manoeuvrability. At low altitude it could turn at 7g at 594 knots [1,100km/h], but just 2g at Mach 1.2 and 40,025ft [12,200m]), for a very poor turn capability at high speeds thanks to a substantial wing loading, features that in time became unsuited to revised Air Force requirements. Guy Mitaux-Maurouard noted, however, how well the variable-geometry wings worked, changes in sweep angle hardly being noticed by the pilot.

Prototype 02 was stored at Istres for a while before a section was removed to serve as an instructional tool at CEV. Today the remains of the airframe reside with the Musée Européen de l'Aviation de Chasse (the European Fighter Aircraft Museum) at Montélimar.

By the 1960s the cost of developing new combat aircraft was growing massively and it is remarkable that Dassault was able to produce this string of fighter prototypes during the decade and into the 1970s. However, of the new types, only the Mirage F1 entered production. The unbuilt ACF takes the story deep into the 1970s and beyond the scope of this book, to a time when completely new military aircraft types were becoming few and far between. The golden age of military aircraft development, when new designs seemed to appear every year was gone, almost certainly for ever.

Airframe

The Mirage G8 was an all-metal aircraft fitted with a variable-geometry wing that could be swept at angles across the range 23° through 70°. It had a large, all-moving tailplane and a single fin plus two substantial ventral fins. Both prototypes were built as two-seaters, but the second was adapted as a single-seat aircraft with the rear position vacated and its canopy covered over. The aircraft housed 2,248 Imp gals (10,220 litres) of internal fuel and Dassault documents indicate that it could carry four 1,700-litre (374-Imp gal) or two 2,000-litre (440-Imp gal) external tanks.

Included in the Mirage G8's planned avionics was a Thomson-CSF Cyrano IV radar and a low-altitude navigation and attack system. Apart from Martel missiles, Dassault papers note that the G8 would have carried two MATRA 530 or Sidewinder air-to-air missiles, or one AN22 nuclear store. The 1,500kg (3,307lb) AN22 would have been loaded semi-recessed under the fuselage, while the air-to-air weapons would have gone under the wings. Both prototypes were flown in natural metal finish with minimal decoration and markings; their noses were painted black.

Surviving airframes

Aerfer Ariete	MM569: Museo Storico dell'Aeronautica Militare, Vigna di Valle
Aerfer Sagittario II	MM561: Museo Storico dell'Aeronautica Militare, Vigna di Valle
BAC TSR.2	XR220: RAF Museum Cosford XR222: Imperial War Museum Duxford
Breguet 1001 Taon	F-ZWVE: Musée de l'Air et de l'Espace, Le Bourget
Dassault Mirage IIIV	01: Musée de l'Air et de l'Espace, Le Bourget
Dassault Mirage F2	01: Centre d'essais aéronautiques de Toulouse, Balma
Dassault Mirage G8	01: Musée de l'Air et de l'Espace, Le Bourget 02: Remains at the Musée Européen de l'Aviation de Chasse, Montélimar
English Electric P.1	WG760: RAF Museum Cosford WG763: Museum of Science and Industry, Manchester.
FFA P-16	X-HB-VAD: Flieger FLAB Museum, Dübendorf
Hawker P.1052	VX272: Fleet Air Arm Museum, Yeovilton
Hispano HA-300	V-1 (51-100): Deutsches Museum, Oberschleißheim near Munich
Ikarus Aircraft	The 451, 451M and T-451MM are all preserved at the Museum of Aviation, Belgrade
Nord 2200	F-WFRD: Until recently with the Musée Aéronautique Vannes-Monterblanc, Brittany. Future uncertain at time of writing
Sud-Est SE 212 Durandal	F-ZWUC: Sections were in store at the Musée de l'Air et de l'Espace, Le Bourget
Sud-Ouest (SNCASO) SO 6025 Espadon	F-WFRG: Most of fuselage survives at the Ailes Anciennes Toulouse
Supermarine Type 510	VV106: Fleet Air Arm Museum, Yeovilton.

Glossary

Note: although fully state-owned companies, the series of Sociétés Nationales de Constructions Aéronautiques (SNCA) manufacturers were operated as private concerns.

A&AEE	Aeroplane & Armament Experimental Establishment, Boscombe Down (UK)
ACF	Avion de Combat Futur
AFC	Air Force Cross
Air Cdre	Air Commodore
Anhedral	Downward slope of wing or tailplane from root to tip
Angle of attack	Angle at which a wing is inclined relative to the airflow
Angle of incidence	Angle between the chord line of the wing and the fore-and-aft datum line of the fuselage
Area rule	Principal law for keeping transonic drag to a minimum. States that cross-section areas of an aeroplane plotted from nose to tail on a graph should form a smooth curve
ASI	Airspeed Indicated
ASM	Air-to-surface missile
Aspect ratio	Ratio of wingspan to mean chord, calculated by dividing the square of the span by the wing area
AVM	Air Vice-Marshal
AWA	Armstrong Whitworth Aviation
BAC	British Aircraft Corporation
Capt	Captain
CAS	Chief of the Air Staff (Royal Air Force post)
Cdr	Commander
CEPA	Commission d'Etudes Pratiques d'Aéronautique (Commission for the Practical Study of Aviation) based at Saint-Raphael. Also known as Escadrille 10S, CEPA was a trials squadron established during 1944 to test and evaluate all new aircraft types intended to serve the French Navy, together with their weapons and equipment
CEV	Centre d'Essais en Vol (French equivalent to A&AEE Boscombe Down)
CFE	Central Fighter Establishment

Chord	Distance between centres of curvature of wing leading and trailing edges when measured parallel to the longitudinal axis
CofG	Centre of gravity
COIN	Counter-Insurgency
Col	Colonel
Critical Mach number	Mach number at which an aircraft's controllability is first affected by compressibility, ie the point at which shock waves first appear
DFC	Distinguished Flying Cross
Dihedral	Upward slope of wing or tailplane from root to tip
DSO	Distinguished Service Order
DTI	Direction Technique et Industrielle du ministère de la Défense
Dutch Roll	A combined yawing and rolling motion
EAS	Equivalent Airspeed (rectified airspeed with a compressibility correction)
ECM	Electronic countermeasures
FFA	Flug und Fahrzeugwerke Altenrhein AG
Flt Lt	Flight Lieutenant
Flutter	A high-frequency oscillation of an aircraft's structure induced by aerodynamic and aeroelastic forces
GOR	General Operational Requirement
Gross weight	Usually signifies maximum weight with internal fuel plus all equipment/weapons aboard, but not external tanks
HSA	Hawker Siddeley Aviation Ltd
IAS	Indicated Air Speed
IMN	Indicated Mach Number
Ing	Ingenieur (engineer)
JATO	Jet assisted take-off
KMF	Kommission fuer militaerische Flugzeugbeschaffung (Swiss Commission for Military Aircraft Procurement)
KTA	Kriegstechnische Abteilung (Swiss War Technical Department)
Lt	Lieutenant
LVK	Landesverteidigungskommission (Swiss National Defense Commission)

Mach Number	Ratio of an aeroplane's speed to that of sound in the surrounding medium – expressed as a decimal
MoA	Ministry of Aviation
MoD	Ministry of Defence – created in the late 1940s to co-ordinate the policy of the three British Armed Services. In April 1964 the MoD was reconstituted to absorb the functions of the Air Ministry, Admiralty and War Office, the Air Ministry (the civilian body that had governed the RAF) ceasing to exist
MoS	Ministry of Supply (UK) – provided stores for the RAF from 1946 onwards. Disbanded and reconstituted as the Ministry of Aviation in 1959
NACA	National Advisory Committee for Aeronautics (USA)
NATO	North Atlantic Treaty Organisation
nm	Nautical mile
ONERA	Office Nationale d'Etude et de Recherches Aéronautiques (National Office of Aerospace Studies and Research)
OR	Operational Requirement
P&EE	Proof and Experimental Establishment, Shoeburyness
RAAF	Royal Australian Air Force
RAE	Royal Aircraft Establishment, Bedford and Farnborough (UK)
RAeS	Royal Aeronautical Society (UK)
RAF	Royal Air Force
RATO	Rocket-assisted take-off (replaced JATO when rockets permanently adopted to give extra take-off thrust). RATO/JATO installations are usually optional/detachable and generally for single use
RATOG	Rocket-Assisted Take-Off Gear
RNAS	Royal Naval Air Station (UK)
SACEUR	Supreme Allied Commander Europe
SBAC	Society of British Aircraft Constructors (now Society of British Aerospace Companies)
Service ceiling	The altitude at which an aircraft's rate of climb falls below a specified figure, for example 1,000ft/min (305m/min)

SFECMAS	Société Française d'Etude et de Construction de Matériels Aéronautiques Spéciaux. In 1955 SFECMAS merged with SNCAN as SNCAN Nord
SNCAC	Société Nationale de Constructions Aéronautiques du Centre. Also known as Aérocentre. Integrated as part of SNCAN in June 1949
SNCAN	Société Nationale de Constructions Aéronautiques du Nord
SNCASE	Société Nationale de Constructions Aéronautiques du Sud-Est
SNCASO	Société Nationale de Constructions Aéronautiques du Sud-Ouest
SNECMA	Société Nationale d'Étude et de Construction de Moteurs d'Aviation
Sqn Ldr	Squadron Leader
STAé	Service technique de l'Aéronautique chargé de la partie technique, industrielle et administrative des marchés d'État. The French state-run Technical Department of Aeronautics
STOL	Short take-off and landing
TAS	True Air Speed
t/c	Thickness/chord ratio
Transonic flight	The speed range either side of Mach 1.0 where an aircraft has both subsonic and supersonic airflow passing over it at the same time
VG	Variable geometry
V/STOL	Vertical/short take-off and landing
VTOL	Vertical take-off and landing
VTO	Vertical Take-Off
Wg Cdr	Wing Commander

Bibliography and Source Notes

A large number of original documents held by national archives, museums and heritage centres were consulted, especially for the British projects in this book. For French subjects the sources were more secondary in nature and feature in the list below. Contemporary issues of the British *Flight* magazine and *The Aeroplane, Air International* and other magazines were consulted, and Phil Butler's series of articles on British jet prototypes in Air-Britain's *Aeromilitaria* also filled important gaps.

Beamont, Hervé, Ricco, Philippe, Bénichou, Michel *Les Dassault à Décollage Vertical: Mirage IIIV: La Voie Était Sans Issue* (*Fana de l'Aviation,* Issues 336 and 337, November/December 1997)

Beamont, Roland *Testing Years* (Ian Allan, 1980)

Brodnjak, Stephen; Markovina, Roko; Miric, Tomislav; Sert, John; and Zadro, Mladen *Soko Aviation Industry Mostar 1951-1981* (NIŠRO, 1981)

Burke, Damien *TSR.2: Britain's Lost Bomber* (The Crowood Press, 2010)

Buttler, Tony *British Secret Projects: Jet Bombers Since 1949* (Midland Publishing, 2003)

Carlier, Claude *Une formule aérodynamique gagnante. La grande aventure des 'Mirage' à géométrie variable* (*Fana de l'Aviation* Issues 536-539, July-October 2014)

Ciampaglia, Giuseppe *Dal Sai Ambrosini Sagittario All'Aerfer Leone: A History of the First Italian Supersonic Fighters Created by Sergio Stefanutti* (Instituto Bibliografico Napoleone, 2004)

Cuny, Jean *Les Avions De Combat Français 1944-1960: I – Chasse Assaut* (*Docavia* Volume 28, Éditions Larivière, 1988)

Cuny, Jean *Les Avions De Combat Français 1944-1960: II – Chasse Lourde, Bombardement, Assaut, Exploration* (*Docavia* Volume 30, Éditions Larivière, 1989)

Cuny, Jean *SE 212 Durandal: Le brève histoire d'une grand famille* (*Fana de l'Aviation* Issue 254, January 1991)

Fayer, Jean-Claude *Prototypes de l'Aviation Français 1945-1960* (E-T-A-I, 2002)

Fricker, John *Upwardly Mobile: Dassault's VTOL Mirage IIIV* (*Air Enthusiast* Issue 58, summer 1995)

Fricker, John *Switzerland's P-16: Father of the Learjet* (*AIR International*, March 1991)

Gaillard, Pierre and Marchand, Alain *Le SO 4000:* (*Fana de l'Aviation* Issues 142-152, 1981 and 1982)

Gaillard, Pierre with Ricco, Philippe *Les Trois Premiers Chasseurs Embarqués à Réaction Français* (*Fana de l'Aviation* Issues 305-308, April-June and August 1995)

Gaillard, Pierre and Marchand, Alain *Le SO 8000 Narval:* (*Fana de l'Aviation* Issues 180 and 181, November and December 1984)

Harvey, RA Sqn Ldr *Farnborough Fiasco: A Test Pilot's Story* (self published, 1997)

Hygate, Barry *British Experimental Jet Aircraft* (Argus Books, 1990)

Jackson, AJ *Blackburn Aircraft since 1909* (Putnam, 1968)

Jones, Barry *British Experimental Turbojet Aircraft* (Crowood Press, 2003)

Liébert, Michel and Buyck, Sébastien *Le Mirage F1 et les Mirage de Seconde Génération à Voilure en Flèche* (*Premier Tome – Projets et Prototypes,* Lela Presse, 2007)

Mason, Tim *The Cold War Years: Flight Testing at Boscombe Down 1945-1975* (Hikoki, 2001)

Matthews, Henry *Prelude to the Sea Vixen: D.H.110* (*X-Planes Profile No. 5*) (HPM Publications, 2001)

Meekcoms, KJ and Morgan, EB *The British Aircraft Specifications File* (Air-Britain, 1994)

Middleton, Don *Test Pilots: The Story of British Test Flying 1903-1984* (Collins Willow, 1985)

Morgan, Eric and Stevens, John *The Scimitar File* (Air-Britain, 2000)

Moulin, Jacques *Le Nord 1500 Noréclair* (*Aviation Français Magazine* Issue 1, December 2004/January 2005)

Noetinger, Jacque *Histoire de l'Aeronautique Français* (Éditions France-Empire, 1978)

Ricco, Philippe *NC 270: Le Bombardier à Réaction qui vola par Procuration* (*Fana de l'Aviation* Issue 349, December 1998)

Salisbury, MW *The Significance of TSR.2* (37th RK Pierson Memorial Lecture, October 1989)

Sartorius, Matthias F *The Perception of the P-16 in the United States: A Historical Analysis* (unpublished thesis, December 2006)

A New Ship-Plane Formula: Aircraft Engineering, April 1949.

The Arsenal VB 10: …un chasseur vraiment unique: Air Enthusiast, July 1971.

Straight to the Target: The Sagittario – Ambrosini's Latest Research Prototype: Flight, 24 April 1953.

Visitor from France: The Breguet 960 Vultur for Carrier Operation: Flight, 15 May 1953.

TSR.2 with Hindsight: Conference Proceedings; RAF Historical Society, 1998.

Index

INDEX OF AIRCRAFT AND AIRCRAFT DESIGNS

INDEX OF PEOPLE